Acclaim for *Neutral Buoyancy:*

"An enticing catalogue of undersea diving experiences, with extended side trips into the sport's history and culture . . . As elemental, entertaining, and stimulating as the environment it traces."
—*Kirkus Reviews*

"Engaging . . . *Neutral Buoyancy* will certainly become cult reading for divers. . . . But perhaps even more impressive is that non-divers will be equally captivated by Tim Ecott's mix of personal odyssey and hard science." —Alexander Urquhart, *Times Literary Supplement*

"Gripping and finely written." —*FHM*

"Unforgettable stuff, vivid, lyrical, and quite brilliantly written. A modern classic about the underwater world that mixes personal memoir with travel, history, and a cast of characters that defy description." —Tony Parsons, author of *Man and Boy*

"Fascinating . . . Vivid descriptions of what's to be seen show skeptics what they're missing: coral as green as 'a fine piece of carved jade,' as scarlet as a 'humming-bird feather' and as pink as the 'petals of a carnation in a buttonhole.' " —*Publishers Weekly*

"Ecott tells the story meticulously. . . . Absorbing." —James Astill, *The Guardian* (London)

"Excellent . . . The author runs the gamut of diving experiences: he includes almost poetic descriptions of the mystic experience of weightlessness and being one with the underwater world, a history of diving, a discussion of hyperbaric physics and physiology, travel narratives of exotic diving locales, and an extremely interesting chapter on Florida's sponge divers." —*Library Journal*

NEUTRAL BUOYANCY

Neutral Buoyancy

Adventures in a Liquid World

TIM ECOTT

GROVE PRESS
New York

Copyright © 2001 by Tim Ecott

First published in Great Britain in 2001 by Michael Joseph, an imprint of the Penguin Group

Published simultaneously in Canada
Printed in the United States of America

Library of Congress Cataloging-in-Publication Data

Ecott, Tim.
    Neutral buoyancy : adventures in a liquid world / Tim Ecott.
        p. cm.
    Includes bibliographical references.
    ISBN-13: 978-0-8021-3907-8
    1. Deep diving. I. Title.

GV838.672 .E36 2001
797.2'3—dc21   2001018840

Grove Press
an imprint of Grove/Atlantic, Inc.
154 West 14th Street
New York, NY 10011

Distributed by Publishers Group West

www.groveatlantic.com

14 15 16 17 18   11 10 9 8 7 6 5

'The sea does not belong to despots. Upon its surface men can still exercise unjust laws, fight, tear one another to pieces, and be carried away with terrestrial horrors. But at thirty feet below its level, their reign ceases, their influence is quenched and their power disappears. Ah! sir, live – live in the bosom of the waters! There only is independence! There I recognise no masters! There I am free!'

Captain Nemo in *20,000 Leagues Under the Sea*,
Jules Verne

Contents

List of Illustrations

Photographs

13 In 1967, Bob Croft was the first man to free-dive below two hundred feet. (Bob Croft)

14 Neal Watson and John Gruener after their record-breaking dive on air to 437 feet and one inch, 1968. (Neal Watson)

15 Umberto Pelizzari can hold his breath for seven minutes. (Tim Ecott)

16 Umberto Pelizzari was the first man to descend to 150 metres without air. (Sector Sport Watches)

Text Illustrations

A   In 1511, woodcuts of divers enlivened an edition of early military strategy by Vegetius.

B   In 1612, Diego Ufano described a 'hood made of greased cowhide, so carefully stitched that water could not enter'.

C   Alfonso Borelli's diver wore claw-like flippers, a 'breathing bag' and a weighted counterbalance.

D   Edmund Halley perfected a workable diving bell which he patented in 1691. (Sketch reproduced by permission of the President and Council of the Royal Society)

E   In 1715, John Lethbridge sealed himself into a 'diving-barrel' made from a hogshead reinforced with iron bands.

F   In 1897 audiences flocked to the Theatre Royal to see *The White Heather*, a melodrama featuring deep-sea divers.

G   Peter Kreeft used his leather diving suit as early as 1800.

H   In 1797, a diving suit of waterproofed leather with a metal helmet was demonstrated by Klingert.

I   Frédéric de Drieberg's 'Triton'.

J   Salvage work on the *Royal George* was the proving ground for the modern diving dress.

K   Louis de Corlieu registered his patent for crêpe rubber hand
    and foot propellers in 1933.
L   The exploits of the Royal Navy frogmen were kept secret until
    the end of the War. (*Illustrated London News* Picture Library)
M   Mr Day's 'Diving Vessel'.

With thanks to the Nigel Phillips Collection and Kevin Casey at
Sub Aqua Prints.

Introduction

Four days after my mother's funeral I went scuba diving for the first time. Using work as my excuse, I escaped from the sombre atmosphere of the crematorium and the silence of an empty house by embarking on a reporting assignment for the BBC in Seychelles. Taking my younger brother with me, we drank in the islands' anodyne beauty and tranquillity. He, unlike me, had long harboured an urge to dive, and in the aftermath of the shock of death I embarked on the underwater adventure with little enthusiasm, largely out of a sense of duty to keep my brother company.

There was a distance between us and the other novice divers, born of sadness, and reinforced by the impossibility of discussing what had happened with people who were total strangers. For the other divers the sport-diving course seemed merely a simple holiday preoccupation, undertaken purely for the purpose of pleasure, or for a badge to show back home.

For most divers the first immersion is an emotional high, a crowning achievement, a conquering of fears and phobias and a passport to membership of the worldwide sub-aqua club. For me, the whole experience was subordinate to the troughs and peaks of my emotional adjustment to the loss of life's central figure. Immediately after that first dive – a mere twenty-two minutes at a depth of thirty-six feet – my diving instructor was clearly perturbed when I told her the experience had been just, well, fine. Alright. No more, no less.

In my case, the excitement of swimming underwater, of confronting aquatic species nose to nose, and of immersion in the big blue rose higher with each new plunge. The journey away from bereavement led to greater involvement with scuba diving, a succession of more advanced training courses, and eventually a job as a dive master, leading other divers on underwater tours. Diving has become my passion, an obsession, and I worship the inner peace that being underwater can bring.

Surfacing from a dive, particularly one which has been physically challenging, I often think it strange that this mind-cleansing, emotionally charged experience is one that my mother never knew I had. It is something akin to the sense of regret I feel that she never met my daughter, born a few years after her passing. How odd, that something so wonderful was not part of our shared experience. In the case of diving, would she approve, I wonder, or worry about the physical dangers of the sport? These are the thoughts that surface at depth.

Bloody Bay Wall, British West Indies

Captain Keith Plaskett tied up the motor yacht, *Little Cayman Diver*, to its mooring buoy on the edge of the reef as the sun was rising. Her bows sat in twenty-five feet of water, and through the gin-clear sea we could make out the coral garden below us.

The captain and his crew assembled our small group of divers in the yacht's main saloon for a safety briefing. 'This is deep water,' he warned, inhaling deeply on the oversized Havana cigar almost permanently clamped between his teeth. 'Don't forget to monitor your depth gauges carefully. The face of the wall is enticing, it can make you want to go down and down. Remember the safety limit.'

'Cap'n Keith', as we learned to call him, had none of the equipment fetishes of the average dive leader. In a torn, oil-stained T-shirt and baggy black swim shorts, he reminded me of an Action Man doll I had been given for Christmas when I was eight years old. A well-used knife, strapped to a muscular calf, and a faded US Navy buoyancy jacket completed the picture. If my Action Man had still been alive, and not the victim of a blazing parachuting accident from my bedroom window, he would have been every bit as faded around the edges as Cap'n Keith. This man had no need to prove himself underwater. At forty-eight, with five marriages down and one in prospect, he liked to break open a bottle of rum in the evening and talk about boats. Considering his history, women featured little in the conversation, but Hollywood couldn't have created a better charter-boat captain.

Minutes after the briefing, we sat on the dive deck ready to enter the sea. Then, one by one, we fell forward off the transom into warm water and looked down. Nothing. The reef was gone.

Thirty yards behind me the bows of the yacht were attached to the shallow mooring, but the stern diving platform had drifted over the edge of the perpendicular reef wall which plummeted into the abyss. Six thousand feet of blue water. At the edge of my vision I could just make out the wall, its sheer vertical face of coral plunging downwards, a mass of life hanging out over the depths, fish moving between its plant growth, and who knew what ready to swim up its face from the reaches of the ocean.

Bloody Bay Wall is one of the world's unforgettable dives. Scarcely a hundred yards off the shores of Little Cayman in the Western Caribbean, the wall is covered by sponges, tunicates, black coral, golden crinoids, flame scallops and sea fans. Beneath, between, around and above these fixed growths, crabs, spiny lobsters, groupers, octopuses, turtles, eagle rays, mantas and sharks patrol the wall, plundering the larder of tinier creatures who shelter in its nooks and crannies.

I emptied my buoyancy jacket of air and sank slowly beneath the calm surface. Looking straight down was to immerse myself in a featureless indigo space. In one direction lay the wall, a reference point to gauge my speed of descent, but above and below there were only shades of blue, bright if I looked up and deepening to black if I looked down. This was the closest I could imagine to sky diving off the side of a cliff. Slower, no doubt, but giving the same sense of freedom, and removal from the normal sensory clues of gravity.

Head-first, I fell gently into this most seductive abyss. My depth gauge showed me to be over one hundred feet down and I halted, hung motionless, scanning the wall one moment then turning away to the big blue the next. Other divers hung above me or closer to the wall, their air bubbles a rising glittering trail to the surface, the bubbles small at first then expanding into hemispherical domes shimmering like mercury as they sought their own element. I swam to the wall and studied it close up.

Cayman waters are among the clearest in the world, free from pollutants, washed by deep ocean swells and unaffected by rain water run-off from land or rivers. On the wall were sponges and sea fans bigger than I had seen in any other ocean. Cayman barrel sponges are rusty amphoras, up to six feet high and with mouths wider than the length of my arm. Up close their surface texture is as smooth as a young stag's antlers at the beginning of autumn, covered with a fine velvet sheath of brown stubble. They were giant tubs fit for Ali Baba's forty thieves.

Ascending the wall, the colours brightened as the spectrum of light was freed from its watery filter. Purple, orange, yellow, green and crimson showed through. Violet vase sponges as richly coloured and intricately woven as a medieval cardinal's robes sprouted from the wall, and peering inside I would find marine worms or brittle stars spreading their tentacles across the brocade.

A week's cruising off Little Cayman passed in a cycle of companionable dives interspersed with tempting meals, non-stop refreshments and spells on the sun deck. After dinner we would kit up again and seek out the shyer night dwellers of the shallow reef, sometimes peering over the lip of the wall into the abyss. The utter dark was broken only by our flashlights, and the blackness was a cocoon, tranquil and not at all alarming, as I had imagined it would be. On our return to the yacht, the chef would surprise us all with what she called a snack. Coconut cake with fruit slices, or ice cream and chocolate sauce with hot tea ensured a peaceful night's sleep. Occasionally, a small bottle of rum would appear. The other divers, all strangers until we met, became good friends. They were relaxing company, knowledgeable about the ocean, and all shared a fondness for its endless mystery.

One evening, Captain Plaskett sat on deck giving me a tour of the starscape above the yacht. Some time close to midnight, he left me alone with my view of the Southern Cross and the Big Dipper, and I decided to sleep on deck. Several times during the night I awoke and stared at the stars as *Little Cayman Diver* rocked gently in the bay. Above me was the sheltering night sky, while below the hull the other space waited for me again.

1. Healing Waters

And, sure, the reverent eye must see
A Purpose in Liquidity.
We darkly know, by Faith we cry,
The Future is not Wholly Dry.
        Rupert Brooke, 'Heaven'

In Italy, a young woman once told me that learning to dive had mended her broken heart. In Spain, the chief executive of an international hotel company said that she dived because no one could telephone her underwater, or ask her to make any business decisions. In England, an engineer told me that he dived in order to experience flight, to escape the ties of gravity. His technical training had made him wish he could fly through the air, like a bird, but on reflection he had decided that to be a fish would be superior. In general, he reasoned, a bird cannot choose to stay motionless in the air. The bird may soar and glide above us seemingly unconstrained by gravity, but is dependent on the wind. The fish can choose to rest in one spot, even with a current flowing, and yet the fish can also move in three-dimensional space. In Switzerland, a man told me that he preferred to dive in alpine lakes rather than tropical seas. He said he found the marine life in warm waters too distracting; there was too much colour, too many things to take in. For him, the joy of diving was the opportunity to see inside himself. In order to examine his own character he needed to be in cold, dark, deep water where diving, just breathing underwater, was an end in itself. In Seychelles, a former professional motorcyclist who was paralysed from the waist down said that diving allowed him to forget his disability for a time. In Papua New Guinea there was an American who told me that diving was his church. What he saw underwater was a clear affirmation of God's presence on earth and being in the sea was the only place he found complete solace. In California, a man told me that an hour underwater was better than any therapy session with a psychoanalyst. A Russian once said to me that, however hard he tried, he could never imagine any creature as weird as those he sometimes found underwater. Whatever space creatures he saw or read about in science fiction were a pale approximation of the variety of life forms he met in the sea.

Diving for pleasure is a young sport. Mass participation in the joy of swimming freely underwater, for no other reason than to be in the liquid world, has only been possible for fifty years. It is easier, cheaper, and safer to learn to dive than ever before. And yet, the prospect of immersion continues to inspire fear. To go underwater is simply not a natural activity. We enter a hostile element where the most basic life fuel, air, is unattainable. To survive, we must take it with us. To confront the liquid world, to enter the element and return to the air world, reinforces our will to live. It provokes joy and contentment in a world where people find less and less time to experience their own personal space.

Throughout history, the motive for going underwater has been to collect and retrieve objects of value, nutrition or decoration. Sponges, mother of pearl, shellfish, items of value lost overboard in a dock, have all been enough to make men and women plunge into the sea. The riches of the oceans have been legendary, and the secrets of the Seven Seas have inspired fantasy and fear. For over two thousand years the aim of going underwater has been simply to work, or to fight. Only recently have we sought out the marine world as free-swimming divers who seek nothing other than the pleasure of being underwater.

Childhood experiences stay with us, and colour our onward journey. Places and people embed themselves in our personality, forever remaining symbols of good or bad times which can be impossible to eradicate. Try as I might, I find it impossible to think fondly of Wales. I can't apologize for it, the country remains for me the place where I began school, and hated it. Shortly afterwards, I contracted pneumonia, which left me a wheezing, bronchitic child forever unwell in the permanently, or so it seemed, damp climate. Fearing for the long-term health of my lungs, my parents were advised to take me abroad, and as my father was in the Army we were able to move to Malaya. There, I taught myself to swim, and spent every day at one of two pools, where my mother would leave my sister and me to amuse ourselves for hours on end.

I have tried to analyse my obsession with being underwater, and conclude that although everyone must draw their own inspiration from any activity, mine has to do with a return to the time when my life seemed totally in balance.

The contrast between Wales and Malaya could not have been more extreme. Just getting there involved a six-week journey by ship from Southampton, a prolonged holiday on which every day brought warmer weather and new adventures. Each stop at a new port was an education. Le Havre, where I saw a *pissoir* for the first time, Lisbon, where my mother wanted to buy a Siamese cat and smuggle it on board ship, and Gibraltar, where one of the ship's passengers was bitten by a Barbary ape. Then the slow, hot crawl as the ship passed through the Suez Canal, followed by more days at sea before reaching Ceylon. There, I had my first entrancing sight of an Indian elephant. One morning at sea we sighted a pair of whales, and there were often dolphins to be seen from the deck in the early morning. These are my impressions of the long voyage, telescoped by boyhood memory.

Once in Malaya, I was transformed by the warmth of the tropical climate and an outdoor life. School was a mere half-day, and every afternoon was a time for adventure in the wild landscape around our house on a hill. There was very little television in that childhood; my only regular viewing was the weekly episodes of *Flipper*. Books were my education, and I would stay awake at night too scared to sleep after reading a few pages of Jim Corbett's *Man Eaters of Kumaon*. In the daytime, giant spiders, scorpions and snakes were always to be found, and my friends and I would invade the jungle armed with sharpened bamboo poles in search of wild pigs. More importantly, I learned to swim. I became a fish.

We lived in Taiping, which was then a very small place, and up in the hills there was an old freshwater swimming pool carved out of the rocks which was filled by a natural stream. The water was always cool and I learnt to dive for coins, which glittered against the bottom of the deep, dark, diving pool. It was shaded by overhanging jungle and in the late afternoon we would listen to the sound of gibbons making their mournful whoop-whooping cry through the trees.

The years we spent in Malaya were a gilded time. My parents were young, and able to enjoy our company without the drudgery of housework or the irksome bills and paraphernalia of cold-climate living. This was the Sixties, and it was party time, but without the Sex, Drugs and Rock 'n' Roll. There were servants to do the chores, and an endless round of dinner parties and social events for which my parents could dress up, my father in regimental mess-kit with the smart red stripe down the legs of his trousers. The women, my mother included, had sets of matched pearls and bouffant hair styles, and lived lives like the glamorous creatures we saw in the short cinema films advertising Peter Stuyvesant cigarettes. People were all sun-tan and white teeth. In the middle of our stay, Father went away to fight in the jungle in Borneo, and we did not see him for six months. I had no thought for the horrors of jungle warfare, and his tales of giant snakes and centipedes in his tent held only excitement for an eight-year-old's ears. When he returned he had grown a beard, an unheard-of indulgence for a British officer, permissible only because the constant humidity in the jungle had given him a skin infection which prevented him shaving. I remember the shock of meeting him at the airport, and my amazement that in spite of this transformation my mother was prepared to kiss him.

Sometimes at weekends we would travel to the coast and take a boat to some small islands, where I could swim in the warm sea. I found my first porcupine fish there, and caught it and placed it in a bucket where it inflated itself like a balloon, a mass of prickly spines with a small, round mouth and two eyes at one end. I let it go. On another occasion I was given a fishing rod, with which I swiftly caught a large horseshoe crab. It was a terrifying sight, like an armoured tank with a long tail protruding from its rear. I cried when I realized I had killed it. So many of my memories from that time are connected with wildlife, from monkeys and wild pigs in the jungle to fire-ants and snakes in the house, bats in caves and fish in the warm sea. Everything in nature was a new discovery, and I was outside all of the daylight hours. I kept scorpions in a jar for a time until I was told to throw them away. On our first night in one house, my mother found an enormous black spider on the wall above my bed. She covered it in DDT powder so copiously that the fumes brought her out in a severe allergic rash. The spider seemed unaffected, so she lifted the upright vacuum cleaner on to the wall and switched it on. The spider was duly sucked into the machine, but Mother feared that it might revive itself and somehow crawl out of the bag. Her solution was to throw the vacuum from the bedroom window on to the lawn below, much to the surprise of the gardener when he found it the following day.

After three years, we returned to Europe and I lost my love for swimming. We moved to Ireland and, although I was wanted on the school swimming team, the prospect of training in an open-air pool was uninspiring. The tedium of provincial life in a wet climate took over, and the years went by in varying shades of grey. It sometimes seems that we never recovered those carefree times near the Equator. But when I dive I am eight years old again, everything underwater a fresh object of enquiry. My parents are in their prime and I have everything I want from life without having to do anything about getting it. Perhaps that is where I return to when I breathe underwater.

2. Clutching at Air

There have been many methods proposed, and Engines contrived, for enabling Men to abide a competent while under water: And the respiring fresh Air being found to be absolutely necessary to maintain Life in all that breath, several ways have been thought of, for carrying this Pabulum Vitae down to the Diver, who must, without being somehow supplied therewith, return very soon or perish.

Edmund Halley, 'The Art of Living Underwater', 1716

Soon after man began swimming and diving in search of food he began to dream of extending the time he could spend underwater. According to Aristotle, there were attempts at supplying sponge divers with air in the fourth century BC. He refers to *lebes* (cauldrons) being lowered to divers on the seabed, from which they would replenish their air supply. In effect, a diver already underwater would simply swim to the cauldron, or urn, and insert his head to take a gulp of air, allowing him to remain at the spot where he was working. For over a thousand years there were periodic claims that it was possible to send air down to a man on the seabed in this way.

In Latin the word for diver is *urinator*, a word with the same linguistic root in ancient Sanskrit as urn and urine, possibly because the liquid we excrete comes from the bladder, a vessel shaped like an urn, and like an urn containing 'water'. A diver plunges head-first into water, inviting comparison with an urn being lowered into a stream to pick up water.

In Chile there are mummified human remains on the Atacama coast which are seven thousand years old. Whale bones and fish hooks carved from mussel shells, found among the mummies, identify the people as shore dwellers making use of the cold current which brings abundant seafood along the Pacific coastline of South America. These people were divers. In all probability they ducked down among the seaweed for mussels and limpets, grubbing around with their hands, half blinded by the salt water. The proof comes from inside the human skulls found preserved in their tribal tombs. In many of the skulls the tiny internal ear bones are thickened with lumpy growths, a morbid enlargement which eventually causes deafness. The condition is known as exostosis, and is caused by prolonged exposure to cold water, usually only after repeated dives over several years. In California, doctors now call it 'surfer's ear', and they have devised an operation to scrape away the offending bone.

Naked divers who could hold their breath have been documented throughout written history, but the first successful use of a mechanical device with which to supply them with air is less easy to date precisely. Alexander the Great is said to have visited the seabed in a glass barrel at the Siege of Tyre in 332 BC inspiring earnest debate about the possibility of constructing an airtight vessel with the primitive construction materials available at the time. Accounts written several centuries after the event say that Alexander saw a sea monster so large that it took three days to pass in front of him, claims which effectively trounce his reputation as a submariner. More weight has been attached to references by the thirteenth-century philosopher Roger Bacon to a bell-like device which allowed divers to work on submerged vessels for lengthy periods. Bacon's descriptions of bells are vague, but the principle is simple.

A man enclosed in a bell can sit or stand on the seabed with his head safely in the enclosed air space above him. He can then reach down or duck down underwater and tie a rope around anything underneath the bell. The object can then be pulled from the sea by men in a boat above. Without a portable source of air, the primitive bell was a huge improvement on breath-hold diving.

Three hundred years after Bacon, reports of more sophisticated diving bells begin to sound plausible, if equally imprecise. Alongside the descriptions of bells, there are various illustrations of leather suits which profess to provide a diver with access to surface air, either through a tube to the surface or by some kind of inflatable bladder carried with him. Without an understanding of the principles of respiration, or of the effects of pressure and the composition of air, early theorists were writing without having actually seen such devices put into effect. They were also unaware of the processes which would cause an enclosed air space to become foul, since they had no idea of the existence of carbon dioxide. The scholarly men who drew and wrote about diving machines could rarely even swim. They did not take into account, for example, that a man trying to breathe underwater through a tube from the surface has to overcome not just atmospheric pressure in the air above, but also the pressure of the water on his chest. To breathe underwater the diver would have to displace a volume of water equal to the volume of air he wished to inhale. The weight of the water makes this a physical impossibility. Sucking through a narrow tube is only possible for the first foot or two, and then becomes increasingly laborious, resulting in potential damage to the lungs, and even haemorrhage.

Wherever men put to sea they lost things underwater. Sailors and passengers dropped things overboard, crates of supplies were tipped accidentally into the harbour and ships themselves were often sunk. And wherever ships were used in battle there was a need to sink the enemy, before they could sink you. While Alexander the Great was watching sea monsters from his glass barrel, divers who could hold their breath were dismantling the booms defending the port of Tyre from his fleet.

Diving as an art of war became something of an obsession during the Renaissance, covert underwater attack the ultimate strategy, if only on paper. The first printed illustrations of a diving warrior were produced to accompany the 1511 Erfurt edition of *Epitome Institutionum Re Militaris*, originally a work by the fourth-century Roman military strategist Flavius Vegetius Renatus. The woodcuts show men in leather or cloth suits, apparently walking underwater, with an air hose leading to the surface. They are suitably armed for combat, and in one picture the soldier wears a metal helmet and visor.

In 1538, the Belgian writer Jean Taisnier relates the story of a diving bell demonstrated in front of the King of Spain. In this account, two Greek divers were lowered into the River Tagus, and emerged quite dry after several minutes underwater in a bell, so dry in fact that they were able to maintain lighted candles inside the bell throughout the dive. In 1551, the Italian mathematician Niccolo Tartaglia published a design for a wooden frame, containing a giant hourglass in which a man could stand encased inside the glass ball. By the end of the century, Buonaiuto Lorini, author of *Le Fortificatione*, had designed several unworkable devices, one of which places a man on a fixed seat with his head in a leather tube which reaches to the surface. It is no more practical than a sketch by Leonardo da Vinci a hundred years earlier which purports to describe a diving suit with which to attack enemy ships, unseen. Da Vinci describes a 'wine skin' to be used to 'contain the breath', which may be deflated to descend and inflated by the diver in order to rise. He advises the diver to carry a sharp knife so as not to become entangled in the enemy nets. Try as one might to give the master inventor credit for such practical instructions, one's faith is shaken on reading that, as part of his armoury, da Vinci advises the underwater warrior to carry with him 'venom of toad, that is, a land toad' and 'slaver of mad dog and decoction of dogwood berries'. These items will be combined with arsenic, sulphur and a little tarantula essence to make a poisonous gas with which to overcome the crews of enemy ships.

While a practicable diving suit was still centuries away, it is clear that by the late sixteenth century the principle and practice of diving bells had been established in much of Europe, with their use being described in Spain, France and Italy. With the increase in numbers of printed books in the seventeenth century, proposed diving devices and sketches of prototypes proliferated. In England, Sir Francis Bacon wrote of the use of bells in his *Novum Organum*, describing a vessel 'made of metal somewhat short of the height of a man'. Diego Ufano's *Treatise on Artillery*, published in Brussels in 1612, describes a diving 'hood', made of greased cowhide 'so carefully stitched that water could not enter through any of the seams'. Perhaps the most inventive armchair theorist of all is the Italian inventor Alfonso Borelli, whose designs included descriptions of 'flippers on the diver's hands and feet in order to swim like a frog'. Borelli also seems to be the first to describe a sort of aqualung, a bag containing air which would be mysteriously regenerated with unspecified chemical components. His work on the way animals move, *De Motu Animalium* (1680), attracted the interest of Robert Hooke of the Royal Society. Hooke's own work, in close collaboration with the experiments of the Irish genius Robert Boyle, was to lay some of the foundations of modern diving science.

Modern, practical diving technology has often been a by-product of other scientific investigation. After the Restoration, the forum for much of that crucial knowledge was the Royal Society. After

A. The first printed illustrations of divers were woodcuts produced in 1511 to enliven an edition of early military strategy by the Roman tactician Vegetius.

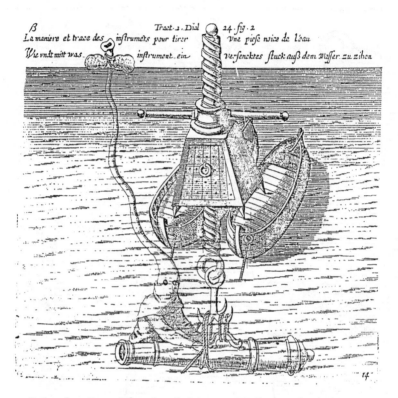

B. In 1612, Diego Ufano described the recovery of objects from shallow water with a 'hood made of greased cowhide, so carefully stitched that water could not enter'.

several years as an informal association of scientific minds, the Royal Society of London for the Promotion of Natural Knowledge was officially granted its charter by Charles II in 1662. Three years later, the Society began publishing its own periodical, *Philosophical Transactions*, a printed forum for the greatest minds of the Restoration, including Christopher Wren and Isaac Newton.

To the modern reader, early editions of *Philosophical Transactions* have much of the appeal of a tabloid newspaper, at least for the breadth of their human-interest stories. All possible topics, from mulberry trees to the anatomy of opossums, from bioluminescence to freakish births, appear in the journal's pages. A grisly tale of a ship's apprentice and a piece of cutlery provides the subject matter of 'An account of a fork put up the anus, that was afterwards drawn out through the buttock'. In similar vein, a paper on 'Henry Axford who recovered the use of his tongue, after having been many years dumb, by means of a frightful dream' is as likely to find a place on the Society's shelves as any of the primary scientific works of the day. In among such things were grander issues, such as the effects of gravity, the nature of matter, the shape of the solar system and even the basics of human biology, topics just beginning to be subject to rigorous empirical method.

Robert Boyle, the Royal Society's great natural philosopher, enlivened the pages of the journal with his experiments to determine the nature of respiration and the laws concerning the behaviour of gas under pressure. Using a vacuum chamber designed by Hooke, Boyle embarked on a series of trials which established that at constant room temperature the pressure in the chamber rose and fell in exact inverse proportion to the volume of air added or removed. His findings became Boyle's Law, which holds that as long as temperature is constant, the volume of a gas will vary inversely with pressure, while the density of a gas varies directly with pressure. In other words, if you think of a balloon filled with air, the amount of air contained in the balloon remains constant once the neck is tied. If the balloon is plunged deeper and deeper into water, the weight of the water will compress the balloon smaller and smaller as it descends. Although the amount of air inside the balloon does not change, the pressure results in it being compressed into a smaller space, i.e. its volume shrinks as the pressure increases. However, because the amount of air inside the balloon does not change, it must necessarily be fitted into less

C. Pre-dating the aqualung by 250 years, Alfonso Borelli's diver wore claw-like flippers, a 'breathing bag' and a weighted counterbalance to adjust his buoyancy underwater.

space, thus becoming denser. The increasing pressure is quite literally pressing the molecules of oxygen and nitrogen in the air closer together. Conversely, if the balloon is inflated at sea level, and then tied at the neck and taken to the top of Mount Everest, it will expand. With less atmospheric pressure, the molecules in the air mixture are able to move more freely and will occupy more space. Boyle's Law is crucial to an understanding of what happens to a diver's air supply as he descends deeper underwater. At depth, bubbles of oxygen and nitrogen released from an air-filled scuba bottle will both decrease in volume and increase in density.

By placing animals in a vacuum chamber, Boyle would subject them to increased pressure, and then release that pressure, famously observing that a viper, so treated, exhibited a small bubble in one eye. Unwittingly, Boyle had caused the snake to demonstrate the solubility of nitrogen under pressure, and witnessed the gas bubbling out of solution as pressure on the animal was rapidly decreased. The mechanism which caused the bubble in the snake's eye – breathing air under pressure – was the same which causes the dread injury to divers popularly called 'the bends'. To Boyle, the presence of the bubble was a matter of curiosity; the disease did not yet exist in man, and its treatment would not be identified with certainty for a further two hundred years.

Robert Boyle's experiments with air did not stop with pressure, but went on to encompass respiration, combustion and the way in which sound is transmitted.

In the history of science, Boyle's 'New Experiments Physio-Mechanicall, Touching the Spring of Air' of 1660 are perhaps the best known. Ten years later, his 'New Pneumatical Experiments about Respiration' make more gruesome reading, particularly to those who willingly immerse themselves in water. Using a vacuum pump to extract air from a 'Pneumatical Receiver', Boyle studied the effects of asphyxiation on birds, snakes, kittens, fish, ducks and rodents. In 1670 he published 'A Comparison of the Times Wherein Animals May Be Kill'd by Drowning, or Withdrawing of the Air'.

For these experiments, Boyle describes tying metal weights to a greenfinch and 'gently' letting it down into a glass filled with water. Boyle writes, 'at the end of half a minute, the strugglings of the bird seeming finished, he was nimbly drawn up again, but found quite dead'. Unsurprisingly, even a 'lusty sparrow' could stand no more than half a minute underwater, prompting Boyle to try his luck with a waterfowl, hoping for greater things. Although ducks seemed designed by nature to cope with immersion better than land birds, disappointingly, 'even this water bird was not able to live in cold water above six minutes; which is but a tenth of an hour'.

Boyle injects a note of compassion into some of the attempts at resuscitation made upon his animal subjects. A newborn kitten, having been reduced to convulsions in a glass jar without air and finally lapsing into unconsciousness, is revived: 'To allow him the benefit of his good fortune, we sent for a Kitling of the same age and litter, which being put into the same Receiver, quickly began to have convulsions, after which he lay as dead.' Again, the kitten is reprieved, and brought back to sensibility by some 'pinching'. The third kitten fares worse, since Boyle explains he had grown 'diffident' after several sessions with the animals. 'When 7 minutes from the beginning of the exhaustion were completed, we let in the Air; upon which the little creature that seemed stark dead before, made us suspect that he might recover, but though we took him out of the Receiver, and put Aqua Vitae into his mouth, yet he irrecoverably died in our hands.'

Frogs and birds suffered suspension in the vacuum chamber whilst partially dissected, alive, with their lungs and hearts exposed so that Boyle could observe the vital organs in the moments leading up to asphyxiation. With the benefit of hindsight it is easy to find such early experimentation grotesque, but at the time, the scientific laws which we take for granted were in their infancy. Remarkably, as the founding fathers of modern science began to publish their findings, there was still no knowledge of the precise components of air. The discovery of oxygen would not follow for a hundred years, but this did not hold up the progress of the diving bell.

While Boyle and Hooke were experimenting with the effects of reduced-air environments, their junior, Edmund Halley, was about to begin his own distinguished career. Immortalized for his accurate prediction of the return of a comet in 1687 which had last been seen in 1608, he worked closely with Newton on the problems of celestial mechanics. In retrospect, Halley's true genius lay in his ability to put large amounts of scientific information into meaningful order. In 1691, he lodged a patent for an improved diving bell, the details of which were not publicly described until he produced a paper for an edition of *Philosophical Transactions* in 1716.

Halley's paper, 'The Art of Living Underwater', sets out the problems as he saw them of the bells constructed at the time. Bells were in use in shallow water throughout Europe, and there had been several notable cases of salvage in recent years. They were successfully used in 1664 to recover cannons from the great Swedish flagship *Vasa*, which toppled over in spectacular fashion at its launch in 1628. Such bells were small and heavy, with barely enough space for a man to work from. Halley was keen to improve on the system, which involved hauling the diver and his bell all the way to the surface in order to replenish the air inside the container. He proposed a method whereby barrels of fresh air could be lowered to the bell, and emptied into it by means of a hose. Stale air would be let out from the top end of the bell through a stopcock. He tells us that air in an enclosed space loses its 'vivifying spirit', and wisely states that he will not go into the precise physiological reasons for this, leaving that to the 'curious anatomist, to whom the structure of the lungs is better understood'. But Halley does understand that current models of diving bells contained only a small amount of air, and while it had been proposed to pump fresh air into them from the surface, the strength of the pumps available at the time was not sufficient to overcome the pressure at depths of more than fifteen feet or so. The deeper a bell descended, the smaller the air space that would be left in which to breathe, as the water pressure would compress the air inside the bell.

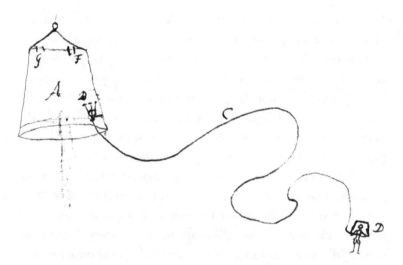

D. In the hope of discovering sunken treasure, Edmund Halley perfected a workable diving bell which he patented discreetly in 1691. His own ink sketch of the design appears in a letter to a fellow member of the Royal Society.

Edmund Halley's bell was bigger and more stable than those of his contemporaries, and he further proposed that a diver might make excursions from the bell wearing a miniature bell on his head. What he suggested was a primitive diving helmet, which would be attached by a leather pipe to the larger bell, although even in 1716 he does not reveal the precise details of this device.

Unlike other scientific brains of the age, Halley tested his improved diving bell himself, descending into the waters of Pagham Harbour in Sussex in the summer of 1691. According to his own account, Halley sat on a bench suspended across the lower reaches of the bell and remained dry except for his shoes. Noting the effects of increased air pressure as the bell descends, he describes the physical sensations produced on the Eustachian tubes during the dive:

The only inconvenience that attends [the descent] is found in the ears, within which there are cavities opening only outwards, and that by pores so small as not to give admission even to the air itself, unless they be dilated and distended by considerable force. Hence, a pressure begins to be felt on each ear, which by degrees grows painful, like as if a quill were forcibly thrust into the hole of the ear; till at length, the force overcoming the obstacle, that which constrains these pores yields to the pressure, and letting some condensed air slip in, present ease ensues.

We know that Halley made several dives inside his bell, and he records using an 'iron pen' to scratch notes upon plates of lead, as well as being able to use a candle to see what he was doing, even though on clear days a glass window in the top of the bell provided sufficient light to read and work by. He also reported the effect of depth upon the colour spectrum, relating the curious phenomenon of blood from a cut finger appearing green rather than red once the diver was sufficiently deep underwater. At thirty-three feet of depth underwater Edmund Halley knew that atmospheric pressure was double that at the surface, since the volume of air within his bell decreased by half at that depth. With each thirty-three feet of immersion an extra atmosphere of pressure is added, so that at sixty-six feet the diver is under the effect of three atmospheres, and of four atmospheres at ninety-nine feet.

Halley's design was patented in 1691, so it is clear that he was working on the idea for at least twenty-five years before he chose to expound on the design in *Philosophical Transactions*. In his patent application it is described as 'a certain new Engine or Instrument never hitherto knowne or practised', even though this was obviously untrue. It is possible that Halley's sea voyages in the South Atlantic, undertaken in order to make astronomical observations, may have made him familiar with the possibilities of underwater recovery. Halley was certainly not the first to publish his findings on bells, but his bell was state of the art, and he proposed that it would be useful in engineering tasks such as the laying of under-water foundations, as well as for the businesses of sponge or pearl diving. Curiously, he does not mention the possibility of hunting for treasure.

Since the recovery of treasure or valuable ironware from ship-wrecks was a lucrative industry, it is likely that many such projects were conducted in secrecy at the time. Halley's exploits in Pagham Harbour are known to have been connected with an attempt to recover the cargo of a merchant ship, and his diving-bell patent was taken out in partnership with three wealthy associates, his financial backers. It seems highly probable that Halley, like many men of the time, was inspired to enter the diving industry by the remarkable adventures of Captain William Phips. His tale is a fantastic adventure, a genuine treasure hunt which had set polite society alight with the prospect of untold riches to be recovered from the seabed.

The Spanish treasure ship *Nuestra Señora de la Pura y Limpia Concepción* left Havana in 1641 as part of a fleet carrying silver and gold from the colonies in South America. The passage from Vera Cruz had already damaged a number of vessels in the fleet, and on a shallow reef off the island of Hispaniola (now the Dominican Republic and Haiti), the *Nuestra Señora* foundered and sank, spilling her five hundred passengers and crew, as well as her bullion, into the water. In 1685, William Phips, an adventurer from New England, mounted an expedition to find the treasure. Rumours were circulat-ing that bullion ships had been lost in the area known as Ambergris Bank, and several sea captains had obtained financial backing from London to find the treasure. They failed. Phips, although not well connected socially, was a persuasive talker, and against the odds obtained backing and a ship from Charles II. Returning to Hispaniola he based himself in Puerto de la Plata, the main port. Letting it be

known that he could pay for reliable information, Phips managed
to find an aged Spanish sailor who was a survivor of the shipwreck.
For a fee, the old man gave Phips as much information as he could
remember about where the ship had gone down.

In 1685 Phips failed to discover the *Nuestra Señora* or its treasure,
and returned to London in the hope of finding more funds. Charles
II had died in the interim, and Phips was forced to mount his sales
campaign afresh, finding a ready ear in Samuel Pepys, then Secretary
of the Admiralty. With cash from the Duke of Albemarle, and
Pepys convinced of his talents, Phips was able to obtain two fresh
ships from the new king, James II, whose outfitting would in part
be paid for by trading cargo in the Caribbean islands *en route* to
Hispaniola.

Using Puerto de la Plata as their base, Phips and his men built
wooden pirogues with which to sail around the treacherous shallows
in search of the wreck. In February 1687, and after almost a month
of searching, the story goes that one of Phips's crew spotted a
particularly pretty 'sea-feather' (probably a fan coral), which he
despatched a native diver to retrieve. The diver reported that the
coral was attached to a strangely shaped piece of reef, which upon
being hauled to the surface with ropes turned out to be a pile of
silver coins. A contemporary of Phips, the writer Cotton Mather,
described the size of the hoard:

Upon further diving, the Indian fetcht up a Sow, as they stil'd it, or a
lump of Silver worth perhaps two or three hundred Pounds . . . and they
so prospered in this New Fishery, that in a little while they had, without
the loss of any man's life, brought up Thirty-Two Tuns of Silver; for it
was now come to measuring of Silver by Tuns.

Much of the silver bullion was caked in coral growth, which
concealed not just silver, but gold, jewels and pearls. For almost

two months, Phips and his crew of native skin divers scavenged the wreck. In June 1687, Phips returned to London with a staggering thirty-two tons of treasure. Investors who had put up one hundred pounds each for the expedition as part of the Duke of Albemarle's company earned a share of the cargo, which totalled almost a quarter of a million pounds.

For William Phips, one of twenty-six children from a poor New England family, the treasure was better than a winning lottery ticket. His life changed, and he became Sir William, first Sheriff, then Governor of New England. King James, too, had shared in the treasure.

The discovery of what became known as the Duke of Albemarle's treasure was to have huge repercussions for the diving industry. Although Phips had used native divers, who retrieved the treasure by skin diving and attaching rope to the lumps of coral crust, a feverish hunt for the perfect design of diving bells began.

The craze for treasure hunting and for investing in treasure expeditions set in, especially since it was known that Phips had left a hoard of gold too heavy to be hauled into his wooden canoes on Ambergris Shoal. Although he returned to the site, word had spread and he found the area awash with prospectors.

In 1695, a pamphlet appeared in London as a direct result of the continuing business in attracting investment in inventions geared towards prospecting for treasure. The pamphlet is anonymous, produced by a 'person of honour', according to the printers, and entitled 'Angliae Tutamen: Or, the Safety of England'. The author rails against the various get-rich-quick schemes abroad at the time, especially the 'diving engines of diverse kinds, all crept abroad since the taking up of Albemarle's Wreck'. The pamphleteer enumerates the types of devices which will allegedly result in success under water:

Some like a Bell, others a Tub, some like a compleat suit of Armour of Copper, and Leather between the joynts, and Pipes to convey Wind, and a Polyphemous Eye in the Forehead to give Light.

'Angliae Tutamen' warns specifically against the squandering of monies in such schemes, which this person of honour regards as a dangerous waste of the nation's assets. Stating that Phips's divers had been 'naked' rather than equipped with elaborate mechanical contraptions, the author warns that most of the inventions trumpeted were ineffective, designed solely to attract shareholders' funds:

These fine Diving-Engines lie by the walls, are at rest, and for ought I know may never more disturb the world with their Noise and Nonsense. 'Tis strange when we reflect what abundance of people have been drawn in . . . allured with the Hopes of gaining vast Riches, by this means.

Strange or not, the number of diving engines and those willing to step inside them was greater than ever. In the eighteenth century, as commerce by sea steadily increased, the usefulness and value of the successful diver would become firmly established.

In addition to the bell, the eighteenth century would see the invention of the so-called 'diving barrel', a brave use of watertight wooden or copper casks into which a man would be sealed and lowered in a horizontal position to the seabed. Poking his arms through watertight holes tied tight by short leather cuffs, it would be possible to salvage objects from the sea floor just as long as the diver had air enough inside the barrel to breathe. The drawback of the barrel system was that if a leak were sprung, rapid death followed, although at least two Englishmen succeeded in achieving heroic deeds with the barrel. One man, John Lethbridge of Newton Abbot, stands out as the most successful.

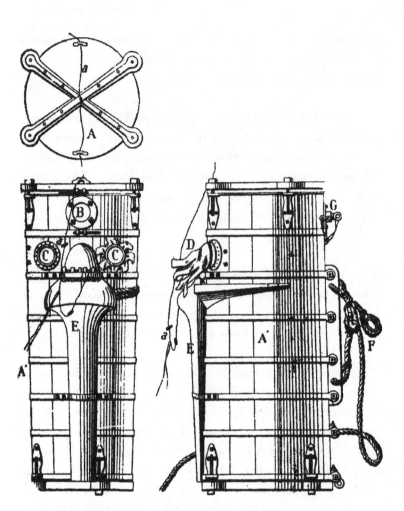

E. In 1715, John Lethbridge of Devon sealed himself into a 'diving barrel' made from a hogshead reinforced with iron bands. A glass porthole, 'B', and two holes for his arms, 'C', allowed him to work underwater as long as there was air inside the barrel.

In 1715, timing his experiment to coincide with a solar eclipse in Devon, Lethbridge had himself sealed into a hogshead (fifty-four-gallon) barrel for half an hour, to prove that it was airtight and that he could survive on the air contained within it. From this he developed a design of wooden cask in which he could lie on his chest, poking his arms out through tight leather sleeves, whilst viewing the seabed through a small glass port. So successful was the format that between 1715 and 1743 (when he was almost seventy), he dived on wrecks in the British Isles, France, Holland, South Africa and the Cape Verde Islands.

Lethbridge's wooden barrel was just six feet long, two and a half feet in diameter at the head, and eighteen inches at the foot. The barrel would be suspended from a ship by means of a rope, and the diver would signal to the surface by pulling on a line dangling within reach. Lethbridge is known to have stayed in the barrel as long as six hours on occasion, and to have reached a maximum depth of around seventy feet. He formed a partnership with another successful barrel diver, Jacob Rowe, and in 1720 the two men successfully raised twenty-seven chests of silver for the East India Company from a wreck in the Scottish Firth of Forth. Successive lucrative dives in the treacherous waters off Cape Verde, West Africa, confirmed Lethbridge and Rowe's reputation. In Table Bay, at the Cape of Good Hope, Lethbridge worked for the Dutch East India Company in the 1730s and 1740s and, according to family records, salvaged at least sixteen major shipwrecks in his long career. In spite of the hazards, Lethbridge lived to be eighty-three and is thought to have recovered over a hundred thousand pounds' worth of salvage (equivalent to more than eight million pounds today) during his lifetime.

For most salvage projects, however, the diving bell continued to be the engine of choice. In *Philosophical Transactions* Halley revealed the secret of his breathing-tube extension device, hinted at in his paper of 1716. He describes the construction of pipes which would lead out from the air space in the main bell to a diver's 'cap of lead'. In the days before rubber, he describes how air pipes could be made from a coiled brass wire coated with thin glove leather dipped in hot oil and beeswax. To complete the seal, 'several folds of sheep's guts' were drawn over the pipes and painted, before a final coating of leather was applied to stop the pipes chafing. Improvements to Halley's original design were also suggested by Martin Triewald, who used a bell over a period of years in Sweden. In 1732, Triewald described a system which placed a 'spiral tube of copper' around the interior of the bell, to which was attached an ivory mouthpiece. The inhabitant of the bell would suck on the tube when he felt the air around his head becoming too hot for comfort, thus breathing air from the lower reaches of the bell, which would hopefully be somewhat less stale. A Scots diver named Charles Spalding is credited with adding a weight which hung directly below the bell, acting as ballast. By means of a pulley, the occupants of the bell could raise and lower the weight, adjusting their buoyancy according to requirements. Although a successful salvor for almost a decade, Spalding perished in 1783 along with his son while working on an Irish wreck, asphyxiated by stale air.

The basic principle of the diving bell would not change, and improvements in design for the simple bell culminated in the work of John Smeaton, another stalwart of the Royal Society, and the founder of the Society of Civil Engineers. In the latter half of the century, he would attach a reliable pump to a square bell to make it a safer and more efficient device, and use it to shift heavy blocks during the construction of Ramsgate Harbour. Smeaton's genius was to add a one-way valve to the air pipe, which prevented the bell flooding if the air supply failed. By constructing a square bell, he had effectively produced a caisson, a dry working space which allowed men to operate in a compressed-air environment. Unfortunately, the air pumps available to Smeaton were too weak to allow the bell-caisson to operate deeper than a few feet.

The diving bell was still in use, with further refinements, at the beginning of the twentieth century, but for divers the comparative lack of mobility of the bell was a major drawback. It was also heavy, and needed considerable manpower to operate it, as well as only being suitable for shallow depths. The dawning century would see a degree of liberation from these constraints with the advent of the diving helmet, allowing men to walk around underwater connected to a surface ship by air hose.

Today, people who cannot even swim can experience life underwater by wearing a type of miniature bell placed over their head and fed with an air hose from a surface pump. This specially designed helmet, like a bell-jar, sits on the diver's shoulders, while excess air bubbles out under its lip, keeping the wearer's head and neck completely dry. In some tourist destinations there are companies offering 'reef-walking' tours, where such devices allow people to have a brief taste of the undersea world. For several years in Seychelles there was one such operation, calling itself 'Jules Verne's Undersea Walk', and the company would allow its customers to stand on a shallow sandy area of an enclosed bay and watch the reef fish, some of which could be encouraged to swim up to the 'diver' with the offer of a handful of breadcrumbs. Such a system obviates the dangers of breathing compressed air, and it requires no specialized training, merely the ability to stand upright and walk across the sand.

In Phuket, in Thailand, a similar type of tourist operation has caused damage to the coral reefs. Reef 'walkers' using the bubble helmets and wearing weight belts to keep them upright are unable to control their buoyancy, and have been allowed to stroll across the coral in some areas, bumping and breaking the fragile structures which they have come to see. It is as though visitors to a garden have gone trampling through a flowerbed in hobnail boots in order to take a closer look at the blooms. On a grander scale we treat coral and the coral reefs of the world with equal disdain.

I have seen green coral as bright as a fine piece of carved jade held up to the light. And I have seen it scarlet as a humming-bird feather or gentle blushing pink like the petals of a carnation in a buttonhole. There is coral with the pale tone of a golden Inca mask and some with exactly the hue of dried lavender. In plates, in tubes, with sharp horns or a head as bulbous as a hooded mushroom, it clusters together on the reef, each species a colonial organism varying in appearance according to its location, depth and the condition of the water around it. Massive, columnar, encrusting, branching and foliaceous are its forms. Some species are aggressive to their neighbours, putting out sweeper tentacles to sting other colonies or simply spreading themselves on to another coral, smothering it. The slow-growing and massive corals are more resilient to storm damage and predation by fish and turtles, while the fast-growing, more fragile colonies are like some underwater hedge, thriving on the pruning they receive when an ocean storm sends the waves crashing on to them. Coral is a sensate collection of individual animals, small polyps sitting in a limestone case which they build by secretion. The hard, bleached coral for sale at souvenir stalls is the skeleton of the living colony. When alive, the polyps emerge to feed on nutrients carried by the sea, including bacteria. Some corals use stinging cells to catch worms or even small fish, while many species rely on algae (*zooxanthellae*) living within the polyps to process sunlight and carbon dioxide off which the coral feeds. If sea temperatures rise too high, killing the *zooxanthellae*, the coral expels the algae and loses its colour. Eventually, unless conditions recover, the coral itself dies, bleached as bones in a desert and prey to a dirty brown carpet of algae similar to something found growing around a sewage outfall.

These fragile places, the tropical reefs which mostly lie between latitudes 30° North and 30° South, cover less than two per cent of the ocean floor. And yet a quarter of all the species of the world's oceans live upon the reefs. Environmental pressures such as chemical and sewage run-off from the land are damaging the world's corals at a terrifying pace, with as much as half of the reefs in the world expected to be at biological crisis point within twenty years.

I once watched a coconut palm which had fallen into the sea smash into a shallow reef with the incoming tide. Like a pile driver, it was driven against the reef with the force of an oceanic battering ram, snapping, grinding and clearing a channel through the coral in minutes. Underwater, I have often watched a family group of the giant bump-headed parrotfish (*Bolbometopon muricatum*) pass over an Indian Ocean reef like a herd of grazing bison. These fish, almost four feet long and with large crowned foreheads, have formidable teeth which are fused into a beak, like a parrot, which they use to bite chunks of coral. As they pass by they excrete copious streams of crushed coral, a sprinkling of fine sand which is all that remains of the limestone coral skeleton when it has been crushed by grinding plates in the fishes' throats. Naturally destructive processes such as these are part of the coral's life cycle, no more calamitous in the long term than the natural pruning of foliage by an elephant in the African bush.

The collection of coral for souvenirs, careless touching of it underwater and trampling upon it are evils visited upon the reef by man. One day, while diving in the Indian Ocean, I watched a yacht drop its anchor on to a patch of staghorn coral. Where the anchor fell it made a neat hole no more than a couple of feet in diameter, a plug neatly drilled into the forest of coral branches. As the boat moved gently at anchor and the occupants lay sunbathing on deck, the wind strengthened fractionally. I watched the anchor chain flex and bow as the boat above began to drift. The hole around the anchor began to widen, and I could hear a snapping, rustling sound as the fine branches of coral were broken off. In a few minutes a path a yard wide and a hundred feet long had been cut through the coral, a neat tramway of destruction unseen by the sailors above. Then the anchor snagged on a brain coral, a huge round ball with a tracery of fine patterned lines resembling the lines on the surface of the human cortex. This obstacle, perhaps twelve feet high and with a girth twice that, was too much for the small anchor to snap. The anchor dragged upwards and over the brain coral, scarring its surface with a broad band where its steel talons clawed against it like a razor slashed across a face in a bar-room brawl. Eventually, the sailors hauled in their anchor and I watched it spiralling upwards on the end of its chain. As it rose, a cloud of coral fragments fell through the water below it. The staghorn coral would recover from this assault, perhaps, in as little as twenty years. Later, a marine biologist told me she thought the brain coral was at least a thousand years old.

Ever since Jules Verne gave life to the character of Captain Nemo, fictional adventurers have made us familiar with the concept of the diving helmet. With his head inside the upturned copper 'goldfish bowl', the diver peers at the outside world through a small round plate-glass porthole, and his body is enveloped in a bulky canvas suit. On his feet, leaden pattens weigh him down, while behind him he trails the vital air hose connected to the surface. The air supply is maintained from the deck of the boat above by a pumping wheel turned by a brawny crewman. Just like an astronaut on the surface of the moon, the deep-sea diver moves slowly around his alien environment, his movements exaggerated and cumbersome. It is an image which survived for over a hundred years, and persists, although there are now just a handful of copper-helmet divers left around the world.

In *The Uncommercial Traveller*, Charles Dickens described the work of deep-sea divers 'in grotesque dress' whom he had seen at the site of the wreck of the *Royal Charter* at Anglesey in 1859. The story had all the ingredients the great reporter needed, melodrama from the loss of five hundred souls in a fierce winter storm within sight of land, and the subsequent recovery of a hoard of gold ingots by brave divers from the wreckage. In 1897, London's Theatre Royal staged *The White Heather*, featuring an underwater duel between the play's hero, Dick Beach, and the villain, Lord Angus Cameron, both wearing deep-sea-diving equipment. The play drew large audiences for almost one hundred performances, and was successfully revived the following year, with playgoers spellbound at the death of Cameron, his air hose slashed by the hero's diving knife. By then, the Victorian public had been exposed to the exploits of real-life diving heroes such as Alexander Lambert, who had recovered the vast majority of gold bullion from the 1885 wreck of the *Alphonso XII* in the Canaries. Lambert was acclaimed as the bravest diver of the time, a bull of a man who travelled the world to attempt salvage jobs other men refused. He is said to have captured a tiger shark underwater in the Indian Ocean, and in 1880 crawled several hundred feet down the flooded workings of the Severn Tunnel to seal a jammed sluice gate. Meanwhile, the popular Victorian magazine *The Illustrated London News* astounded readers with gruesome tales of divers recovering corpses from under the ice after a skating accident in Regent's Park, and of the miraculous recovery of stolen watches thrown over Blackfriars Bridge by a thief attempting to hide the evidence of her crime. Helmeted divers braving the murky waters made good copy, and provided great scope for newspaper illustrators.

The value of the helmet diver as a dramatic hero persisted. Less

THE GRAPHIC

AN ILLUSTRATED WEEKLY NEWSPAPER

No. 1,452—Vol. LVI.
Registered as a Newspaper.

SATURDAY, SEPTEMBER 25, 1897

THIRTY-TWO PAGES

Price Sixpence
By Post, 6½d.

LORD ANGUS CAMERON AND DICK BEACH FIGHT FOR THE POSSESSION OF THE MARRIAGE RECORD ON THE SUNKEN YACHT

"THE WHITE HEATHER" AT THE THEATRE ROYAL, DRURY LANE

DRAWN BY W. HATHERELL, R.I.

F. In 1897, audiences flocked to the Theatre Royal to see The White Heather, *a melodrama featuring deep-sea divers, a breed who already personified the ideal of Victorian adventurers.*

than fifty years after Victorian audiences gasped at the sight of Dick Beach, Hergé's iconic cartoon character, Tin Tin, wore standard diving dress in the hunt for Red Rackham's treasure. For a time, the feature-film industry contrived to insert everyone from John Wayne to Bob Hope into a diving helmet, with varying degrees of dramatic or comic success. The diver in his hard hat was a knight in armour battling the sea and whatever monsters it might contain. The dramatic possibilities were endless. No sooner was the diver on the seabed than the giant tentacle of a monstrous octopus would snake out and grasp him, a tentacle which would usually be hacked off with the help of a large knife, the diver's most useful tool. Giant clams would enclose the unwary diver's boot, pinning him to the seabed while a hungry shark circled in the background. If nature did not supply the threat, then an entanglement of the air hose would provide the drama. Or, unbeknown to the diver, the audience would see something happen to the man pumping him air, a fight on deck or an attack on the boat, forcing him to abandon his station at the revolving wheel.

Helmet or hard-hat diving is what we think of when we hear the phrase 'deep-sea diver'. The helmet system is still used today, although the modern hat is a lightweight affair, with none of the visual appeal of the burnished-copper domes which caught the imagination of Victorian authors and, later on, Hollywood directors. Before astronauts made space the final frontier, the deep-sea diver was the archetypal hero.

Like almost every aspect of the development of modern diving technology, the right to claim the invention of helmets has been subject to dispute. Lawsuits were launched and patents registered to prove ownership of the various systems proposed to allow a man to breathe underwater. Edmund Halley registered the patent for his diving bell long before he published details of its design, and John Lethbridge and Jacob Rowe are said to have gone into partnership so as to avoid legal disputes over their diving barrels.

The first man to build a bell, barrel or helmet and use it successfully may never be accurately determined. In the scheme of things it may not matter much, since history is apt to recognize those who apply new technology, rather than conceive it, particularly if they turn the invention into a commercial success. The refinement of the diving-helmet system is no different.

The first helmets were simply miniature bells, placed over the head and resting on the diver's shoulders. The advantage of a diving helmet is that it overcomes the problem of breathing through a tube clamped between the teeth and sucking air from the surface. If the diver's head is enclosed in its own air space (a rigid helmet), the pressure of the surrounding water has no effect on the air within it. Air can then be supplied through a tube to the helmet, and as long as the air pipe is reliable, the air needs only to be pumped into it at sufficient strength to overcome the surrounding water pressure. The insertion of a glass window, and the addition of an air feed supplied by a bellows, were just adaptations of the ancient technique of sending an urn down to a free-swimming diver on the sea bed. Like the urn and the diving bell, the first helmets were open at the neck, allowing excess air to escape under the rim in a stream of bubbles. To keep the water level from rising within the helmet as the diver went deeper, the pressure of the air being pumped from the surface would have to be increased. The drawback of the open design was that once the diver bent forward (or fell over) the air inside could escape, and he could easily drown.

As early as 1774, a diving helmet that allowed a man to walk around freely underwater was demonstrated in front of the King of Sweden. Few details exist of how the device worked, but it was likely to have been a waterproofed dress of leather, supplied with air from the surface through a leather pipe. The early pipes were constructed in the same way as those described by Halley a hundred

G. On the Baltic coast at Barth, Peter Kreeft used his leather diving suit as early as 1800; the diver was supplied with air from a pair of hand bellows.

years before, oiled leather tubes kept open by an internal brass coil. A similar means of construction was applied to form a headgear of waterproofed leather in several early attempts at a helmet. By 1775, in Paris, Fréminet had invented what he termed a 'hydrostatergatic machine' which allowed him to walk underwater, again a leather jerkin and integral hood moulded around a metal frame. The same technique allowed the German diver Peter Kreeft to demonstrate yet another version of the same idea off the Baltic coast of Mecklenburg in 1800. Once again, the King of Sweden was witness to the latest diving invention, which, according to a friend of Kreeft, was 'not among those castles in the air which some inventors work so hard at building'. Kreeft's helmet and leather jacket were sewn together, protecting the diver from the frigid waters of the Baltic.

One spectacular-looking diving suit, tested on the River Oder in 1797 by another German, Klingert, went so far as to claim that the diver could carry with him a reservoir of air rendering him partially independent of the air supplied through the always suspect leather pipes. Klingert's device aimed to protect the diver's body in a metal cuirass, leaving the arms and legs free to move. The snag with this system is, of course, that those parts of the body not contained within the air-filled portion of the dress are subject to the effects of water pressure, and the differential between the compressed air inside the helmet and the rest of the body results in a 'squeeze', preventing the diver going much beyond fifty feet. So, as the diver descends, the parts of his body not inside the helmet are subjected to greater pressure than those within. The same effects hindered the barrel divers cocooned in their wooden caskets; their arms, operating outside the barrel, were squeezed painfully by hydrostatic pressure, effectively limiting the ultimate depth to which the divers could descend. The solution to the problem is to increase the pressure of air being pumped to the

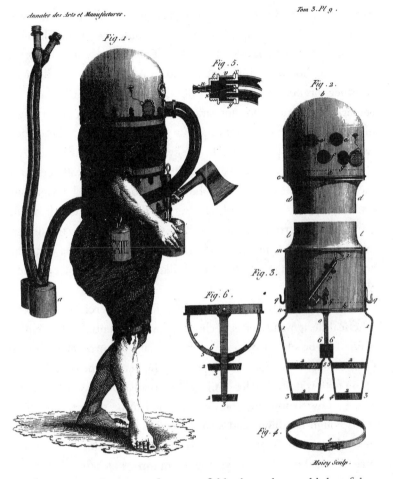

Annales des Arts et Manufactures .   *Tom 3. Pl. 9 .*

Fig. 1.   *Fig. 5.*   *Fig. 2.*   *Fig. 3.*   *Fig. 6 .*   *Fig. 4.*

Moisy Sculp .

*H. In 1797, a diving suit of waterproofed leather and a metal helmet fed
with air from the surface was demonstrated by Klingert in the River Oder.*

diver's helmet so that it equates to and compensates for the water
pressure on the rest of the body.

Diving suits of various designs proliferated between 1770 and
1820. Fréminet in Paris, Klingert, Schultes and Kreeft in Germany,
and Tonkin and James in England all produced apparatus which

may have worked adequately in shallow water. In America, there are reports of a suit capable of a forty-minute dive being demonstrated in Philadelphia as early as 1819. Copper body sheaths, brass reinforcing hoops, leather jerkins and iron helmets were all tried. Another Frenchman, Frédéric de Drieberg, designed a device remarkably similar in appearance to the modern scuba set, incorporating a metal air cylinder worn on the back. The device was supposed to pump air into the cylinder from a pair of bellows also on the diver's back. The bellows handle was affixed to a metallic crown, which could be pulled to and fro by vigorous nodding of the diver's head, causing the bellows to suck air down a tube leading from the surface. Known as the Triton, the device may have worked, but required its operator to keep up a constant and tiring nodding motion not dissimilar to the actions of a pecking chicken.

To produce a working diving helmet for commercial use, a more practical design and better technology were essential. The helmet needed to be attached to a waterproof suit, to protect the diver from cold and abrasion, and to prevent the peril of the open helmet filling with water at angles of tilt greater than about twenty degrees. The air hoses supplying the diver needed to be robust enough to stand rough handling, and strong enough to contain air pumped through them at great pressure. To overcome the increasing pressure as the diver descended, the air pumps themselves had to be efficient and strong.

Stronger air pumps, waterproof cloth and a decent metal helmet which could be attached to the suit only became possible in the nineteenth century, as engineering and machining skills improved with the Industrial Revolution. The most successful application of innovative technology was the adaptation of a fire-fighter's leather smoke helmet for use underwater. Using prototype helmets, Charles and John Deane, two brothers from Deptford on the

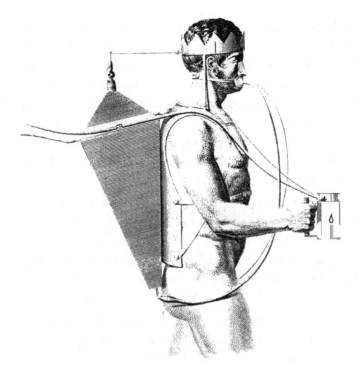

LE TRITON

I. Frédéric de Drieberg's 'Triton' required the diver to draw air into his tank from the surface by nodding his head in a metal crown which was connected to a pair of bellows.

Thames, began salvage diving in the 1820s. By 1829 they were able to put them to good use to salvage the wreck of the *Carn Brea Castle*, which had sunk off the Isle of Wight with a cargo of copper. The successful recovery of the cargo brought them to the attention of Lloyd's underwriters and several years of profitable work in diving salvage followed. Charles Deane, the original inventor of the smoke helmet design, had sold his patent to his employer Edward Barnard, and together they had tried to interest the Admiralty in the design. The Admiralty did not see the usefulness of the idea, and for a time the invention was set aside, although several diving helmets were manufactured for the Deanes by the London gunsmith Augustus Siebe. Following a number of successful commercial salvage dives, Charles Deane finally obtained a contract to dive on the wreck of the *Royal George*, which was causing a hazard to shipping at Spithead, Portsmouth.

The *Royal George,* like the great *Vasa* in Stockholm (1628), was a casualty of peacetime, having capsized in 1782 while being repaired of a minor leak. Ironically, the ship was a veteran of several battles against the French, and was Admiral Kempenfeldt's flagship. A thousand people died when she sank, including a large number of women and children who had been visiting the ship in port, making the disaster one of the greatest maritime tragedies in British history. The loss of the *Royal George* stunned the nation, and was a serious blow to the Royal Navy. One of only three one-hundred-gun ships of the line, she had been due to sail for Gibraltar, which was under siege by Spain. The ship's loss was immortalized in art and literature of the time, as well as in a poem by William Cowper:

Toll for the brave —
The brave! That are no more;
All sunk beneath the wave,
Fast by their native shore.

A land-breeze shook the shrouds,
And she was overset;
Down went the Royal George,
With all her crew complete.

Apart from the loss of life, and ship, the *Royal George* was a major hazard to the crucial naval base at Spithead, home of the British fleet. In death, her hulk would be a menace to the fleet for over half a century. She sat in sixty feet of water, fouling anchor lines and posing a serious threat to shipping manoeuvres at the port. Explosives and grappling hooks failed to clear the wreckage from the harbour. In the summer of 1832, Charles Deane dived on the *Royal George* using improved equipment made by the Siebe Company. Over the course of several summers, Deane managed to retrieve thirty of the ship's valuable guns.

By now, an important addition to the diver's suit had come in the form of waterproof canvas, thanks to the patented design of Charles Macintosh. It had been developed as a result of a chance discovery by a Scottish medical student named James Syme, who published an account of what he called 'a valuable substance which may be obtained from coal tar' in 1818. The substance was naphtha, and when mixed with melted India rubber it made a liquid which could be painted on to cloth. This rubber solution could be sandwiched between two layers of canvas to make a waterproof diving suit, or indeed a Macintosh raincoat. Years afterwards, Syme was to remark that his discovery gained him 'little credit and no profit, except the confidence which results from struggling with a difficulty'. The Macintosh process of waterproofing was phenomenally successful, and a precursor to the more versatile process of vulcanization. By 1857, the Macintosh company was advertising vulcanized rubber items in its nautical collection, including a diving dress remarkably similar in appearance to a modern diving suit. Other rubber products included inflatable boat cloaks, life belts and all types of foul-weather gear.

Using Macintosh's patented material, a canvas suit could be attached to a diving helmet by means of a neck plate, or corselet. Holes in the neck of the diving suit fitted over bolts or studs in the corselet and then a flange made of copper would be placed over the studs, trapping the suit material between it and the corselet. A washer, originally made of leather, went between the metal corselet and the helmet which was in turn screwed on to bolts on the corselet. To provide stability underwater, a pair of forty-pound leaden weights were hung over the corselet, back and front. This arrangement produced the 'closed diving dress', production of which fell to the firm of Augustus Siebe, an immigrant German engineer and gunsmith living in England. Siebe improved upon the Deanes' original design, perfecting rubber cuffs for the diving suits which made a watertight seal and allowed the diver to adopt any position underwater.

Work on the wreck of the *Royal George* was to inspire further advances in diving, when the task of finally removing her guns and timbers from the seabed was entrusted to Colonel (later Lieutenant General) Charles Pasley, a military engineer from the Corps of

J. Salvage work on the Royal George *at Spithead was the proving ground for the modern diving dress.*

Royal Sappers and Miners. Under instructions from the Admiralty, who were weary of civilian contractors promising much and delivering little, Pasley took command of the operation to clear the seabed. In 1839, using soldiers, not sailors, he set about systematically demolishing the wreck, a task which would not be complete until 1845. Throughout the process, not a single diver was killed, although several were injured badly enough to prevent them diving again. Basic safety procedures, such as divers operating in pairs, and the regularization of an effective system of rope signals were laid down by Pasley's team, and his methods led to the establishment of the first naval school of diving.

Systematic improvements to the original Deane designs for diving helmets were carried out during the intervening years, and having established its credentials on the *Royal George*, it was to the firm of Augustus Siebe that the Admiralty turned for manufacture. Siebe, later Siebe-Gorman, would be established as the pre-eminent manufacturers of diving equipment in the world. Testimonials from treasure seekers and salvors adorn the early Siebe equipment catalogues, literature which describes the proprietor as 'the father of the diving dress and helmet', and points out the firm's position as sole contractors to the British Admiralty for diving apparatus. By the turn of the century, Siebe would be supplying diving equipment not only to the British Navy but also to many others, including the navies of Russia, Japan, Portugal, Spain and Italy.

For a century and a half, many of the great innovations in diving would come from the work of the firm. From rubber catheters into which the fully dressed diver could urinate, to underwater lamps and telephones, Siebe's could supply it. And they would be at the forefront of diving research in the lead up to the First and Second World Wars. Diving, submarine warfare, mining and aviation were all natural areas of expansion for the firm's expertise. The company motto was penned:

Everything for Safety Everywhere,
On the Land, at Sea, and in the Air,
Underwater and beneath the Ground,
Wherever Danger's Likely to be Found.

With the gradual perfection of the closed-dress diving helmet, man was equipped to enter the deep. Supplied with fresh air from increasingly efficient air pumps and reliable hoses, the diver was at liberty to walk around on the seabed, examining the scene through the windows in his helmet. To maintain an upright position and to overcome the buoyancy of the air-filled suit, he would wear lead weights around his neck and on his feet, as much as two hundred pounds in total, once the closed dress was devised. Within the confines of his waterproof canvas suit he wore thick woollen undergarments and was fairly well protected from the chill of immersion.

It seemed as if the barriers to deep-sea diving had been all but removed, but in many ways the voyage of discovery was just beginning. The sea had by no means been conquered, since the main physical laws governing the human body under increased pressure were yet to be understood.

Fiji, South Pacific

In the Somosomo Straits between Taveuni and Vanua Levu, I saw a banded sea snake surface for air like a living snorkel. Its stream-lined body seemed impervious to the strong currents for which the Straits are famous, and I watched it resume its exploration of the reef below me as I sank towards the shelter of an overhanging ledge covered in soft corals. Nearby on the sand another tubiform creature poked its head from its burrow, a bright blue ribbon eel

(*Rhinomuraena quaesita*), with its jaws and eyes picked out in vivid yellow and two tiny flaps like flags sticking up from the end of its snout. The flaps waved in the current and as I knelt close by the eel emerged from its home bit by bit, like the lead in a propelling pencil. Eventually it protruded several inches from its lair, a small thin creature with jaws agape, testing and tasting the current for food scraps. I could study it as long as I did not move, but when I did it disappeared backwards into the hole in a flash.

The reefs of the Straits, whose local name means clear water, belong to the *Tui Cakau*, Chief of Somosomo, and he has the right to banish divers and fishermen from the area. It is a privilege he rarely enacts, since both groups pay him for the use of his territory, either in cash or in kind. Divers come here to marvel at the luxuriant growth of soft corals fed by nutrient-rich currents and the hosts of reef fish which thrive in them.

Setting off from Taveuni in the early morning, we had passed through the 180-degree meridian which cuts through the island and the sea here. Our skipper, Tyrone, made a joke about diving tomorrow today, and said that later we would be going back to the shore yesterday. I sat up front in the wheelhouse of the diving boat as he pointed out the long, low shape of Vanua Levu in the distance to starboard, while to port there were the green forested slopes of Taveuni. The sea was flat calm, but as we headed for the reef Tyrone told me that it was almost full moon and the currents would be particularly strong. We discussed the local dive sites and he told me he was writing a book about the history of Fiji. He was proud of the islanders' warrior past, and it emerged that he hated the foreign names imposed on the reefs by visiting divers. 'Once an American journalist came here,' he lamented. 'She called one of our dive sites the "Rainbow Reef" because it had so much coloured coral and now that's all people want to see.' Tyrone had his own favourite reef, which the locals call the *Uto ni Niu*, 'Heart of the Coconut'. There, he said, there was a natural whirlpool which sometimes traps a floating coconut on its surface and keeps it there. The nut can only escape from the current if it sprouts a shoot which will stick up high enough to act as a sail to catch the wind.

Tyrone was right about the current, and as I entered the water with two other divers we were carried away from the boat at speed. Swimming down into the lee of the reef we found calm, and looked up to where thousands of fish stood headfirst into the current plucking their nourishment from its flowing larder. The reef was a parapet sheltering us from the force of the current, and swimming up to its shallow lip was to be pushed away like a leaf in the breeze.

One afternoon I took a small plane from Taveuni to Savusavu. When flying, we can sometimes look out into an unbroken expanse of sunlit blue sky. If you stare into the distance and let your eyes drift out of focus you can wrap yourself in its immensity. It is a sensation that approximates to the feeling of diving in blue water. Flying over Fiji's Koro Sea I was in that perfect space. I pressed my forehead hard against the perspex window of the aircraft until it was warm and clammy, and gazed down at the sea. The height of the aircraft flattened the waves below me and the channel was a giant quilt of blue and brown, green and grey with white wavecaps standing out in long streaks like stitches. Even on the seemingly smooth surface I could make out the lead lines like stretch marks betraying the presence of currents. As the island came into view, the fringing reef on the eastern edge of Vanua Levu decorated the sea with perfect bow-shaped breakers, tassels on the quilt. We were too high to make out the fish below the waves, but I knew they were there.

Fifty-eight minutes after landing at Savusavu I am underwater again. I have travelled from the tiny airport to the yacht-club marina in the small town and taken a fast boat out to the reef I had studied from the air. I swim down into a submarine canyon between two massive heads of plate coral beyond Lesiatheva Point and look upward towards the sky. Now I am on the other side of the blue mirror. My head is full of bisections: thoughts of under and over, yesterday and today astride the meridian, wet and dry, air and sea and flying and diving. For a moment I flip over and swim on my back and compound the topsy-turvy state of my world.

The late-afternoon light is weak underwater and there is a plankton bloom, the proliferation of microscopic life which considerably reduces the visibility. I glimpse a hammerhead shark streaking up the wall of coral, one rolling white eye socket twitching against the grey skin of its flattened head. Now there are batfish (*Platax teira*) above me, fifty or more spade-shaped silver orbs, twisting their disc-shaped bodies in the current. It is difficult to focus on an individual fish in the gathering dusk as they catch the light for a moment, then disappear. They remind me of sequins on the bead curtains sometimes seen draped across shop doorways in the tropics. This is the time of day when the sea seems on edge. The dying of the sun will usher in a changing of the guard underwater and the night feeders will come up from the depths to prowl the reef. I shiver and signal to Jack, my dive buddy, that we should return to the boat.

Late that evening I walk through Savusavu and find myself alone on the dust road leading out of town along the shoreline. The road is invisible and I must walk slowly to find my way safely home. There is no division between the sea and the night sky and pinpoints of light shimmer down low as if the stars are touching the water. As I move further along the road and away from the sounds of Savusavu town I hear voices and laughter coming across the bay. The tiny lights are not stars, but lanterns held by men and women in a hundred small fishing boats and canoes. It is the season for mackerel and the Fijians are luring them into nets with their lamps, confusing them with false moonlight.

3. Organic Gold

And one ran and filled a sponge full of vinegar, and put it on a reed, and gave him a drink, saying, Let alone; let us see whether Elias will come to take him down.

And Jesus cried with a loud voice, and gave up the ghost.

Mark 15, 36–7

Since civilization began, the sponge has been part of human life, valued for its natural absorbency, its pliability and its texture. A good-quality bath sponge can soak up eight times its volume and twenty-five times its weight in water and yet release it all when squeezed. In pottery it is still used for smoothing wet clay and in the beauty industry for applying cosmetics, while interior designers recommend it for achieving sophisticated paint effects.

It is certain that the earliest divers went in search of sponges. In the Mediterranean the creature's domestic duty was recorded by Homer, who in the *Iliad* described Hephaestos wiping the sweat from his body with a sponge, while in the *Odyssey*, Penelope's maidens used sponges to clean the dining table for her suitors. Aside from tormenting Christ on the cross, Roman centurions used sponges to prevent their metal helmets rubbing sores on their heads as they marched, and mediaeval robbers tied sponges to their feet to allow them to creep up noiselessly upon their victims.

When the modern diving helmet went into commercial production in the 1850s, it was the Mediterranean sponge divers who took it up and used it with the most disastrous consequences. Even more so than navy salvage divers, or Victorian engineers, the artisanal divers were driven by the desire for profit, and the need to dive as deep and as long as they could to bring in their cargo of soft gold. In the Greek Islands and around the Levant hundreds of divers were killed, and thousands crippled by the bends. Without access to the latest scientific theories on what caused the disease, they resorted to witchcraft and superstition to protect them underwater. On some islands divers were forbidden to eat cheese before diving, while others believed that fasting throughout the day would prevent an attack of the bends. The sight of an afflicted diver was so common in Greece that folk dances were created in which the participants dragged their limbs and beat upon their torsos, mimicking the agonizing symptoms of the bends.

The invention and perfection of the diving helmet sent sponge production into a new era. A report produced by the United States Fish Commission in 1897 stated that there was 'scarcely a civilized habitation in the country in which the sponge is not in daily use. Besides its very general employment for toilet purposes, it is utilized everywhere in the arts, trades and professions and in domestic life.'

Sponge supplies were considered so important in the early twentieth century that for many years the American government was worried that over-fishing of the natural sponge was depleting its stocks, and there was official concern that national requirements might not be met. By the outbreak of the Second World War high demand and falling natural supplies meant that all sponges sold in America were reserved for military and industrial use. So crucial were supplies of natural sponge that various countries experimented with attempts at cultivating artificial sponge beds, especially the

Japanese, who utilized captured Pacific islands as testing grounds for the technique. The process involves tying small scraps of living sponge to a rope or wire fixed to the seafloor with a weight. By choosing a lagoon with a good tidal flow of nutrients, the growth of the sponges can be accelerated, and harvesting the fully grown sponges is easier than searching for randomly seeded wild specimens.

In more peaceful times the humble sponge travelled from the poorest of Greek fishing villages to the most sumptuous bathrooms of Paris, New York and London. It was equally welcome in the servants' quarters, mopping the floor in the maid's pantry, or in hospitals, where it was used to soak up excess blood in the operating theatre. Until the advent of synthetic materials in the twentieth century there was simply no adequate substitute for the natural sponge. And yet many people still confuse the sponge with that other desiccated bathroom artefact, the loofah. The loofah is made from a gourd plant, and is dried vegetable matter, while the sponge is an animal.

The bathroom sponge is yellow, soft and fluffy when dry. The appearance is artificial: it has been killed, stripped of its skin, cleaned, bleached, dyed, trimmed and dried. Taken fresh from the sea, it has the consistency of raw liver. What we use is really the skeleton of the animal. In its natural state underwater, the sponge may be hard or soft, and almost any shade of brown, blue, green, red or yellow. Sometimes it is as black as coal. Certain types may be poisonous to the human touch and many harbour bacteria and parasites which make them inedible to fish. It passes water through its body in huge quantities, and filters the sea clean of debris, even human waste. Tiny whip-like fronds sweep water through the sponge's myriad pores, filtering everything in the liquid that passes through it and trapping whatever it wishes to eat, including 90 per cent of bacteria found in the water. The sponge has another talent unique in all of the animal kingdom. If it is passed through a sieve, or even mashed into pieces in a kitchen blender, and then replaced in salt water it will regenerate itself, slowly reforming into a functional animal.

On a deep wall in the Caribbean I saw my first large barrel sponge. After exploring a shallow reef flat, I swam down through a narrow chute which led me out on to the face of the wall. On a small ledge at the exit point of the chute I saw the sponge standing like a giant cooking pot, a brown cauldron as tall as a man and with a neck so wide I could have stepped inside.

Like most divers, I had seen many small sponges, fleshy lumps of rubbery material which seemed interesting only if they happened to shelter a small colourful crab or shrimp. I knew that, like coral, they were living organisms which could easily be harmed by the touch of a human hand, but in general they seemed so completely inert, so lifeless to the eye that I didn't look at them closely. The sponges I had seen were usually irregular balls or elongated tubes. Sometimes they were cones with slender bases standing out from the furry growth on the edge of a reef like an ear trumpet protruding from an old man's very hairy ear. Often there would be several sponges of different species growing together in a clump, one variety with long, delicate, scarlet fingers poking through another, which resembled a moth-eaten green and yellow cushion. In the bright light of a torch, the colours would come to life, often outstripping the corals and even the fish around them in their glory. But the life of the sponge itself was a mystery to me. Questions about sponges to local dive guides were generally answered in the same way: 'It's some kind of sponge, look inside and you might see a banded coral shrimp living there.' I suppose asking divers about sponges is rather like asking ornithologists about trees. Trees are the things birds sit on, not necessarily intrinsically interesting.

This large barrel sponge was different. Its bulk was impressive, its texture fascinating and the sheer magnitude of its girth bewitched me. It stood almost six feet high, and if I hovered in the water column beside it I could barely stretch my right arm from one edge of the lip to the other. The temptation to know what this knobbled brown body felt like was too strong. Throwing my principles to the bottom of the reef wall, I reached out with my fingertips to touch the sponge. The surface was smooth, velutinous and yet firm. Like the feel of cartilage under flesh.

On every successive dive I sought out these giant barrels, virtually ignoring the fish around them, content merely to hang above them peering into their maw, stretching out my arm to gauge them against the other specimens I had found. My question to the other divers at the end of a dive was inevitably the same. Did you see the size of that sponge? No one seemed to share my fascination. I couldn't understand it, I was blind to the sponge's lack of charm. I was infatuated.

On one dive, I found a turtle nibbling on the edge of a barrel sponge. The turtle, big-eyed and innocent, occupies a special place in almost every diver's heart, and yet my attention was focused on the sponge. How much damage would this reptile do to this seemingly helpless barrel? How long had it taken for the sponge to generate the bite-sized chunk missing from its lip? Did the sponge feel anything? I needed to find out more.

When I returned home, I read as much as I could find in the fish books about sponges. Their biological name is *Porifera*, meaning simply 'pore-bearing', and it is the pores in the surface of the sponge which are its claim to fame. The fleshy walls of the sponge are riddled with pores, channels through which the animal draws and expels the water around it. Cells in the walls of the pores filter out anything from the water which the sponge can consume, and it is the fine construction of the channels and the soft texture of the dried tissue of a small number of sponges which make them useful in the bathroom. The sponge is in essence a colony of tiny cells of different types, some for feeding, some for pumping water, but many of these cells are capable of transforming themselves so as to perform any of several bodily functions when needed. The sex life of the sponge is even more arcane: they may reproduce sexually or asexually, shooting out clouds of sperm or eggs into the sea. One sponge may choose to distribute sperm one day and eggs the next. Other species produce buds within their skin which migrate from the parent and grow into individual sponges elsewhere.

I found out that the giant barrel sponges were *Verongula gigantea*, and that they preferred clear water with little strong current. It seemed they grew very slowly, no more than a quarter of an inch a year. At that rate, the sponges I had seen in the Caribbean were three hundred years old.

I went to the Natural History Museum in London and found that there were hardly any sponge specimens on display in the public galleries. They were clearly not considered a sexy animal in the bright new world of interactive museum display. Disappointed, I made further enquiries, and was told I could make an appointment to talk to someone in the zoology department. Clare Valentine, Curator of *Porifera*, was the person I needed to see. She is responsible for the largest collection of sponge specimens in the world.

In the bowels of the Natural History Museum, there is a labyrinthine maze of passageways and storerooms, and, just like an iceberg, the unseen portion of the museum is larger than that visible above. Down here, there is none of the splendour of Robert Fowkes's grandiose exterior design with its striking blue brick and intricate terracotta reliefs of animals and plants. It is more like the basement of a Victorian hospital, with nooks and crannies harbouring all manner of items no longer deemed fit for public gaze. In one large room there were a dozen old wooden cabinets stuffed full of disintegrating specimens. There were elephant fish and sharks, stingrays and turtles. Against one wall there was a sturgeon, the fish exploited for the rich eggs we call caviar. The live fish are elegant creatures under severe threat from pollution and over-fishing in their native Russian waters. This dried individual showed cracks in its delicate snout and its distinctive bony tail was sagging. Nearby, two giant tortoises, distant cousins from the Galapagos and Aldabra, stood side by side, dilapidated and battered, with skin in tatters and their stuffing hanging out like worn-out toys. On top of a tall cupboard I spotted a Coelacanth, the so-called fossil fish once thought extinct but 'rediscovered' in the 1930s in the Indian Ocean and now known to be one of the oldest surviving species on earth. Demand for the specimens was so intense at one time that museums offered fishermen from the Comoros Islands cash rewards of thousands of dollars in return for a dried specimen. This Coelacanth sat gathering dust in isolation on top of his cupboard, retaining a little dignity away from the higgledy-piggledy crush of the specimen cabinet.

Clare guided me through the maze of passages to the rooms containing the sponge collection. Row upon row of large cardboard boxes sat in stacks almost to the ceiling. This was the dry collection, whole sponges collected over a century and a half of zoological expeditions. A manila label in neat copperplate handwriting dangled from the handle of one of the boxes just out of reach. It said 'Crawshay's West Indian Sponges'. I asked if I could take a look. Inside there were eight or nine sponges, fairly small in size and all a uniform shade of dirty grey. They were unappealing to the eye, mere husks of the creatures I remembered seeing underwater. Without their skins, and without being bleached and trimmed for commercial sale, they were as dull as old grey socks. In another room, Clare showed me what she called the wet collection.

Hundreds and hundreds of antique glass specimen jars filled with formaldehyde, inside which there were scraps of sponges. Floating morsels. And then there were the slides, thousands of specks trapped between glass plates ready for examination under the microscope.

'We're not exactly sure how many specimens we have, somewhere between a hundred and fifty thousand and a quarter of a million,' Clare explained. 'Some of these jars date from the *Challenger* voyages.'

The round-the-world voyage of HMS *Challenger* marks the very beginning of modern oceanography for most scientists, a three-year journey which began in 1873 and covered almost seventy thousand nautical miles. The whole ship was a floating laboratory, and a team of scientists collected over thirteen thousand animals and plants from the Atlantic, Pacific and Antarctic Oceans, a collection so extensive that the official report of the voyage took twenty years to prepare. Modern researchers are still using many of the specimens, including the sponges, and newly found organisms can most easily be compared to the existing examples in the museum for accurate identification.

Away from the mountainous collection of dry and wet specimens, the curator's office contained a small library of sponge-related documents. I read as much as I could, returning to the museum on more than one occasion to consult Clare Valentine. I learnt that living sponges can be soft and slimy and might smell like meat when pulled from the sea. Some are wrinkled, some are smooth and some are hairy. They can be amorphous lumps covered in knobs, lobes, or fingers. They might be clumps of flesh creeping over a coral head like spilled cement, or tall stalks rising from the coral like slender trees. There are sponges which bore into coral, rooting themselves fast in the limestone skeleton of the reef. The teardrop crab plucks small pieces of sponge and attaches them to its shell, where they form a living suit of camouflage. There was a mass of information about how diverse and intriguing the animals are, but on one thing the experts were all agreed. Individual sponges are hard to identify.

Human interest in the sponge has not stopped in the bathroom. In the 1950s, extracts of sponge were used to treat leukaemia, and there is intensive current research into chemicals from some species which may be useful in the fight against cancer. Scientists say that the sponge family contains the widest diversity of biologically active compounds of any marine phylum, and the pharmaceutical companies have been targeting sponges as possible sources of new drugs for several years.

According to a report in the *British Medical Journal* of 1932, the sponge, 'like water voles and female plaice, does not show senescence'. Could the ordinary sponge, ignominiously used for exfoliating beautiful women throughout the centuries, hold the secret of eternal youth?

A German researcher in the nineteenth century quoted Aristotle, who described the sponge's ability to grow back from the stump left behind when a diver pulled the animal off the seabed. The Greek expertise in sponge dealing has been long established. However, whenever the modern trade in sponges was mentioned, I found numerous references to a small town in America. According to the experts, Tarpon Springs, on the Gulf Coast of Florida, was at the centre of the international sponge trade. One report claimed that sponges on sale to tourists in Greece were often imported from America, and even Mediterranean sponges were exported to Tarpon Springs for preparation and packaging. They would then be shipped back to Greek wholesalers in Athens, who would pass them on to souvenir shops in the islands. This surely outstripped the selling of coals to Newcastle. Tarpon Springs deserved a visit.

*

The most ancient fossils come from the sea. Three hundred million years before the dinosaurs lived on earth, there were sponges in the ocean. Two hundred years ago, naturalists classified sponges as plants, because they believed they did not move. Some do. A sponge has no mouth, no digestive tract and no anus. Not even a nervous system, and certainly no brain, and yet it is an animal. Although most sponges do not generally move about, they are all multi-cellular, and their cells function in an integrated way. Crucially, like all other animals, their cells and tissues are bound together with collagen, a complex protein that is not found in plants or fungi, for example, which utilize pectin. The number of sponge species in the world today is still a mystery, with the latest research indicating that there are at least twenty thousand varieties, four times as many as previously estimated. They live in every ocean, and in freshwater as well as salt. Today, the annual world trade in sponges is valued at around fifty million dollars, and most of that business is controlled by a small number of Greek businessmen, a mere handful of wholesalers who buy the raw natural sponges from producers in the Mediterranean, the Caribbean and the Gulf of Mexico.

From the deep waters off Libya and Tunis in North Africa to the Dodecanese Islands of Greece, and on the shallow reefs of the Bahamas and Cuba, men still risk their lives to dive for sponges. In the Gulf of Mexico and the Florida Keys, hooking sponges from small boats can still bring a good income to a poor immigrant family from Haiti or the Dominican Republic. They are carrying on a tradition which began in Greece before written history was recorded.

The Greek sponge beds are found all over the Aegean, in the Cyclades, the Sporades and the Dodecanese Islands. Traditionally, the sponge boats, simple wooden affairs with five or six men aboard, would leave home twice a year, staying close to home in winter but sailing as far as Tangiers in summer in search of the best sponges.

The age-old method of sponge collection was to station a man in the bows of the boat with a wooden viewing tube, perhaps just an old bucket with a glass bottom, which he would use to peer at the seabed. When a likely spot was found, the boat would anchor and the diver would be readied for his work. Stripped naked, he would pick up the trigger stone, a heavy piece of slate or marble which would be rounded at one end and have a hole drilled through its middle. Through the hole would pass a rope, which would be tied tight to the stone, with the loose coils unravelling behind him from the deck as he dived. He would prepare himself for the dive with a prayer and then plunge from the deck holding the trigger stone in front of him like a miniature surfboard. The carved front end of the stone meant the diver could tilt it in front of him as a primitive aquaplane, steering his fall to the seabed so as to land as close to the sponges as possible. A sharp knife or a hooked spear would serve to rip the sponge from its fastening on rock or coral, and if there were several specimens to hand he would use a small net bag to carry his catch to the surface. Leaving the trigger stone on the seabed to be hauled up afterwards, the diver would pull himself back up the line to the boat. Naked divers often went to a hundred feet with this method, and sometimes more.

This method of diving persevered in the Mediterranean well into the twentieth century, even after the diving helmet was put into use. For most divers, such equipment was too expensive to buy, and the naked diver could earn a good living without it. These divers were often deaf, their eardrums perforated by the constant attack of water pressure as the heavy trigger stone pulled them to the seabed. To equalize the ears by holding the nose and blowing against the Eustachian tubes, as a recreational diver learns, would waste time, and would mean letting go of the stone with one hand.

Tarpon Springs, Florida

They say you don't have to be Greek to succeed in the sponge business. But it certainly helps.

Tony Lerios was a boat builder from the tiny Greek island of Kalymnos. In 1913, he emigrated to America, joining his father Theophillis and several hundred other men from the Dodecanese Islands who had recently set up home in the small Gulf Coast village of Tarpon Springs. In turn, these men would send for their wives and siblings, cousins and friends, gradually establishing their own community, which the local residents dubbed Greek Town. The new arrivals came mainly from Kalymnos and Halki, but also from Hydra, Spetses, Symi and Aegina, poor islands where life at the beginning of the twentieth century was completely centred on the sea, and what could be brought from it to eat or to sell. The islanders came in search of a fresh start in the New World, but they brought their ancient culture with them, and a skill that would make Tarpon Springs rich. They were sponge divers, and they came to harvest the sponge beds of the warm waters of the Gulf of Mexico.

Tony Lerios died in 1992 when he was a hundred years old, but his workshop beside the Anaclote River, a small estuary leading into the Gulf, is still there, virtually unchanged. It is a simple wooden building nestling in the shadow of the road bridge, and in sight of the shrimp quay on the other side of the docks. The workshop is crammed with his old tools, and the paraphernalia of a lifetime spent fixing boats and making equipment for the sponge divers of Tarpon Springs. On a hot summer's afternoon I walked into the workshop to meet Tony's grandson, Nick Toth, who carries on the family tradition of making diving helmets by hand. I had spoken to him by telephone from London after seeing an

advertisement for his diving helmets on the Internet, and I journeyed to Tarpon Springs to meet him. He was my only contact in
the tight-knit Greek community, and I hoped he would lead me to
the men who control the sponge industry.

Meeting someone for the first time after only establishing telephone contact is always intriguing. Nick was younger than I had
expected, a strongly built man with thick hair and a neat beard,
already grey in the way very dark men can be at an early age. He
spoke slowly and with natural modesty as he explained the detail
of his work in a meticulous way, perhaps because he thought I
couldn't understand any of the machinery. I learned later that he
had been interviewed on local television and radio a number of
times, and he was well practised in taking visitors through the
process of making a diving helmet.

Inside the workshop there was a strong smell of engine oil.
Every flat surface was covered in a mixture of metal shavings, oil
rags, rivets, grommets and valves. Put together and burnished
with care, they would make up the detail of a traditional diving
helmet.

With only the breeze from the river coming through the doorway
to keep him cool, Nick uses a short-handled wooden mallet to beat
copper sheeting into shape on a cast-iron mandrel, or block. Two
hours of strenuous hammering are needed for one breastplate, and
Nick has the forearms of a blacksmith. On top of the breastplate,
which rests on the diver's shoulders, he will solder a brass neck
ring on to which the copper helmet, which he calls a 'pot', will be
screwed. The neck ring is machined on a lathe over eighty years
old, the same lathe that Tony Lerios taught Nick to use when he
was still a schoolboy. Around the edge of the breastplate are the
brails, fastenings on to which the canvas diving suit is attached and
held in place. Four glass portholes, or lights, allow the diver to
look forwards, to his left and right, and finally upwards towards

the boat which supplies him with air from the pumps above.

After around a hundred and forty hours of meticulous workman-ship, Nick will have created a fully functional diving helmet which has changed little in design since his grandfather began making them a hundred years ago. Nowadays, the helmets are bought by collectors, pieces of fine craftsmanship to be put on display, items which are significantly over-engineered in comparison with most modern equipment. But these are not replicas: Nick Toth's helmets are as fit for service underwater as any made at the height of the diving industry in Tarpon Springs.

'I don't know if what I'm doing is art, or craft, or just plain engineering,' Nick said simply. 'I know it feels good to work here with the same tools, in the same place that my grandfather worked all those years. He had a place in the community, and I guess I see this as helping keep the community alive.'

The Greeks came to Tarpon Springs by invitation. In the 1870s, Tarpon Springs had been a resort for winter visitors from the Northern states, well-to-do families who had made their wealth in the great industrial cities like New York, Chicago and Philadelphia. They used their money to build large wooden houses around the central lake, a natural pool known as Spring Bayou which is fed by the Anclote River. With weeping willows by the lakeside, and tall shade trees draped with Spanish moss along the residential streets, it was the perfect place to escape the rigours of the East Coast winter. And Tarpon Springs was served by the railroad. Many of the grand houses are still there, and the grandest of all cluster around the streets adjacent to Greek Town.

Nick took me on a tour of the village, cruising slowly through the gracious streets in an old Buick with wide bench seats and a slick interior. At his recommendation, I found a room in the Spring Bayou Inn, an imposing house built in 1905, its style typical of the shingle mansions around the Bayou. It had original sash windows under a steeply pitched roof with boxed eaves, and a distinctive round corner tower above the wide verandah at the front of the house. Inside, immaculate hardwood floors and highly polished banisters, porcelain door handles and etched glass panels completed the Victorian vision. It was easy to imagine genteel life in Tarpon Springs a hundred years ago.

It was John King Cheyney, Nick explained as we drove, a wealthy Quaker from Philadelphia with property interests in the small town, who first realized that there was a new fortune to be made in the waters offshore from Tarpon Springs. Cheyney knew that the waters of the Gulf of Mexico were rich in natural sponges, and that the old-fashioned methods of fishing for them were leaving a treasure trove of excellent specimens untouched in the deeper waters offshore.

American fishermen had pulled sponges from the shallow waters along Florida's coast since the 1840s. The established method was known as hook-boating and was the same technique used by spongers further south in the Florida Keys and the Bahamas. Using a long pole with an iron tip, a fisherman would simply reach down into the water and skewer the sponge with the pole, hoisting it to the surface to be thrown into the bottom of the boat. It was a technique only suitable for shallow water, and the number of sponges that could be retrieved successfully was small. Cheyney realized that the United States was the world's largest consumer of natural sponges and that less than half that demand could be met from domestic production.

The turn of the century witnessed a large expansion in industrial manufacturing in the United States, and the price of sponges increased accordingly, an increase fed partly by the fledgling motor industry. In Chicago, the great automotive factories alone needed hundreds of tons of sponge for cleaning and polishing the hundreds of thousands of new vehicles which were rolling off the automated production lines. Only a natural sponge for washing, and a chamois-leather cloth for drying and polishing, could do the job effectively. In an era when virtually our every need is met by synthetic materials, it is hard to imagine the reliance of previous generations on natural substances. It is said that there were over a thousand industrial uses for natural sponge, and until synthetic substitutes went into mass production after the Second World War, nothing could compete with the material for absorbency and efficiency.

In 1891, John Cheyney formed the Anclote and Rock Island Sponge Company, with headquarters in Philadelphia. The sponge business in America was one in which the Greek community of New York already had a hand. John Cocoris, an ambitious young buyer from New York with no capital of his own, told Cheyney that the way to take sponges from deep water was with a diving suit. To do it, he would need men experienced in the use of the suits, but they would also have to be men who knew about sponges. Greek divers were what he needed.

In 1905, Cocoris brought a five-man crew from the island of Aegina to test out his theory. Within a year the word had spread through the sponge islands like wildfire, and five hundred men had arrived from Greece to work in the sponge trade. The spongers of the Dodecanese were not only skilled divers; they had an ancestral relationship to the sponge industry which could be traced back to the very roots of Mediterranean civilization itself. The character of the sleepy Victorian resort was to be changed for ever, and Tarpon Springs was to become the largest sponge-trading centre in the world. Soon John Cheyney was just one of several suppliers shipping over a million dollars' worth of sponges from warehouses in Tarpon Springs. Greek Town was the centre of the industry, and its main street was named Dodecanese Boulevard.

*

Early the next morning I walked back into Greek Town from the Bayou. Not all of the town's successful businessmen were Greek, but many were, and the local historical society is proud of its archives listing who owned what and where. Armed with a map produced by the Tarpon Springs cultural centre, I was able to find the Alissandratos house, and the Faklis department store. I also found the home of the Cretekos family, who according to local records were cousins of the family of Maria Callas. The young diva used to come to Tarpon Springs from New York during the winter, and elderly residents say they remember seeing her playing on the lawn in front of the house, though there are no reports of her singing annoying the neighbours.

In general, the Greek families did not have the grandest homes, and they clustered together in simpler one-storey buildings closer to the sponge docks. Wall signs announce the beginning of the main drag, and a plethora of souvenir shops cater for the day-trippers who come to see what is left of the old Greek Town. Signs for 'Katzaras – Shells' and 'Bouzouki – Gifts' signal the approach to Dodecanese Boulevard.

Although it was quite early, there was already a steady stream of families and elderly tourists wearing sun-visors walking up and down the Boulevard when I arrived. They strolled towards the docks and the signs leading them to the St Nicholas sponge-boat tour, stopping to look at the curio shops selling Greek pottery and tablemats decorated with photographs of the Acropolis. The menu in the window of Costas's Restaurant advertised Mama's Greek Style Home Cooking. Pastry-shop windows along the way displayed more Greek food, sweet pastries and breads, baklava and kadaifi or the sweet milk tarts called galatoboureko. Every other shop had strings of bright yellow sponges hanging in the doorway, and at the end of the main street was the original Sponge Exchange, a market square where the boats would deposit their cargo of damp sponges for public auction at the end of a voyage. Originally the sponges were stored here by the dealers as they awaited shipment to packing warehouses, and kept in a series of cement rooms built into the walls of the market square. The rooms were like prison cells, simple square chambers with a locked metal grille for a door, allowing the sponges natural ventilation in the dry air. Most of the storerooms have been converted into tourist boutiques and now they sell not only sponges but also the full panoply of seaside souvenir kitsch. There are bags of shells and dried starfish, petrified seahorses from Indonesia and sea urchins from the Pacific – a depressing catalogue of Third World plunder from the ocean.

Opposite the Sponge Exchange there was an original wooden sponge boat, a gaff-headed yawl named *St Nicholas*. For five dollars I could sail upstream and watch a helmet diver in full costume jump overboard into the Anclote River to look for sponges. I paid my money and joined the tour. The *St Nicholas* motored upstream away from the docks for a few minutes and the skipper explained the basic working of the diving equipment, and how many years it took for a boat captain to learn to operate a sponge boat safely. I went to the back of the boat and saw that the propeller was encased in a metal wire cage, a safety precaution to prevent the diver's air hose being cut if he was swept under the stern by accident. A young diver clad in an orange canvas suit and heavy lead boots was introduced to the passengers. He said his name was John Michael Stellianos, and he told the assembled trippers that his grandfather had been a diver in Greece. Until recently he had been working for IBM in Cincinnati, but now he wanted to return to his roots and try life as a sponge diver.

Once inside his copper helmet, and armed with a sponge hook resembling a short-handled trident with curved prongs, young Stellianos clambered down an iron ladder and dropped into the water. We followed his progress from the stream of bubbles which erupted on the surface of the estuary as he walked along the bottom. Five minutes later he surfaced, and clambered back on deck. On the tip of his trident there was a soggy brown clump of natural sponge.

Not far from the sponge dock I found a small museum, irresistibly entitled Spongerama. Inside, the history of Greek sponging was illustrated in a series of dusty glass cases. Behind the glass there were diorama scenes made up with plaster models of fishermen and men in helmets engaged in sponge diving. According to the museum display, more than a dozen varieties of natural sponge had been traditionally collected for domestic and industrial use. Dried specimens and photographs were provided for every type. Some of the names were self-explanatory, the Hardhead and the Grass sponge, the Yellow and the Finger sponges, but others had more mysterious, musical appellations, like the Manatapas and the Zimocca. Some were easily identifiable as the soft, rotund bathroom-type sponges, while others were coarser, wire-like fingers of what looked like dried breakfast cereal. The Elephant's Ear was flat and vaguely unpleasant in appearance, more like a cauliflower ear than something belonging to a pachyderm. The Turkey Cup and the Turkey Toilet took their names from their country of origin rather than any association with the eponymous feathered fowl. In some countries they were better known as the fine Levant variety, and were long valued by surgeons in staunching blood during operations. It seems they absorbed blood efficiently but did not break up and leave pieces of themselves in the wound. The best sponge, they say, is the Sheepswool, soft and super-absorbent yet resilient, strong enough to last four or five years if rinsed well after use.

After leaving the sponge docks I walked back along the river to Nick Toth's machine shop.

'How was Spongerama?' he asked with a friendly smile. I

confessed that I had probably seen enough of the touristy Hellenic experience laid on by the shopkeepers of Tarpon Springs. I had seen some small boats with freshly caught sponges at the quayside, but the rewards of selling souvenirs and kebabs clearly outstripped the town's function as a sponge dock. I needed to know more about the genuine sponge business.

'Come on,' he said. 'Let's have lunch.'

We walked back along Dodecanese Boulevard, and down a side street. Even a few yards off the main tourist thoroughfare the atmosphere was different. On the corner of Maragos and Athens Street we passed the Taverna Diogenis, shut up and deserted even though it was lunchtime. Next door to the taverna was a simple room with bare linoleum on the floor. There was no sign outside, no sandwich board to lure the wandering visitor inside, but there was a small bar at one end close to the door. As we walked in I noticed that the place was busy, and the sound coming from the tables was the low murmur of male voices. There wasn't a woman in sight, and the chatter was punctuated by the sharp clack of draughts pieces being slapped down at every table. Nick explained that we were in John Klonaris's coffee shop, a place where men came to relax, away from their womenfolk. Everyone inside knew everyone else, and I wasn't sure I would have come in without a local escort. The faces around us were clearly Greek, dark-skinned men with thick black moustaches in the Mediterranean style, and the names of the men who greeted Nick were the traditional and invariably saintly choices, Tony, Michael or George. Underneath the kitsch façade of Dodecanese Boulevard it struck me that there was a real community with a strong Greek identity, hanging on to its heritage by its fingertips.

Nick ordered some beer, and we sat down at one of the plain Formica-topped tables. The men around us were mostly elderly, and they concentrated on their game intensely.

'You see that man playing over there?'

I identified a large man with a patch of pure white hair around the base of his skull. He was quite bald on top, his head and face evenly sun-tanned around a pair of laughing eyes.

'That's Mr Billiris,' said Nick, taking a swig of his beer. 'If you want to know about sponges, you have to talk to him.'

The next day I set out early before the sun became too strong, walking along the edge of the Bayou, the lake where Greek boys traditionally dived for a gold cross during the Epiphany celebrations. Here, as the whole town looked on, the Greek Archbishop would throw the small cross into the lake and all the adolescent boys would swim for it, the lucky victor receiving the cleric's blessing for the year ahead. The lake was deserted, and the water when I dipped my hand into it felt cool. The willows trailing their fronds above its surface in the pale light made it seem like an English summer morning. I walked on, studying the big houses and gradually moving away from the wealthy part of town.

Within half an hour it had begun to warm up and I had reached a less idyllic spot, a collection of old buildings squatting close to the river with battered pick-up trucks parked in the shade of the trees. A silver-roofed corrugated iron building stood on the corner of the road, and inside I could see five or six men sitting on metal chairs arranged in a circle. They seemed to be arguing about something, although they were speaking Greek and I could only judge the mood by their tone. Large black letters high up on one side of the building said simply SPONGES, and I saw that in the back of one of the trucks there was a pile of them tied up in a net. I walked closer to the building and the raised voices dropped when they saw me staring in at the scene. I waved and said 'Good morning', ostentatiously brandishing my camera and photographing the building. A hand was raised in greeting, and then the argument resumed. I moved along, and paused at the river bank, where there was a small rotting motor cruiser tethered like a mangy dog to the wharf by a blue nylon rope. There was an atmosphere of decay here, and a brooding sultry heat which made the town suddenly seem very much a part of the Deep South. I checked my watch. Nick Toth had been as good as his word, and I had an appointment with Mr Billiris, but my tour had taken longer than I had planned, and now I was going to be late.

A painted wooden sign hung on the front of the old clapboard warehouse. The lettering was faded by the Gulf Coast sun, but I could just make out the words *George Billiris, Sponge Merchant International*. A narrow doorway faced directly on to the street, and I stepped inside. As my eyes adjusted to the shade of the warehouse I saw that the interior of the building was crammed with dried sponges. A narrow passageway led down the centre of the warehouse and on each side of it there were vertical wooden partitions enclosed with chicken wire. Each partition was divided horizontally at eye level to provide an upper and lower level to the container, and in each wire enclosure there were bright yellow bath sponges of every size and shape. As I stood there, a doorway opened in the wooden wall to my left and a small gnomish man appeared clutching a sheaf of papers.

'Excuse me,' I began, 'I'm looking for Mr Billiris.'

'George?' the gnome grumbled, pulling the door to the office shut behind him with a bang.

'I believe so.'

The man snatched a pair of wire-rimmed bifocals down off his bald forehead to peer at me, sizing me up before he gave anything away.

'Nick Toth arranged for me to see him, and I'm sorry I'm a little late.' The man was impassive. 'I'm from England,' I offered lamely as some kind of justification for my visit.

'In there,' he finally grunted with a backward cast of his shining pate, then he bustled off down the passage between the rows of sponges. I tapped on the door before cautiously opening it. A pile of cardboard boxes obscured my view of the interior, so that I had to step inside in order to see if anyone was there.

A large old metal desk filled one half of the small room, and the man I had seen in the coffee shop the previous day sat behind it, pressing a telephone to one ear and shuffling a mound of manila folders in front of him. He waved at me to come in and sit down in an old swivel chair in front of the desk. He carried on talking into the telephone for several minutes, while I examined the room in detail, keeping half an ear on the conversation, which was peppered with talk of cargo delivery dates, and F.O.B. sponge prices. I had no choice but to listen, and I assumed that if the conversation had been a secret I would not have been invited to sit. Occasionally Mr Billiris broke into French, and then a Greek phrase would slip into the conversation but the bulk of it was in English. I noticed that the pile of boxes near the door were labelled POISON in large letters, with the words MURIATIC ACID underneath. Apart from the metal desk and the chair I was sitting on, both of which I judged to be at least thirty years old, the office was scarcely furnished. In one corner behind the desk there was a large wooden filing cabinet, and the walls were decorated with several tattered posters of Greece. Suspended on a string over the window shutters there were a dozen small sponges which had been dyed in varying shades of green, blue, purple and red. There was no computer in evidence and, apart from the international phone call being conducted on the other side of the desk, there was no sense that I had found the hub of the international sponge trade. Finally, the phone call ended and George Billiris rose from his chair and extended a large firm hand in greeting. His face had the youthful sheen of an even tan, and his eyes were a piercing shade of light blue.

'I'm sorry to have kept you,' he said. 'One of my wholesalers is having a problem, he's new in the business and I want to help him out with a deal. Sit down. Now, how can I help you?'

After some small talk, I explained that I wanted to know about the sponge-diving business, and that I had been told he was the man I should talk to.

For two hours, George Billiris explained the fine detail of the international sponge trade. He told me about the history of sponging in Tarpon Springs, and how his own grandfather John Billiris had come to America from Kalymnos. John's son, Michael, took over the business in his turn and now George was the third generation of the house of Billiris. Now in his seventies, he has no children of his own to carry on the business.

'I didn't get married until I was past fifty,' he said. 'I loved being on the sponge boats too much. There's nothing like working on the water, you feel better when you wake up at sea. We used to compete boat to boat, just like in Greece in the old days when they competed island by island to see who was best. My father used to say to me, "Come on, George, are you gonna' let that guy beat you?!" He'd encourage me to bring up more sponges than the next man, and that was when I was fourteen years old.'

I wondered if he thought the town could survive as a Greek attraction for very much longer. George paused, and put his large brown hands face down on the desk in front of him. 'We're losing our Greek customs slowly,' he said wearily. 'Once upon a time tourists came here to see the sponge docks, and that was it. Sponges and Greeks, they go together. Always have done. This is the only place in the world where you can come and see so much of the old sponge trade, and I don't want it to be some kind of theme park. The young people are better educated, so they don't want to go to sea, risk their lives, leave their wife and kids behind for weeks at a time. But we can only survive as an authentic community if we keep on dealing in sponges. But even some of the Greeks here don't understand that. Why, only the other day a woman in a tourist shop told one of my boats not to leave the wet sponges near her shop, 'cos she said they smelt bad! I said to her, ''Think about what you're saying for a minute – without sponges you wouldn't have any customers!'' But she didn't get it. She just didn't get it.'

George Billiris is frightened that Tarpon Springs will lose its identity if it loses the sponge trade, and he is doing everything in his power to keep interest in the business alive. George explained that there were only a few thousand natural sponge producers in the world, and only a handful of dealers left like himself. From Tarpon Springs he and a couple of other large-scale buyers ship finished sponges to Paris, London, Frankfurt and Athens, and he confirmed what I had read in London, that many of the sponges sold to tourists in Greece had been fished from the Gulf of Mexico.

In the warehouse, George Billiris showed me how the natural sponge was prepared for packing and export. The boxes of poisonous acid I had seen in his office were part of the process. By the time the sponges reach the warehouse they have usually been dried in the sun and the wind by hanging them on a rope strung across the boat's deck at sea. The rubbery skin of the sponge has been beaten with a mallet and pulled off so that the soft tissue, *spongin*, underneath is exposed. Once ashore, the sponge must be cleaned further and beaten again to remove any debris inside it. Then it will be soaked in fresh water and dried again to remove the evil-smelling skin tissues still clinging to it. Finally, it will be trimmed to shape and then dyed in a secret mixture of acid to make it acceptable to the retail trade.

As we talked, George Billiris led me into the depths of the sponge warehouse. We walked between the chicken-wire stalls where thousands of sponges lay, graded according to size and type. The best quality were the Rock Island Sheepswool, which as I'd learned at Spongerama were durable yet soft, and found only in a small area of the Gulf of Mexico. We squeezed past the man whom I had spoken to outside George's office. His bifocals were now perched on the tip of his nose, and he was recording the details of finished sponges with a pencil in a handwritten ledger.

'This is Manny,' said George.

Occasionally, Manny would pick up a sponge and hold it up against a wooden board, into which circular holes had been cut, each of different diameter. 'This is how we measure the sponge,' George explained. 'Our buyers work in inches, and we know that the buyers in Chicago want ten and a half inch sponges. In Cleveland it's eight and a half inches, and California only seven inches. It's just habit, I guess. Basically, the bigger the sponge the more it's worth.'

'Your business isn't exactly hi-tech,' I joked, drawing a baleful glance from Manny as he wrote in his ledger.

'Look, Manny is eighty-five years old,' George replied. 'And there just isn't any way to speed up this business. The only way to judge a sponge is to look at it with the human eye. And it takes a lot of years to judge a sponge by sight.'

Shafts of sunlight filtered through small skylights high in the roof, and there was the constant hum of electric fans circulating the air amongst the stacks of sponges. In the centre of the old building a set of double doors on either wall had been thrown open to let in the fresh air, the best way of drying the sponges without bleaching them too harshly in the sun. Halfway between the two sets of doors, three men sat in the middle of the warehouse. The softened light from a roof pane was muted by a miasma of fine dust in the air, throwing the trio into soft focus. In front of them was a large plastic tub full of dried sponges, grey and dull-looking like the ones I had seen in the Natural History Museum. The three men were elderly, and they didn't look up from their work as we approached. With one hand they would pick a sponge from the tub and hold it up to the light. Then they would begin to trim it with a pair of metal shears, hand-sprung sheep shears made in Sheffield and unchanged in design for centuries. The sponges were being trimmed to make them a uniform shape, more pleasing to the eye, and easier to hold comfortably in the hand.

'A sponge is like a woman, either beautiful or ugly,' said George. 'But we can always improve it.'

He took a large sponge from a rack close by and beckoned me over to a small band-saw mounted next to a bench. Perched on a high stool, he examined the sponge for half a minute before switching on the saw and pulling the sponge towards the humming blade.

Above the noise of the saw I had to lean close to him to hear what he was saying. 'This is a large wool sponge,' he shouted. 'It cost me twenty dollars at the market, but I can cut it into four, maybe five commercial-grade sponges each worth twice that. Look here, you see the middle of the sponge – it's decayed. I cut that out, trying to maximize the thick growth around the outside.'

The old man worked quickly, applying a lifetime of experience to trimming the wool sponge. Just like a diamond cutter working out which angle to cut at to bring out the most fire within the stone, he stopped occasionally, peering down his nose at the lump of fibre, visualizing the line he would draw across it with the band-saw. He was concentrating on it, like some three-dimensional puzzle. Afterwards, the sponge would go into the tub, where the three men with their shears would fine trim it to get the perfect shape. Then it would be bleached and dyed bright yellow for the retail trade. George switched off the band-saw. 'Natural sponges are grey,' he said. 'They look dirty and people don't like it. When you bleach them and dye them you weaken them, and they don't last so long. But that's business.'

George Billiris said he was going out to lunch, but told me I was welcome to stay in the warehouse as long as I pleased. The men trimming the sponges were happy to talk to me and I drew up a spare chair as they worked. 'Curly' Spaniolos and 'Piggy' Lontakos were slightly older than George, in their mid-seventies, while the third man, Mike Boulafentis, was ten years older. They worked methodically, the snip-snipping of the metal shears a constant musical accompaniment to their chatter. They remembered the days when there were two hundred sponge boats in Tarpon Springs, and they remembered the bad times in the 1940s when a blight came and wiped out the sponge beds for over a decade.

'That's when people started going into other things,' Curly recalled.

The men wore white T-shirts, and as they talked they would pick up a rubber mallet and batter the sponges before they trimmed them. A light spray of water and fragments of coral, sand or shell would fly from the sponges and spatter the white cotton midriff of the shirts, and then the shears would deposit a layer of sponge snippets on top of it all. Curly had the deepest voice I think I have ever heard, and forearms covered in tattoos from his days in the Navy. 'Most of the young guys from Tarpon went into the Service,' he growled. 'That's when we showed everyone we were 100 per cent American, I guess.'

'That's right,' Piggy chipped in. 'Back then you had to stay here, marry a Greek girl and keep it that way. But after the war everything relaxed, and now it doesn't matter who you marry or whether your kids speak Greek so much.'

The hours went by, and gradually the midday heat in the warehouse wore off. I sat among the sponge flecks watching thick brown fingers flexing the shears as deftly as a barber's nasal scissors while the three men told stories about the heyday of Tarpon Springs. All of them remembered the day Hollywood came to

Tarpon Springs. *Beneath the 12-Mile Reef* was one of the first films shot in Cinemascope, and one of the first major roles for the young Robert Wagner. During the making of the film in 1953, a crew and cast from Twentieth Century Fox virtually took over the town. The film used the old rivalry between the Greek community and the original Florida sponge fishermen as a backdrop for a love story between Wagner and actress Terry Moore. Much of the dramatic tension revolved around Wagner, as Tony Petrakis, falling in love with a girl who wasn't Greek, and the commercial rivalry between the sponge divers and their 'American' counterparts in the shrimp fleet. With the added drama of underwater scenes and sponge-diving action, the film has become a minor classic, at least locally, and it certainly helped the tourist business.

The reality of life on the sponge-diving boats was sometimes even more dramatic than Hollywood could depict. Piggy recalled a friend of his who came back from a sponging trip with a bad case of the bends. 'They were working on him all night, sitting on his arms and legs, rubbing his chest and stomach trying to massage away the pain. He was only eighteen when it happened, but until the day he died the muscles on one side of his face were twisted. He always looked like he was smiling.'

'You had to watch out for the air hose,' Curly added. 'A friend of mine was drowned when the boat's propeller cut the air line. And they still have accidents today. They've got new lightweight diving gear, but it's still surface supplied and sometimes they just stay down too long and get a "hit".'

The Greek divers developed their own schedules for beating the bends. They knew, solely from experience, that no two men were equally susceptible to the disease, and a fit, lean diver with a lot of experience could sometimes emerge safely from a dive at a depth where other men would have suffered a debilitating attack. They knew that a tired man was more susceptible than a fresh one, and that the effort of fighting against a strong current would make a man more susceptible to the bends. On board the sponge boat, the diver was king. He was cosseted and protected, fed and watered before the other crewmen and given as large a share of the purse as the skipper when the cargo was sold. Without the diver, no one made a living.

A good diver can earn between fifty and a hundred thousand dollars a year from sponging. The best method is still to go out into offshore waters and walk along the seabed in an upright position while breathing air through a hose fed from the surface. Now, an electric compressor has replaced the heavy two-man pump that sat amidships on the old sponge boats, and instead of a copper helmet the diver wears a modern mask and regulator attached to the air hose. Scuba diving is not recommended for sponge collecting since the diver can quickly become separated from the boat and drift out of sight of the crew, and swimming horizontally is much less efficient against the current than walking upright attached to a line from the boat.

According to George Billiris, the sponge industry is ecologically efficient. 'We've been doing it for two thousand years, and there's still sponges out there!' he laughs. 'And the old methods always ensured a supply of sponges. When you clean them on the boat you trim them and throw the waste back in the water. When it hits the bottom it will seed itself and grow back into a whole sponge in about a year. And don't forget, the diver always leaves a tuft of sponge on the rock where he pulls it off. That too grows again, and usually within a year you can go back and find a sponge in the same spot, but maybe 20 per cent bigger than the one you pulled up.'

George says he can sell as many sponges as his divers can bring in. 'The beauty of a dried sponge is it doesn't go stale, it doesn't have to be fed and watered like livestock. If the price falls you hold back your stocks and they sit there in the warehouse minding their own business waiting for the market to recover.'

The number of sponge fishermen and divers has fallen drastically in recent years. The natural sponge is still a valuable product, but few men want the risk and uncertainty of a trade which is weather dependent, and offers little in the way of insurance or guarantees when something goes wrong.

Pollution and over-fishing in certain areas are more of a threat to the sponge trade. In the 1940s, a bacterial infestation swept through the Mediterranean, then the Caribbean and finally up into the Gulf of Mexico, virtually wiping out the sponge trade. Most of the Tarpon Springs sponge fleet went out of business, and only a few families clung on, relying on restaurants, souvenir shops and the tourist appeal of the town's Greek atmosphere to stay solvent.

In recent years the sponge beds have recovered, and there is excess demand for good-quality natural sponges worldwide owing to the difficulties of harvesting the animal from the sea in large quantities. The sponge has so far defeated attempts to grow it in large numbers under artificial conditions, so, for the foreseeable future, demand will exceed supply. Biological prospecting, the craze for identifying and isolating potentially useful pharmaceutical compounds from natural organisms, looks set to increase demand for the humble sponge, especially if its anti-carcinogenic potential can be unleashed. But now, there are less than a hundred men working the sponge boats full time in Tarpon Springs. In Greece, the men of Halki and Kalymnos want jobs in the tourism industry, and fewer and fewer men in the Caribbean want to fish for sponges for similar reasons. Meanwhile, the godfathers of the sponge business are now in their seventies and eighties. The race is on to pass on the secret of sponge harvesting to a younger generation.

Desroches Island, Amirantes

I swam along on my back with my arms spread apart as if on a crucifix. Stretching my arms to their limits, I was unable to match the wingspan of the creature above me. Three or four inches above my face, its white belly filled my vision and I was mesmerized by a row of gently pulsating gill slits. The pale flesh quivered as it pumped water through the openings in its underside, and through the slits the private inner surfaces of the beast were briefly visible. I hardly dared breathe in case the air bubbles from my diving equipment startled the animal which had allowed me such an intimate embrace. After a minute I gave up trying to match the manta ray's pace and dropped back. She swam away from me without hurrying, and then returned, circling our small group of divers for more than ten minutes. We watched her watching us, mesmerized by the easy beat of the smooth black wings, rising like a rider's cloak in the wind. Circling, staring, effortlessly drawing nearer, the ray seemed intent on establishing contact. None of us moved, each diver hanging, arms folded across the chest, waiting, watching, corralled by the dancing form. Finally, she was amongst us, all eyes upon her and all interest in the rest of the reef suspended. And then, someone gave in to impulse and tried to touch the muscular cape. Our communion ended, and with one wing beat she was out of reach. In a few seconds the manta had left our range of sight, its dimming shape no more than a tracing-paper outline, fading slowly into the surrounding blue of the ocean.

4. Straightening the Bends

In the worst cases the diver began to feel faint a few minutes after return to the surface; soon he became unconscious and his pulse disappeared; and in a few minutes he was dead.

J. S. Haldane, *Respiration*

In 1869, a bulletin from the French Academy of Medicine described a list of symptoms which the author, Dr Gent, felt should preclude a man from employment as a diver. He ruled against:

Men with short necks, full blooded and florid complexions.

Men who suffer from headache, are slightly deaf or have recently had a running from the ear.

Men who have at any time spat or coughed up blood, or have been subject to palpitation of the heart.

Men who are very pale, whose lips are more blue than red, who are subject to cold hands and feet, with what is commonly called a languid circulation.

Men with bloodshot eyes, and high colour in the cheeks showing the interlacement of numerous small but distinct blood vessels.

Men who are hard drinkers, and have suffered repeatedly from venereal disease, or who have had rheumatism or sunstroke.

The conditions which might cause the symptoms described are strikingly familiar to modern divers. Heart and circulatory disease, asthma, lung injury and alcohol consumption are still regarded as contra-indications for diving, and anyone wishing to learn to dive will have to answer a medical questionnaire designed to reveal a history or pre-disposition to weakness in such areas. The ears, the lungs and the circulatory system are those parts of the body most crucially affected by changes in pressure during diving. Any problems in these areas are likely to be exacerbated by a combination of the effects of increased pressure on descent underwater, and then decreasing pressure of ascent on the human body. Experience of venereal disease is no longer a subject on which the prospective diver will be questioned.

The advent of efficient air pumps allowed helmet divers to go deeper than ever before, but the barrier to depth is not just the supply of air, but what happens to air and the portions of the body which contain it. With the increased use of compressed air in naval salvage and marine-engineering projects, a new and mysterious disease had come to light. Popularly known as 'the bends', it has been described as the first modern disease, a direct result of technology developed during the Industrial Revolution. Its first victims were not just divers, but engineers and tunnel workers who spent their working days in compressed-air environments.

Non-divers will frequently cite the bends as one of the few terms they know regarding the hazards of descending into the sea. Its reputation as an affliction is as alarming and sinister as the man-eating shark. The bends is certainly a serious threat to life and most definitely to limb, and it remains an important consideration for even the most infrequent diver. Although the scientific causes are now firmly established, the disease remains a secretive and unpredictable thing even today. Whereas the risk of shark attack is almost always negligible, and usually avoidable, the only sure way to avoid the risk of the bends is not to dive.

The bends was first properly described as 'caisson disease', since it was observed in workers who had been exposed to increased air pressure for long periods during the construction of bridges, tunnels and deep foundations. In order to keep water at bay from the site where they were digging, 'caissons' or sealed metal chambers were lowered into place and pumped full of air to keep them dry. Similar in concept to John Smeaton's diving bell, used in the early 1800s for harbour construction, caissons were widely adopted by Victorian engineers when they began spanning the great rivers of the fast-growing conurbations of the nineteenth century. Hugh Snell, a doctor who studied caisson disease, observed that 'Wherever compressed air is going to be used on an extensive scale, a small hospital close at hand should be provided.'

Calculations available to the earliest modern engineers told them that the pressure to which we are subjected at sea level is equivalent to a 'weight' of air of 14.7 pounds per square inch. Edmund Halley knew that atmospheric pressure at sea level (the weight of the air above us) is almost exactly equivalent to the weight exerted by thirty-three feet of seawater. A man who is thirty-three feet underwater is therefore subject to twice the pressure he feels at the surface, i.e. 29.4 lbs per square inch. At sixty-six feet another atmosphere of weight is added, making him subject to three atmospheres, and so on, with pressure increasing by a further atmosphere with each thirty-three foot increment of depth. If the caisson is sunk into the sea, then to keep it dry at a prescribed depth underwater requires an air pressure equivalent to these atmospheric values. Working in a mineshaft, or on tunnel foundations, the air pressure needed depends on the level of the water table. In the latter half of the nineteenth century, it was tunnel diggers and engineers who experienced the bends, rather than divers. Divers were fewer in number, and on the whole were not going very deep underwater, therefore avoiding the bends more by chance than by design.

Caissons were essentially gigantic steel air locks, metal shafts sunk into the ground with a hatch at the top which the tunnel workers climbed through and then closed behind them. Air pumps at the surface, originally nothing more than bellows, had been immeasurably improved since the advent of the steam engine, and supplied air which pressurized the caisson sufficiently to keep any ground or river water out. After several hours' hard physical labour in these increased atmospheric pressures, some workers complained of limb and joint pains, symptoms which at the time were ascribed to rheumatism or arthritis. In some cases, physicians thought that a man's susceptibility was a factor of his nervous disposition. A French engineer, Charles-Jean Triger, described such maladies in the 1840s, following caisson work in coalfields near Lyons, but a virtual epidemic of the disease among American bridge-builders was to spur interest in the causes and treatment of this crippling affliction.

The scale of industrial expansion in the United States dwarfed many of the civil-engineering projects being undertaken in Europe in the nineteenth century. A new bridge for the Mississippi in 1868, and shortly afterwards the beginning of the Brooklyn Bridge across New York's East River, entailed the construction of caissons which were deeper than those used anywhere before. In Mississippi the caissons extended a hundred feet underground, while in Brooklyn they reached a depth of almost eighty feet. On each project several men died, and dozens more were crippled from the bends. Another massive construction project in New York, tunnels under the Hudson River, resulted in almost four thousand cases of the bends. The disease, which the French had simply called *mal de caisson*, became 'the bends' because American tunnel-workers compared the painful contortions of its victims to a forward-leaning pose adopted by fashionable women of the era, known as the 'Grecian Bend'.

Men with the bends would complain of a variety of symptoms: itchy skin, a red rash, violent headaches and blurred vision. Pains in the joints made them scream, and often they lost all feeling in their legs. They were left with permanent weaknesses of the limbs, and sometimes paralysis. Breathlessness and palpitations were common after-effects of a day underground. Severe cases would take to their beds and lapse into unconsciousness and die. For many men, surviving the initial attack was only the beginning of their torment. Paralysed, they would remain bedridden while pressure sores developed and festered, and without antibiotics, they eventually died in agony from septicaemia or gangrene. Doctors were baffled by the disease, since some men would work long hours under the same conditions and seem unaffected, while others collapsed after only a short time spent in the caisson. Even more strangely, the victims of caisson disease only suffered these symptoms after they left the caisson, not while working inside it. Gradually, doctors and engineers realized that if the speed at which men left the caisson was slowed, and if the pressure under which they worked was gradually reduced as they returned to the surface, the cases of the bends also fell. Although several physicians surmised that working in a compressed-air environment was having an effect on the caisson worker's bloodstream, the precise cause of the bends was still a mystery. The caisson workers were suffering the same injury that the viper in Robert Boyle's 'air receiver' had experienced two hundred years before. The cause was nitrogen bubbles.

The precise mechanisms involved in producing the symptoms of the bends were discovered by Paul Bert, a French physiologist with an interest in aviation medicine. Just as depth underwater increases pressure on the human body, so ascent into higher altitudes exposes us to lesser atmospheric pressure. Therefore, the effects of pressure on the human body were of scientific interest not just to divers, but also to those who ventured up high mountains, and into the sky in balloons.

Bert was fascinated by what he termed 'the considerable influences which changes in barometric pressure can exercise on living beings', and pondered how it was that communities were able to live in the Himalayas, or the Andes, at altitudes which would make most individuals from sea-level faint. In 1878 Bert's seminal work, *La Pression Barometrique*, established that barometric pressure acts on human beings by diminishing the tension of oxygen in the air, resulting in climbers and balloonists becoming unconscious at high altitude, a condition which Bert proved could be remedied by providing them with supplies of oxygen. The causes of altitude sickness are not precisely the same as the bends, but the relation between physiology and gas exchange under differing atmospheric pressures was for the first time being clearly explained. Bert proved that the nitrogen in the atmosphere we breathe was harmless at normal pressures, but that under increased pressure, as when diving or working in a caisson, the nitrogen would dissolve into the body tissues via the bloodstream. Sudden decompression, the release of pressure, allows the nitrogen to return to its free state too rapidly, with disastrous consequences.

Nitrogen is known as an inert gas, one which the human body does not use in the metabolism. Unlike oxygen, the entire proportion of nitrogen in the air around us is inhaled and exhaled without it taking part in the gas exchange performed by our lungs and bloodstream. And yet, nitrogen makes up the largest portion of the air we ordinarily breathe, around 78 per cent of the total. At increased atmospheric pressure, whether it be due to depth underwater or compressed-air atmospheres like those in a caisson, the density of the nitrogen and oxygen in a given volume of air increases. In simple terms, when pressure increases, there are more molecules of oxygen and nitrogen crammed into the same amount of space. In these circumstances, excess nitrogen passes through the bloodstream and into the body as a solution, especially into fatty tissues. Paul Bert did not discover the fine details of this process, but he pointed his finger at the right culprit in the case of nitrogen's role in the bends.

Once in the tissues, nitrogen does nothing, and no appreciable effects are felt, but when the pressure is released, the nitrogen comes out of solution in the form of bubbles. This is the same process so easily observed in a bottle of carbonated water. Releasing the screw top allows the gas to bubble out. In the human body, if the pressure induced by depth is released too rapidly these bubbles will be large, and when they invade the central nervous system they cause tissue and nerve damage, resulting in the symptoms described as the bends. Bubbles in the joints are especially painful, while those in the spine and brain may cause paralysis, or a fatal stroke. Bert established that if the pressure can be released slowly, then the bubbles will pass out of the body tissues and into the bloodstream at a rate and size at which the body can return them to the lungs safely. Once allowed into the blood at a safe speed, the nitrogen will be released from the body through respiration in the normal way.

In the 1870s, recompression chambers were built by several doctors involved in treating construction workers, and sometimes they were able to halt or cure the symptoms of the bends, but the treatment was randomly carried out and crudely measured. The construction workers knew from bitter experience that temporary relief from the pain of the bends could be obtained by going underground again; however, the return to the surface would very often worsen the affliction. Establishing a precise schedule for safe decompression from depth would not follow for another twenty years, and cases of the bends continued to afflict caisson workers and divers, without any reliable treatment being available to them in the interim. A contemporary of Bert wrote simply that 'Friction, massage and hot baths may be tried as a palliative, and a small injection of morphine to relieve severe pain.'

By 1905, the problems associated with helmet divers working underwater had become a preoccupation for the British Navy. The security of the Empire depended on the safety of the fleet, and divers had become an essential part of keeping her ships afloat. They repaired ships at sea, inspected anchorages and maintained harbours. By then at least ten thousand copper-helmet diving suits were in use worldwide, most of them made by the Siebe Company or their main rivals, Heinke. A large proportion of those diving suits had been supplied to the Royal Navy, but divers had been restricted to maximum depths of around one hundred feet, the safety limit for the equipment in use at the time.

Although it was once considered an impracticable and ungentlemanly weapon for the Royal Navy, the submarine had become a reality of modern warfare, and the possibility of an enemy using them to launch a self-propelled torpedo at British ships had become a new threat in the last years of the nineteenth century. Improvements in submarine technology had at last led to the creation of a British submarine fleet in 1901, and it was this that provided an added stimulus to research into deeper diving.

The loss of an A-Class submarine close to the Isle of Wight in March 1904 in less than sixty feet of water provoked alarm at the Navy's inability to raise the wreck from the seabed or rescue any crew. The A-1 was the first totally British-designed submarine, and her loss with all eleven crewmen was an embarrassment to the Admiralty, if nothing else. In the summer of 1905, another submarine of the same type, the A-8, sank off Plymouth, killing another fourteen men. If divers were to be involved in any realistic rescue procedures then their working depths would have to be increased, and proper procedures introduced for getting the diver back to the surface without risking the bends. In 1905, the Admiralty Committee on Deep Diving was formed, and John Scott Haldane, a prominent Oxford physiologist and a Fellow of the Royal Society, was appointed as its chief investigator. Haldane was already a respected medic with a driving desire to improve working conditions for the common man, and he was politically well connected. His elder brother Richard, having been a prominent Liberal MP for twenty years, became British Secretary for War in 1905.

J. S. Haldane's original interest was in air quality, and in ascertaining what it was that caused miners and factory workers to expire when they were exposed to contaminated air. In 1896, an underground explosion at a Welsh coalmine killed fifty-seven men, but on personally examining their bodies, Haldane discovered that only four had perished in the blast itself; the rest had died from carbon monoxide poisoning. He set out to study the lethal gas, and, largely as a result of his work, the miners learnt to carry caged mice underground to warn them of the presence of its deadly fumes. Haldane's work encompassed anything and everything connected with the physiology of respiration, and he willingly used himself as a guinea-pig in many of his potentially lethal experiments. Through his studies, he made the fundamental discovery that it is the build-up of carbon dioxide in the human bloodstream which stimulates us to breathe. With his knowledge of breathing gases, and as a specialist in human respiration, it was logical that he should be chosen by the Admiralty to apply himself to the problem of nitrogen absorption in the human tissues, the cause of the bends identified by Paul Bert almost thirty years earlier.

While other men were formulating theories on paper as to how to avoid the bends, Haldane used Bert's work as a foundation for a rigorous programme of experiments to find out the precise effects of increased atmospheric pressure on human physiology. He dismissed Bert's use of the term 'caisson disease' as 'somewhat misleading, and much better replaced by "compressed-air illness" '.

Haldane constructed a steel decompression chamber at London's Lister Institute and proceeded to subject goats, pigs, rats and mice to increased atmospheric pressure. By rapidly decompressing these creatures inside the chamber, Haldane would simulate what happened to a diver breathing compressed air underwater and then ascending to the surface. In effect, he gave the animals the bends. Haldane's post-mortem examinations revealed not just that nitrogen bubbles had formed in the animals' nervous systems, but that bubbles were much more prevalent wherever there was fatty tissue. The animals which died were most often those with a greater percentage of fat in their bodies, areas which Haldane knew received a less efficient supply of blood circulation. Now something made sense. Engineers had reported that fat men had died more commonly than others from the bends after working in the caissons. Older, more overweight divers also seemed to be more prone to the disease, and Haldane observed wryly that increasing professional experience coincided 'with the increase in waist measurement which accompanies the onset of middle life'. In short, 'middle-age spread' was potentially fatal to divers. Haldane deduced that not only was the fatty tissue absorbing more nitrogen than other tissues; it was then releasing it more slowly.

From there, Haldane went on to conclude that the length of time spent under pressure affected the severity of decompression sickness, and that the formation of bubbles depended on the body tissues becoming 'saturated' with nitrogen. The longer a person spent at depth, the longer it would take to 'de-saturate' his tissues of nitrogen. Haldane proposed that the body tissues which stored nitrogen most effectively, the fatty areas with poor blood supply, must be allowed to de-saturate by half the amount of nitrogen contained within them before any more pressure was released by ascending to a shallower depth. This, he said, would avoid the formation of bubbles large enough to cause the bends. A man diving to a depth of one hundred feet could safely ascend to fifty feet, wait as long as necessary to allow the nitrogen in his body to diminish sufficiently, and then go back up to twenty-five feet, and so on. How long a 'safe' ascent would take had to be worked out with great precision. It had been thought that a slow descent and a slow return to the surface were the best means of avoiding the bends, but as Haldane points out, 'very slow methods are impracticable on account of changes of tide and weather. The whole physiological side of compressed-air illness had therefore to be reconsidered.'

In developing his theory of staged decompression, John Scott Haldane was applying two crucial laws of physics, established in the eighteenth century, to the problem of the bends. According to Dalton's Law, the pressure of a given volume of air is equal to the sum of all the pressures of each gas within the mixture. In other words, the pressure of one atmosphere of air is made up of the sum total of individual pressures of oxygen, nitrogen and the other gases within the mix. Each gas contributes a proportion of the total pressure. Henry's Law additionally states that the amount of gas which can dissolve in a liquid is proportionate to the pressure of that gas. In diving, therefore, as pressure increases, more gas will be dissolved in the liquid bloodstream and from there find its way into the tissues.

In August 1906, after experimenting with men in his compression chamber in London, Haldane was ready to attempt a sea trial with divers in full equipment. The cool waters of Loch Striven and Loch Ridden on the west coast of Scotland were chosen for the dives, and two men from Haldane's experimental team volunteered for the operation. They were a young Naval Lieutenant, Guybon Damant, an educated man with little diving experience, and an older man, Petty Officer Andrew Catto, who had several years of underwater work behind him. So far as anyone knew, no helmet diver had ever been deeper than one hundred and ninety feet, and only for a few brief minutes under exceptional circumstances. Over successive days Haldane sent Damant and Catto deeper and deeper into the Scottish lochs. First, a hundred and thirty-eight feet, then a hundred and sixty. The next day, both divers reached a hundred and fifty feet, and then dived progressively deeper until they had both made successful descents to a hundred and eighty feet underwater with no ill effects. Each man knew what was expected of him: a gradual ascent to the surface, pausing at intervals on the rope line which they had followed to the bottom of the loch. With typical thoroughness, Haldane made Catto and Damant do heavy work underwater, making them pull on ropes attached to weights to simulate the effort of a working diver. While diving, Haldane had the men take samples from the air inside their helmets, so that he could analyse the purity of the air they were breathing. Among his findings were that the Royal Navy's air pumps were not as efficient, or as well maintained, as they ought to have been.

On the final deep dive of Haldane's field trial, Lt Damant reached a depth of two hundred and ten feet, or thirty-five fathoms as it was measured at the time. This was about as deep as a diver could effectively function with the hand-operated air pumps in use with the Navy. On the return trip to the surface he paused for several minutes at one hundred and ten feet, fifty feet, then twenty-five feet, and made a final stop ten feet below the surface. He had set a new record for a safe helmet dive breathing compressed air, and proved Haldane's theory of staged decompression. Record or not,

Damant's diary entry on the moment when he reached the floor of Loch Striven is hardly celebratory: 'Quite pitch dark – hands too cold to feel much but could not detect any solid on bottom, nothing but mud.'

Haldane's genius was not just to apply the laws of gas physics to the issue of decompression sickness, but to devise a set of mathematical tables which would allow divers to calculate how long they would need to ascend from a dive of virtually any depth, and in how many stages. From this, divers adopted the principle of 'decompression stops', the system of ascending up a weighted line to a prescribed depth and simply waiting until their bodies had been given sufficient time to release a safe amount of nitrogen from their tissues before proceeding any shallower. All divers using compressed air apply the same principles today, although sport divers plan their dives so as to avoid compulsory decompression stops, and hence further reduce the risk of the bends.

Haldane's decompression tables gave precise decompression times for any dive down to a maximum depth of two hundred and four feet (thirty-four fathoms), and in 1907 they went on sale at a cost of just sixpence. However, the barriers to deep diving involved more than the price of a set of decompression tables. Not only was the diving equipment itself quite expensive, but supporting a diver underwater required a large team of helpers and crew, not least to man the air pumps. According to Royal Navy records, a diver at thirty fathoms below would need a team of eighteen men to turn the large wheels driving air through the hoses which snaked down to his helmet. Such dives were rarely attempted; a portable steam pump would have made things easier, but the advantage of the hand pumps was that they could be operated under almost any conditions. In any case, the sheer physical effort of working at such a depth also meant that most divers could only work for a few minutes. When necessary, however, Haldane's decompression tables made deep diving safe, and largely removed the dreaded threat of the bends from the diver's mind. Twenty-five years after publishing his diving tables, Haldane was able to claim that, in the Royal Navy at least, 'compressed-air illness has practically disappeared except in isolated cases where from one cause or another the regulations have not been carried out'.

Men working underwater no longer needed to trust to chance and their own constitution to save them from crippling injury. Haldane's tables became the adopted standard for all Royal Navy divers, and although they would be revised and improved over the years, his work laid the basis for all diving tables formulated afterwards.

County Down Coast, The Irish Sea

Years before I learnt to dive, I lived in Ireland, on a coastline where I could look across the water and see Scotland on a clear day. As the crow flies, it was a clear run across the Irish Sea to where Damant and Catto made their record-breaking dives, although I didn't know it at the time. The edge of our garden fell off steeply through gorse bushes to sharp rocks along the shore, and there was no beach to speak of. Between the rocks there were pools and inlets where thick kelp blurred the line between stone and water and at low tide blood-red beadlet anemones lay on the black granite like oozing warts. With the ebb of the tide even the helpless kelp seemed to suck and slither along the rocks, and underfoot they were greasy with its snail-wet fronds. Dulse, the tough red seaweed that was dried and sold as a snack in local villages, grew in the shallower pools, and as the tide receded there was always the gentle popping sound from the air bladders on the yellow-brown bladder wrack which hung like beaded hair on the upper shore. In summer the inlets were seductive, and on rare days when there was no wind or current to bestir the sand, the water could be as clear as glass.

One warm day I collected some friends and drove them along the coast to where I knew there was good swimming from the rocks, and a high ledge on a spur of granite which made a perfect natural diving board. A series of rocky fingers led out some distance from the shore so that we could dive into deep water without having to wade through the greasy kelp in the shallows. Between the rocks the ravines were filled with enough water at high tide to make a decent swimming pool, though even in summer the water was not warm and no one wanted to be first to jump in. The water was like a magnet to me. Standing on the granite ledge I was determined to get everyone into the water, to smother them in its crystal light and make the most of the bright clear space. I wanted them to understand how rare it was to be able to see the sandy bottom so clearly and have the underwater landscape revealed to our gaze. Today there would be no lurking dark shapes beneath us as we swam, no imaginary terrors lying just out of sight in the grey murk. We had no masks or goggles, just swimsuits and towels to dry ourselves afterwards.

I jumped from the high rock and sank deep into the cold ravine. I had, as usual, forgotten to hold on to my spectacles, and the force of the dive pulled them from my face. I surfaced and trod water, marking the spot where I knew the glasses had fallen, thankful that there was clear sand below me. Only then did I discover that none of my companions could free dive deep enough to retrieve them. Without my glasses I could not drive us home, and none of the others had a licence. We were miles from the nearest village or telephone box, and I had university exams coming up soon. Without my glasses I could not work or even read effectively, and I couldn't even afford to buy a new pair. Time and again I dived to the bottom hoping to get within six inches of where the glasses had lodged, but my eyesight was too poor to find them. We were stuck.

As I harangued my friends for their useless swimming abilities, and they me for my stupidity, a man in a rubber suit and scuba gear appeared from underwater a few yards from where I was bobbing. He stared at us for a moment and started to swim out to sea. I shouted and he turned, popping his head out of the water. I explained what had happened and he disappeared beneath me, emerging a minute later with my glasses. The diver was alone, and with a wave of his hand he disappeared again, submerging like Nereus having deigned to visit the air world to perform a good deed for the day. In all my years of walking this stretch of coast I had never before seen a diver, or even met anyone else swimming.

Diving can be disappointing. People travel to particular diving destinations in order to see certain things: new fish, bigger fish, sharks, manta rays or deep walls of coral. They may want safe, easy diving or more challenging conditions such as strong currents which sweep them through submarine canyons at high speed. There are never any guarantees that a particular species will be around at the time you visit the dive site, and a diver needs to dive often in one spot in order to say he knows it well. Over a number of years I dived one small reef in Seychelles over fifty times. I knew individual fish on the reef, and could easily spot fresh damage to individual pieces of coral. Very often I would hear visiting divers pronounce that they did not want to visit the same dive site twice in one week. 'We've been there already,' they would say. This is as illogical as saying you have seen a sunset on a particular beach once, and don't need to see it from the same place again. The point is that we spend only a brief period underwater, usually barely an hour at a time, and the probability that we will see everything of interest in that moment is nonsensical. Could you stand in a forest and see all the birds that visit a tree in one hour of one day in the year and say you know that tree?

In the same way, diving in tropical waters will not always result in a better experience than diving in the English Channel. Many tropical resorts have contributed to pollution and siltation of the coral reefs offshore so that destinations once famous for their fish life are now a poor imitation of their former glory. Cooler waters sometimes offer more.

In Britain we grow accustomed to subtle light. We notice gradations of illumination never seen in the tropics, and our temperament is affected by how much light we receive at different times of year. The mood of the sea around the British shore is endlessly mutable, absorbing and repelling the sun and sky in a shifting plate of limpidity. Even in high summer it is rare for the sea to be both calm and completely clear. When I dive abroad in clear blue water I never lose my sense of wonder that the sea can be so naked. I stare at it endlessly. My body thirsts for immersion. When I jump into it I am in balance again.

Many British divers have told me they miss our waters when they dive in a warm clear ocean filled with colourful tropical fish. They enjoy tropical diving as an occasional activity, but they revel in the mystique of the cool temperate seas around our own coastline, and enjoy the challenges it brings: strong currents, deeper dive sites and poor visibility. It is not, I believe, just a case of making the sport of diving itself more complex, or more technical, or of making their own activity seem more dramatic. These divers are like the English gardeners who take foreign holidays but say they would quickly tire of an endless summer. They love the scents of the northern spring and autumn in different but equal ways, and they enjoy the clearly defined march of the seasons which bring variety and rhythm to the year.

I often wonder if there is a discernible identity to the underwater places I visit, a connection with the land nearby or an atmosphere which mirrors the country which lays claim to the territorial waters in which I am diving. Is the Great Barrier Reef in any sense Australian? Or are the underwater Florida Keys American? Obviously such national identities are ultimately artificial, on land as well as in water, but the essential spirit of any country is surely an identifiable thing. Once I have dived somewhere I am imprinted with the underwater atmosphere of the place, and often associate what I have experienced with its landbound identity. I believe there is a feel to every underwater landscape, and it may be in stark contrast to the nearby shore, but it is connected to it, and we must use the land as our starting point in order to get there.

The Cornish coastline is usually regarded as one of Britain's most attractive diving areas. Its mild climate in summer and its position at the south-western tip of England gives it a toehold in the rich currents sweeping north and east through the Channel and up into the Irish Sea. When I first visited the coast to dive it was late August, and the sea should have been at its warmest. Our plans were overtaken by the guaranteed irregularity of the English summer. A storm blew up, and it rained for most of the three days we were there. We were cold on land, let alone in the sea.

In spite of the weather, my buddy and I managed to achieve several good dives and saw some remarkably colourful anemones, a nice kelp forest and the impressive wreck of a coal carrier sunk sixty years earlier and now home to impressive schools of big fish. David, my regular buddy at the time, was an extremely experienced South African diver who had dived all over the world, including a spell in the Antarctic on a research vessel. I felt happy underwater with him, since I reasoned he always knew best, and nothing about diving in British waters seemed to worry him unduly. One afternoon he spied a large lobster on a shipwreck, and caught it with his bare hands. It weighed sixteen pounds and had pincers almost a foot long. Back on the diving boat I tried to persuade him to release it, but he argued that to reach that size it must have been fifty years old, and no longer of reproductive age. To me, that made killing it worse. I kept thinking about it surviving all that time, possibly having been alive since the end of the War, and then meeting its end through an unlucky encounter with two divers. David had the decency to eat his lobster, and said it tasted very good, but I would rather have seen it alive and left it there, the ancient guardian of the shipwreck. I feel exactly the same way about big game fishing. Why select a rare and magnificent fish from the ocean, stick a hook in its mouth, or perhaps its eye socket, and fight it to the point of exhaustion and call that sport? I can see no difference between game fishing and big game hunting. Choose an animal, kill it with superior technology, a gun or a carbon-fibre rod, have your photograph taken with it, and then show that photograph to other people. These are exercises in ego, not skill.

One day, when the weather deteriorated further, we were forced to dive in Falmouth Estuary, a relatively sheltered spot, but not the best diving that the rugged coastline has to offer. As David and I flipped over the side of the diving boat into the water, the sky was grey, and it had begun to rain. It seemed warmer underwater than above; at least we were out of the wind. There was nothing remarkable about the dive site, no shipwreck to explore, no kelp and no impressive fish life; it was simply sheltered from big waves.

As we sank slowly into the dull water we found ourselves beside a perfectly flat mud bank which sloped off at an impressively regular angle into the deep. No rock or patch of seaweed broke up the surface. The bank was dark silt-grey, and apparently lifeless. All over the surface there were dead scallop shells, the detritus of fishing boats which had scoured the bank clean of life, or so it appeared. Around us the water was a monochrome expanse, a colourless backdrop of ash-dull nothingness. Not a fish or plant, a shell or a speck of colour or movement was to be seen.

Usually, just being underwater is enough for me, the ease of movement and the rhythmic sound of my air bubbles are soothing and the weightless hovering is its own reward. Simply to allow myself to breathe underwater I have used scuba equipment to scrape algae off swimming-pool walls, and enjoyed the experience; it is still diving. In Cornwall, we were about a hundred feet down when I remember looking up and seeing nothing but mud to one side and dark water on the other. There was merely a faint patch of grey light further up the slope where the surface should have been. High above us the rainstorm had intensified, soaking up the sunlight and effectively cutting us off from its rays. David ferreted in the mud ahead of me and then he ascended a little and dropped back so that I couldn't see him for a moment. I was close to the mud, my face just inches away, using it as my reference point in the void. It was soft and friable, a mountainside of fine dust which could afford me no grip.

The angle of the mud bank made me feel dizzy with its massive insubstantiality. Illogically, I began to imagine myself rolling down the slope, clawing at the soft surface and wrapping myself in a choking slurry as I dropped towards an eternal pit. I had a sense of panic at the thought that there was nothing visible alive anywhere around us. For the first time in my life the sea had become an utterly hopeless and sterile environment. It was as though we were already dead things. In a wasteland. When we left the water I felt as if I had returned from Hell.

5. Advanced French

*At the end of my varied career as a sailor and an inventor, the thing
which gives me the greatest pride is that I was the first to plunge into the
sea, swimming freely underwater without any connection or tie to the
terrestrial world.*

Yves Le Prieur, *Premier de Plongée*

Neutral buoyancy is a state of equilibrium. It occurs when an object
in a liquid is weighted so precisely that it neither sinks downwards
nor floats upwards. A neutrally buoyant object hangs suspended in
the liquid like a bubble frozen in a block of ice. This balance
between floating and sinking is what scuba divers seek to achieve,
which brings them as near to a sensation of weightlessness as can
be experienced without going into space. This liberation from
gravity's tiresome pull frees not just the body, but also the mind.

Divers often call the ocean 'inner space', likening their experience to being an astronaut floating in the cosmos, even calling
themselves aquanauts or oceanauts. The comparison of deep space
with deep sea is not just a neat linguistic juxtaposition of opposites:
of above and below, high and deep, two threatening and airless
environments. Being underwater is more than that, less other-
worldly, more an immersion in one's own thoughts and reactions,
and a confirmation of the diversity and richness of this earth's life.
Total immersion in water does strange things to the mind, but

divers are slow to talk about it, especially to non-divers, perhaps wanting to keep that part of their adventure a secret.

Scuba diving is not, as Jacques Cousteau famously put it, 'an entry into the Silent World'. The sound of one's own breathing is amplified and compounded by the demand valve from the scuba tank. Air bubbles escaping from the regulator mouthpiece make a constant burbling noise. Coral reefs crackle, like ageing bones. Many fish and crustaceans make pops and grunts, slight sounds, muffled to the human ear, but they add to the noise none the less. The silence that divers seek is more internal. Diving makes you think and allows you to think alone.

Underwater, the noise of my own breathing reminds me that I am an unnatural visitor to this world. A sibilant, sucking, respirator sound fills my throat and mouth, lips unflatteringly stretched around the neoprene mouthpiece supplying me with air. The air filling my lungs is compressed and chilled, cooling me faster than the conductive properties of the sea around me. Ninety feet above, there is a blue canopy dappled with silver and gold haloes as sunlight hits the waves. Up there, the world is real, filled with conversation, relationships, decisions, plans to be made.

Underwater, there is freedom from everything terrestrial. For me, *inner space* more accurately describes the place my mind goes when underwater. The mental release that neutral buoyancy brings is even more valuable than the interaction with creatures of the deep.

SCUBA – the Self-Contained Underwater Breathing Apparatus – has made recreational diving accessible to anyone in reasonable health and with the inclination to do it. But in historical terms, scuba represents just one phase in the struggle to explore and conquer the marine world. Only in the span of one lifetime has there been a commercially successful breathing system available which allows a swimmer to attach an air cylinder to his back and swim down under the sea purely for pleasure.

If he set his mind to it, Yves Le Prieur was one of those men who could build anything he wanted. If something was broken, he could fix it, and he was always ready to improve on other men's machines. In 1925, while serving as a Captain in the French Navy, he attended an industrial exhibition at the Grand Palais in Paris. There, amongst the latest mechanical inventions, he saw a large glass tank in which a diver was demonstrating a prototype blowtorch to cut sheet iron underwater. In the tank the diver was using a simple breathing device, a rubber tube held clamped horizontally between his teeth and connected to a hose which in turn led to a pressure pump, very similar to a bicycle pump, on the surface. On his face the diver wore a pair of goggles resembling wire-rimmed spectacles, and his nose was pinched closed by a strong rubber clip. The diving device was a system invented by his compatriot Maurice Fernez a dozen years earlier, and used extensively by Mediterranean shell and sponge divers as a cheaper alternative to a copper-helmet diving suit. The crowds around the diving display shifted and moved on, but Le Prieur stayed put. He stared transfixed at the diver, struck by the freedom of movement the man enjoyed in the display tank.

In the Navy, Yves Le Prieur had tried the traditional diving helmets and lead-soled boots which the seamen used for fixing ships' hulls and inspecting propellers, but what he saw in the exhibition tank was something else entirely. The underwater welder was wearing only a swimming costume. He was virtually free to move up and down wherever he wished, a merman freed from the shackles of heavy equipment. His arms could stretch and move unencumbered by a canvas suit, he could turn his head and look up or down without being confined inside the metal dome of a helmet, while his feet were free of the leaden-soled boots which rooted the Navy divers to the seabed.

Although the mechanic in the Paris exhibition tank was free of the heavy diving equipment used for underwater salvage and repair, he was still dependent upon the hose to the surface for his supply of air. Deep-sea divers had been working in the same way for a hundred years, always hampered by heavy equipment and a fragile air line stretching like an umbilical cord to a boat above. The air line kept them alive, but it also posed a hazard, a potential entanglement which might trap the diver by wrapping itself around a shipwreck or be caught by a ship's moving propeller and slashed, with predictable results. The air line also fed a continuous supply of air to the diver, which was trapped inside his helmet and canvas suit, inflating it gradually like a balloon and making him more buoyant. To prevent himself from suddenly floating to the surface with fatal consequences, the diver had to periodically tap his head against an exhaust valve on the inside of the metal helmet to release excess air from inside the suit. He walked upright underwater, heavily weighted down so as to compensate for the buoyancy of the canvas suit and copper helmet. He also needed the weight, as much as two hundred pounds in total, so as to work in underwater currents which might topple him over.

Yves Le Prieur finally walked away from the Grand Palais, his mind buzzing with an obsession. He would find a way to dive like the underwater welder, but he would somehow do away with the air hoses which tied the diver to the surface pumps. Then he would go where he pleased, swim freely underwater and see the underwater world as a man-fish.

Le Prieur was already forty years old when he attended the Paris exhibition, and had served in the French Navy for several years in the Far East. Whilst stationed in Tokyo before the First World War, he had learnt Japanese and studied ju-jitsu. He became the first foreigner to publish a book on how to learn the martial art, and while working as a translator at the French Embassy in Tokyo, achieved the distinction of becoming the first man in Japan to fly an aeroplane.

Le Prieur had never seen an aeroplane of any description until his father posted him a magazine from France which contained news of the latest developments in the new and exciting world of aviation. In the magazine there was a detailed drawing of a biplane, and an article explaining that the secret of successful flight was to use lightweight materials. Le Prieur decided he would try this new craze out for himself. He had the drawings of an aeroplane, and looking around him he saw that Japan could provide an endless supply of a suitably strong but lightweight construction material. Bamboo. He would build an aeroplane in the grounds of the small cottage he was renting in the diplomatic quarter of Tokyo. After a few days, he ran out of space, and managed to obtain permission to move his project to the grander confines of the French Ambassador's garden.

As Le Prieur worked on his bamboo creation, he realized that on his naval salary he would never afford the price of an engine to make it fly. Determined to persevere, he decided to build the plane as a glider to the same design, and find a car to tow him into the air. Interest in his project spread around the diplomatic community, and after several weeks Le Prieur was ready to try out his biplane. The Ambassador invited a selection of local dignitaries and fellow diplomats to an afternoon garden party to watch the device take to the air. Embarrassingly, there was too little space in the Ambassador's garden for the glider to pick up sufficient speed for lift-off. Le Prieur sat grounded in his machine as the assembled crowds looked on, distinctly underwhelmed by the possibilities of this new technology.

Attempts to find a vehicle with enough power to get the glider off the ground proved impossible until a wealthy Japanese baron offered the use of his own car, a machine with a remarkable forty horsepower engine. In December 1909, Yves Le Prieur set up his biplane in a public park, and with some difficulty managed a short flight no more than twenty feet in the air before landing safely, if precariously, using ailerons controlled by pieces of string. Other flights followed, and Le Prieur decided to leave the Navy and become a flier.

On his return to his home town of Lorient in France, Yves Le Prieur informed his father that he wanted to take up flying. His father dismissed the idea out of hand, predicting that aeroplanes were a passing fad, and that nothing useful would come of them. Unwilling to upset his widowed father, Le Prieur enrolled in the School for Naval Engineering. There, Le Prieur's aptitude for invention was put to good use, and he went on to design accurate mechanical range finders for ships' artillery, an artificial horizon for an aeroplane cockpit and an incendiary rocket for bringing down zeppelins.

Le Prieur had a particular talent for adapting and improving existing technology, and the sight of the diving display at the Paris exhibition fired his imagination. Using the proven Fernez diving system, he hit upon the idea of attaching the diver's mouthpiece to a bottle of air, and found the perfect solution in a new product being used by the French motor trade. The Michelin Company were using compressed air in bottles to inflate the latest pneumatic car tyres, and Le Prieur attached one to the Fernez mouthpiece.

Le Prieur was not only an inventor; he was also a man with the means to put his ideas to the test. He contacted Maurice Fernez, who gave him permission to use his device as the basis for his new idea. In the summer months of 1925 he experimented with the Fernez equipment at his villa in the South of France. By the following summer he was ready to demonstrate his new invention, the 'Fernez–Le Prieur' device, to the public at a Parisian swimming pool. Attaching the three-litre Michelin air bottle to his back with leather straps like a rucksack, and wearing a pair of swimming goggles, he had the foundations of the modern aqualung. Now he was free to swim underwater.

'I felt as happy as a boy', Le Prieur wrote afterwards, 'who has been given a magic toy which would allow him to live underwater as easily as a fish.'

Le Prieur was not the first to conceive of disconnecting a diver from his surface air supply. In 1825, an English inventor named William James had proposed fitting a coil of metal tubing around a helmet diver's waist which could sustain him with air for a limited period, although it seems certain the device was never tested. In 1860, two Frenchmen, Benoit Rouquayrol and Auguste Denayrouze, had invented a commercially successful diving suit which included a compressed-air reservoir as an emergency back-up device. For short periods of time, and at shallow depths, a diver could unplug himself from his air line and move around the seabed using the reservoir of air carried in a metal canister on his back. It was the Rouquayrol–Denayrouze helmet design which inspired Captain Nemo's diving suits in Jules Verne's undersea epic 20,000 Leagues Under the Sea, published in French in 1870, and translated with huge success into English three years later. The use of a self-contained air supply had also been used successfully in fire-fighting helmets, and equipment designed to allow men to escape from mining disasters where air was fouled by gas or chemical explosions. Such equipment had in turn been adapted to make emergency breathing bags for submariners, although the bags used provided a very short supply, only enough for the sailor's ascent to the surface. A Japanese company had demonstrated what they called a 'peerless respirator' in 1918, but, although it allowed a diver to breathe underwater, its operation was technically complicated and impracticable for sustained effort at depth.

In general, until Le Prieur demonstrated his new invention, divers were artisans, rough, uneducated men who carried out dangerous tasks and were paid accordingly. They were useful workers, scraping the bottoms of ships encrusted with barnacles, freeing propellers from entangled lines or even recovering treasure from sunken wrecks.

Underwater naturalists and photographers had begun experimenting with deep-sea-diving helmets in order to see the underwater world for the first time, but they too were using the device as a practical means to an end. No one dived for the sheer pleasure of being underwater, and no one swam freely underwater while breathing. Yves Le Prieur moved in different circles. After the First World War, he was promoted to the rank of Captain, and he had made close friends with Jean Painlevé, a pioneering producer of scientific films whose father had been Prime Minister of France. Painlevé, who wanted to film marine life, was intrigued by his friend's invention, and together at St Raphael on the French Riviera they would found the world's first diving club. The *Club des Scaphandres et de la Vie sous l'Eau* was its polite title, but informally it was known as the *Club des 'sous l'eau'*, a slang term for drunkards. The club was somewhat exclusive: the year was 1934, and few ordinary people took holidays or had the resources to invest in one of Le Prieur's diving inventions.

Yves Le Prieur continued to improve his diving device, moving the air cylinder from his back to his chest, a position he considered safer since the cylinder would not accidentally bump against an underwater obstruction without the diver noticing. A valve to regulate the air flow out of the Michelin cylinder and a pressure gauge to monitor its contents could also easily be seen by the diver when worn on the chest rather than behind him. By the time he patented his new diving device in 1933, the name Fernez had been removed from the design. Public demonstrations in the Paris

Trocadero followed, and various gimmicks were displayed by fellow members of the St Raphael club, including an underwater bicycle with lead tyres to keep it underwater, and Le Prieur's latest idea, an underwater gun fired by compressed air. The gun, named the 'Nautilus' in honour of Jules Verne, enjoyed limited success in underwater hunting as it was too powerful, perhaps as a result of Le Prieur's naval munitions experience, and generally blew its target to pieces.

Archive film taken of Le Prieur's diving equipment by his friend Painlevé shows him at play on the Riviera, or performing somersaults in an elaborately designed underwater set at the Trocadero. To draw in the French crowds, a suitably attractive female swimmer who could hold her breath underwater joined Le Prieur, playing the role of mermaid.

The disadvantage of the device as conceived by Le Prieur was that the air flowed continuously out of the Michelin bottle, and at any depth below ten metres would be exhausted in ten minutes, perhaps sooner. To regulate the air flow, the diver would turn a manual valve at the top of the cylinder, but without a more finely tuned airflow control the device was useful only for a brief underwater excursion, and many people dismissed the invention as a plaything for the idle rich. Others took the invention more seriously, and the Navy adopted Le Prieur's diving equipment for its potential use in underwater salvage and inspection. The Paris fire brigade also used the equipment to retrieve corpses from the Seine.

When Le Prieur and his wealthy friends took to the sea for their excursions, they swam with plimsolls on their feet, and wore Edwardian-style one-piece bathing costumes. In 1935, an article in the *Paris Soir* newspaper appeared about the St Raphael 'underwater-swimming club', and shortly afterwards Le Prieur received a letter from a fellow naval officer named Louis de Corlieu, who was anxious to join the club and try out the new sport. De Corlieu was no idle supplicant; he too was an inventor, and told Le Prieur that he had a patent for something he called 'life-saving propellers'. De Corlieu had designed the first rubber foot fins, or flippers, and by 1933 had registered the patent for both hand and foot propellers in eight countries. De Corlieu offered Le Prieur's underwater-swimming club several sets of his propulsion devices free of charge, anxious, he said, to take the design out of the drawer and into the water where it belonged. Louis de Corlieu also offered to give the club members instruction in the latest swimming technique, the crawl, which in his own words would allow them to move as easily and 'happily as fish in the sea'. Yves Le Prieur took up the offer.

Equipped with foot propellers, Le Prieur could now glide with ease underwater. Then he added a further refinement to his system. Instead of tight-fitting goggles, which would press against the diver's eyes with increasing water pressure at depth, he attached his breathing cylinder directly to a mask, which covered most of the face. Instead of two small goggle lenses, the diver now looked through one plate of glass, and excess air flow escaped around the face from the edges of the rubber mask pocket. The air inside the mask acted as a cushion, keeping the mask from pressing uncomfortably against his face. Now, Yves Le Prieur looked like a modern scuba diver.

Underwater, the scuba diver is a weightless nymph, soaring, gliding and hovering wherever he chooses. Out of water, divers in full equipment are ungainly, swaddled in rubber and weighed down by a backpack festooned with an air cylinder and its attendant air hoses, dials, and the clips and buckles which keep them all in place. A wrist-mounted computer which calculates depth and time underwater and automatically displays decompression times has

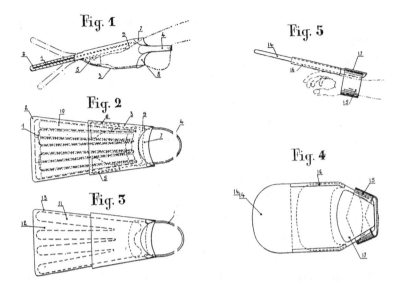

K. *Louis de Corlieu registered his patent for crêpe rubber hand and foot propellers on 6 April 1933, inventions he saw as devices for life-saving.*

become standard equipment, used in addition to a back-up system in the form of a diver's watch and depth and air-pressure gauges. In Britain, we often carry a spare air cylinder in addition to the main supply, a so-called 'pony' bottle with just enough air to get to the surface and allow for a decompression stop on the way up. A knife strapped to a calf, a torch or two, and a reel of nylon line to clip on to a fixed point as a marker at the start of a dive all have to be fitted into the ensemble, as well as an inflatable safety buoy, which can be used on the surface to signal our presence in choppy seas. The diver begins to resemble a robot, his flesh invisible and his body disguised by dehumanizing excrescences. Back pain after a day carrying such equipment around is not uncommon.

For many years I was uninterested in scuba diving, mostly because I felt the equipment was ugly, a bulky restrictive tangle of daunting technology which seemed the very antithesis of what being underwater should represent. Even the prospect of squeezing oneself into a wetsuit in the promise of protection against the chill of the sea held no appeal. People imagine that a neoprene wetsuit flatters the physique, compressing any unwelcome flesh into shape just like a corset. In fact it seems to do the opposite, creating extra padding and rolls around even the most lithe of figures. One winter's day at university, I was propositioned by a diver from the sub-aqua club who offered to give me a bear hug whilst wearing her wetsuit. She was a large person whose charms had been wasted on me, and she clearly felt that the offer of a rubberized encounter might provoke some greater affection. I could imagine nothing worse and declined the offer as decently as I could.

In cool or temperate waters, the wetsuit must be tight-fitting so as to trap a layer of water effectively between the neoprene and the body. The diver's own body heat will warm the layer of water sandwiched against the skin and insulate him from the cooler water outside the suit. If the sea temperature requires a thick wetsuit then it is usually also necessary to wear thick neoprene bootees, gloves, and a hood in addition to the body suit. Fully attired, above water it is difficult to breathe with ease, and the effort of struggling into the suit makes me pant like a dog. A strong belt weighted with lead pieces or lead shot counters the increased buoyancy of the rubber suit. Once equipped, I can stand up and hobble in feet encumbered by fins to the side of the boat and attempt a graceful entry into the sea. Like a seal, floundering and slow on a rocky shore, I know I will undergo a metamorphosis when I heave myself into the water. As the bubbles and froth of this explosive invasion of the water's surface dissipate, I am free again. The weight and discomfort of the equipment disappear, and all I am conscious of is the functional efficiency of the items which will allow me into the liquid world.

*

At the same time as de Corlieu and Le Prieur were tinkering with their swimming inventions in the capital, and on occasional sojourns to the Riviera, another equally important but informal association was developing. Skin diving, the art of catching fish armed with a homemade harpoon and a pair of goggles, was in its infancy as a hobby. The French Riviera in the Thirties had all the right ingredients to inject fresh impetus into the new sport – warm water, and a large concentration of leisure travellers looking for a new diversion.

One of the first men to practise the art of skin diving for pleasure was an American journalist named Guy Gilpatric. In the early 1930s he contributed a series of articles on the art of spear fishing to Philadelphia's *Saturday Evening Post*, a paper specializing in health and fitness developments. His occasional despatches from the South of France were popular enough to inspire the first book on pleasure diving, *The Compleat Goggler*, published in 1938. In it, Gilpatric describes fashioning his own underwater mask from a pair of flying goggles, whose ventilation holes he stopped up with putty. Over successive summers, Gilpatric and others developed increasingly effective goggles and then masks through which to view their prey – the tasty grouper and octopus who made their homes along the rocky coastline. Other designers, modelling their designs on goggles made from polished tortoiseshell by pearl divers in Japan and the South Pacific, took up the challenge. They soon discovered that two separate lenses resulted in distorted vision underwater, since it was impossible to keep the small lens cups in exactly the same horizontal plane – a distinct disadvantage when judging one's distance from a targeted fish. The early gogglers used homemade harpoons and had no flippers to propel themselves through the water. They experimented with weights around their middles to allow themselves to sink faster in pursuit of fish, and with simple snorkels made of rubber tubing fastened around the face with elastic bands.

In 1937, a Russian émigré named Alec Kramarenko, living in

Antibes, spent several months taking rubber moulds of his own face in an attempt to build a more comfortable face mask which would fit everyone. He patented a rubber mask which covered both eyes and sat across the bridge of the nose, with a single-plate glass lens which overcame the problem of distortion but brought with it another equally distressing phenomenon. The rubber skirt around the mask pressed against the forehead and nose, creating a hermetic seal. As the diver went deeper underwater, the increased pressure forced the mask against the skin, leaving painful red welts and causing the eyes to bulge painfully behind the glass. An alternative design, the full-face mask, allowed the breath-holding skin diver to exhale into the mask to counteract the squeeze of water pressure as he dived. It did not, however, permit the diver to relieve the excruciating pain on the ears. As he dived, increasing water pressure on the outside of the ears and differential pressure on the Eustachian tubes at the back of the throat had to be equalized in order to avoid a ruptured eardrum. This time another Frenchman, Maxime Forjot, came up with the solution, a mask in which the rubber skirt covered only the eyes and nose of the diver, a design patented in 1938 which allowed a diver to grasp his nose between finger and thumb and blow out gently with the mouth closed. This technique clears the ears by pushing air up the Eustachian tube to counteract the inward pressure of water on the outside of the eardrum. An Italian physician first described this technique, known as the Valsalva manoeuvre, in the eighteenth century. The Valsalva is an adaptation of a natural reflex, which increases the efficiency of the abdominal muscles and is also experienced when lifting a heavy weight, or in childbirth to expel a baby from the uterus. It can also be described as a mild version of what you do when straining during a heavy bowel movement. With brow furrowed, jaws clenched and lips pursed, the abdominal muscles force air into the throat.

Gilpatric found the whole idea of the sport faintly amusing, and the tone of *The Compleat Goggler* is self-deprecating. It is a book full of jokes, and features recipes for cooking the fish caught with the new spear-fishing equipment. To prepare octopus, he advises tenderizing with a mallet. 'Beat him hard. Beat him plenty. Beat him some more.' Gilpatric mocks everyone on the Riviera: the English, the French, the Germans and himself. However, for many spear fishermen back home in California, *The Compleat Goggler* would become a bible, and the techniques Gilpatric described would shape the development of skin diving in the years leading up to the Second World War. Gilpatric himself would not live to see the sport grow, dying in a suicide pact with his wife when they discovered she was suffering from cancer.

In Europe, in happier times, two young men stood on the shore and watched Guy Gilpatric skin diving at Antibes. They would take up spear fishing as a result of seeing him in action, and copy his equipment to spear their own fish. Independently they would go on to become the first household names of the modern sport of scuba diving. They were Jacques Cousteau and Hans Hass.

In June 1939, Yves Le Prieur received a visit from a young naval lieutenant, who introduced himself as Jacques-Yves Cousteau. In his own words, Le Prieur was 'only too happy to meet a young man with just as much enthusiasm for diving as myself'. The young officer wanted to see the diving equipment which the French Navy and the fire brigade of Paris had ordered, and he wanted to hear from its inventor's own lips how it functioned. Le Prieur and Cousteau had much in common, even a similarity of physique, both men thin but wiry types with distinctly Gallic noses and dark hair brushed straight back off the forehead. More importantly, they shared a naval background, and, like Le Prieur, Cousteau had travelled widely in the Orient. Coincidentally, Cousteau and Le Prieur were both frustrated aviators. While Le Prieur had abandoned flying to please his father, Cousteau had been forced to give up his place in flying school after a serious car crash, suffering injuries which almost cost him the use of both arms, and causing after-effects which stayed with him throughout his life.

Le Prieur found Cousteau cordial, and extremely enthusiastic about the possibilities of free-swimming divers exploring the undersea world. In 1942, with France occupied by German troops and the French Navy out of action, the young officer came to see Le Prieur again, this time accompanied by his wife, Simone, and one of his diving companions, Frédéric Dumas. Le Prieur invited the trio to stay for lunch and the talk was all about diving. 'Cousteau showed me his first diving device,' Le Prieur wrote later, 'but I felt it was unsafe, and advised him to use it with a mask which covered the whole face, not just with a breathing hose held in the mouth.'

Cousteau told Le Prieur that he had been experimenting with underwater photography, and explained that he had been constructing watertight cases for use with a cheap cine camera. Cousteau had been filming simply by diving down while holding his breath, and he was keen to find a safe way of staying underwater long enough to film more extended sequences. Yet again, the two men found common ground. Le Prieur's inventive talents had also led him into the world of film, not least through his association with Jean Painlevé, and one of Le Prieur's latest schemes was a watertight camera system, and a prototype cage which he hoped could be used for filming sharks underwater. One of Le Prieur's many preoccupations was his fascination with the world of film, and he had invented a transparent screen which could be used to create special effects for the movies. The device was used in the 1932 version of *King Kong*. Disastrously, Le Prieur had let his patent on the invention expire, having been assured by experts in Hollywood that the system was inferior to one already in existence.

Jacques Cousteau was also an avid film fan, and an aspiring film-maker. He had even managed to visit Hollywood during a round-the-world voyage in the Navy, a visit on which he managed to wangle a meeting with Claudette Colbert and Douglas Fairbanks. When the Cousteaus left Le Prieur's house in Paris, all was well, and Jacques promised to keep Le Prieur abreast of his future research into new diving equipment.

For Le Prieur, diving experiments had been interrupted by the War, but in Cousteau's case, the hostilities would provide the means to an end, an ideal opportunity to develop and improve his diving skill. With the French fleet scuttled at Toulon, he was on armistice leave from the Navy and able to set up house in the small Mediterranean fishing village of Bandol, where he and several friends could practise their underwater film-making. 'The first requirement of diving was to feed our band of twelve,' Cousteau wrote afterwards. 'We ate few fish. We calculated that in our weakened physical condition an undersea hunter would burn more calories chasing and fighting a fish than his portion of the game would restore.'

Simone Cousteau, whom Le Prieur described as a charming woman, was indirectly to hold the key to the next stage of diving history. Her father, another ex-Navy officer, happened to be a director of the Air Liquide Company, the main French manufacturer of industrial gases. Through his father-in-law, Cousteau was able to arrange a visit to Paris in December 1942, to meet Emile Gagnan, a senior engineer with Air Liquide. Gagnan had been wrestling with the problem of designing a valve which would allow motor vehicles to use natural gas as a substitute for petrol during the War. What was needed was a valve to control the flow of gas from a bag on the vehicle's roof, which would only dispense gas to the carburettor when the engine required fuel. Cousteau explained that he needed something which would allow compressed air to be delivered in the same way, not to a car engine, but to a man's lungs via a breathing tube. Gagnan found the answer. A new valve, which would allow the diver to receive air only when he sucked on the mouthpiece attached to the hose leading from the cylinder, would solve the snag of Le Prieur's continuous-flow device. Gagnan's valve worked in two stages: the first comprising a spring-loaded valve at the neck of the compressed-air bottle, which reduced the pressure of the flow of air to a manageable strength; while the second – a rubber membrane or diaphragm contained in the diver's mouthpiece – only released this lower-pressure air when the diver breathed in: the so-called demand valve.

Cousteau experimented with Gagnan's invention by diving in what he describes as 'a lonely stretch of the River Marne' close to Paris. After a few days and several minor modifications, they had a working scuba system. Instead of the ten or twenty minutes of diving possible with Le Prieur's device, Cousteau's regulator allowed the diver as much as an hour in shallow water. In 1943, the first regulators were delivered to Cousteau in the South of France, a moment he records in *The Silent World*: 'no children ever opened a Christmas present with more excitement than we did when we unpacked the first "aqualung".'

In 1943, Jacques Cousteau and his friends in Bandol made several hundred dives with the new invention, testing it with experienced skin divers Frédéric Dumas and Philippe Tailliez, as well as with Cousteau's wife Simone. They used it to make underwater cine films. Emile Gagnan and Jacques Cousteau christened the new device the 'Aqualung'.

Within a few years, the demand-valve regulator would be the world's first successful commercial scuba system. For Yves Le Prieur, the Cousteau–Gagnan device was something of a surprise. The Navy abandoned his invention in favour of the new system, although Le Prieur believed that the regulator held in the diver's mouth made him liable to drowning if he passed out underwater. Le Prieur's continuous-flow system supplied air into a full-face mask, allowing him to breathe whether conscious or not, and the air pocket around the face allowed him to talk underwater to other divers. With typical thoroughness, Yves Le Prieur improved his own breathing system to regulate the supply of air, and his system also included a pressure gauge attached to the air tank so that the diver could monitor his remaining air supply, which the aqualung did not. Even so, the patented Cousteau–Gagnan design swept all before it. 'I never heard from Cousteau again,' Le Prieur wrote years later, 'only of his fame.'

The harsh reality is that perhaps a thousand of Yves Le Prieur's scuba systems were manufactured and sold, whereas Cousteau's system became the world's most powerful brand name in diving. The Aqualung was easy to use, and it allowed virtually anyone with a mask and fins to become a diver. Like Hoover and the vacuum cleaner, the name of the brand and the generic tool became interchangeable terms. When Cousteau began to sell his under-water films for international distribution after the War, the success of the Aqualung was guaranteed, and media attention focused on the man who told the story of diving so vividly in his book *The Silent World*, co-written with Dumas and an American journalist, James Dugan. Magazine and newspaper articles, including a particu-larly profitable relationship with *National Geographic*, were com-bined with Cousteau's charismatic personality and a talent for filming diving expeditions to the far-flung corners of the world. When television came into its own as a mass medium in the 1960s, Cousteau was a natural star, and his gentle French accent and carefully scripted delivery made him an international household name. The adventures of Cousteau and his ship, the *Calypso*, inspired a generation to take an interest in, and formulate an affection for, the sea.

Since Jacques Cousteau died in 1997, his reputation within diving has been somewhat revised. Like almost all modern heroes, he has not been allowed to rest in peace. With the benefit of hindsight, journalists and former colleagues began to pick over the private life of the man who had seemed the epitome of the daring adventurer. They criticized his techniques of filming wild animals and questioned his scientific method, painting him as a self-publicist who hogged the limelight at the expense of other pioneers in diving.

In California, Cousteau's son Jean-Michel now runs Ocean Futures, an organization dedicated to fostering positive relationships between man and the ocean. I went there to ask him about his father's contribution to diving.

'My father was not the first to invent the technology of scuba,' Jean-Michel told me, 'but once he got on to television, he brought the ocean into people's homes. Even *The Silent World*, which was a major book and film success, only reached a few million people, but once he started making the television series in the mid-Sixties, I would venture to say he had, maybe, an audience of one billion people in a hundred and twenty countries.'

Did his father see himself as an environmentalist?

'Not at first, it's true. But I think he made people wake up to the fact that we are dependent on the ocean. He brought the underwater world into their living rooms, and that hasn't gone away. I think he was in the right place at the right time, and his driving force was always his curiosity. The scuba technology was just another result of his obsession with looking for something new. All his life it was the same. If he knew the answer to something, it didn't interest him any longer. His curiosity was insatiable, and infectious.'

From *Life* magazine to *National Geographic*, Cousteau's exploits made irresistible copy. He travelled the seven seas, dived for treasure, and even experimented with building houses on the seabed. Filming manta rays in the Indian Ocean, sharks in the Red Sea or octopus in the Mediterranean, he provided readers with populist forays into the mysteries of the oceans. In 1951, *National Geographic* published a photo-feature on Cousteau and his 'Fish-Men', which provided huge publicity for the forthcoming book, *The Silent World*. In its first year of publication it sold almost half a million copies worldwide. Captain Cousteau was made. Among the international fans mesmerized by the story of undersea exploration was Ian Fleming, the creator of James Bond. He became a life-long admirer of Cousteau, and dived with him; Cousteau's experiences were no doubt the inspiration for many of 007's most thrilling underwater escapades. Cousteau's own film, *World without Sun*, won him a Hollywood Oscar (1965), as did his documentaries *World of Silence* (1956) and *The Golden Fish* (1959). For over a decade, the television series *The Undersea World of Jacques Cousteau* was a blueprint for marine-documentary makers, and essential viewing for any child or adult with an interest in the sea. Films, television series and books all reinforced the Cousteau image, making him the most famous scuba diver of all time.

In October 1943, Jacques Cousteau and his two closest diving companions decided to make a test to see how deep a man could dive with the new aqualung system. The trio, Cousteau, Frédéric Dumas and Philippe Tailliez, called themselves 'The Three Mousquémers', making a pun on the French word for sea (*mer*) and the adventure story entitled *The Three Musketeers*.

Dumas was chosen for his fitness and experience to descend feet-first down a rope line anchored in two hundred and forty feet of water. He was the strongest swimmer of them all, and he pulled himself down the line to a depth of two hundred and ten feet, the deepest anyone had gone with the new aqualung. Dumas returned safely, tying his weight belt to the line to mark his depth. Returning to the surface, he reported that once below a hundred feet he had felt happy and carefree, almost as if he were drunk. Dumas was suffering from what Cousteau and his friends called 'rapture of the deep'. It is still one of the most serious hazards of diving with compressed air.

Four years after Dumas set his record for deep diving with the aqualung, the Mousquémers were officially diving for the French Navy, and had formed a unit known as the *Groupe d'Etudes et de Recherches Sous-marines* (the Undersea Research Group). The GERS was used for mine-clearance work, mapping underwater obstacles, and anything else useful to the postwar reconstruction of the Navy. In September 1947, tests were ordered on the possible maximum depths at which divers using the scuba system could work. Near to the Navy base at Toulon, Maurice Fargues was chosen to make the first dive.

Chief Petty Officer Fargues was known as a tough sailor, an experienced helmet diver who had great physical strength. He attached a rope safety line to his belt and clasped a lump of pig-iron in one hand as ballast to help him descend an anchored line leading into the depths. At intervals on the descent line, Fargues paused to scribble his name on marker boards attached to the rope, marks which would verify the depth he had reached. Occasionally he would pull on the safety line attached to his belt, signalling to the men on the ship above that all was well. After four minutes, the line went slack. The sailors above hauled on the line, dragging the diver to the surface. He was unconscious. For several hours the crew tried to revive him, but Fargues was dead. Despite his strength and his experience he had fallen victim to nitrogen narcosis. While they worked on Maurice Fargues' corpse, someone pulled the descent line to the surface. At three hundred and ninety-six feet they found a childish scrawl on one of the marker boards. Fargues had attempted to write his name on it, perhaps seconds before he passed out. He had earned a place in the record books as the first man to die using the aqualung.

The physiological causes of nitrogen narcosis are now well documented. All novice divers learn that diving with compressed air presents two major hazards: the bends and narcosis. And yet divers continue to be fascinated by depth. To non-divers, it is as illogical as the obsession some people feel when driving a sports car. They simply want to say they have driven faster than the next man. Deep diving often appeals to the same mentality. But there is a poetry in deep-water diving which seduces otherwise logical and sensible men. Errol Flynn, the swashbuckling actor, wrote in his memoirs that deep diving terrified him, prompting him to take risks he would never have entertained in his film career. 'I must go down,' he wrote. 'It is the indescribable beauty down there that makes you want to go and hold it. It is an exercise in quick reflexes. Your mind sharpens, it snaps, it works like an automatic pistol . . . then I am living – and if not, I am dying as one who has, just before, been living intensely.'

Freeport, Bahamas, 1968

Two men in scuba equipment step off the side of a charter yacht and swim down a weighted rope line into the clear, blue water. At the bottom of the line they attach a metal clip to the rope and begin to swim back towards the surface. Heavily weighted, the downward journey has taken them less than three minutes, and they have reached a depth of four hundred and thirty-seven feet, and one inch. The divers do not know it. They cannot think straight, and they feel drunk.

The divers are suffering from nitrogen narcosis. Knowing that this would happen, they have strapped their regulators on to their faces so that they will not spit them out and drown. It is as much as they can manage to signal to each other that they must now swim back up the line.

They do not know how long they spend at maximum depth, perhaps a few seconds, perhaps half a minute. To reach the surface and avoid the bends, it will take the two divers one and a half hours of slow ascent, most of that time spent hanging on to the rope line at sixty feet. As they swim into shallower water their heads become clearer, they can think again and they know they must adhere to the plan they made for safe decompression. They feel cold and tired. Once out of the water, the rope line is pulled up after them, and only then do they learn that they have set a new world depth record for diving breathing compressed air. Over the next thirty years, at least ten divers will attempt to match their achievement. They will all die.

The two men were Neal Watson and John Gruener, both at the time in their late twenties and extremely fit athletes. After diving and training together for over four years, they calculated that they were both physically and mentally strong enough to subject their bodies to the effects of the deep. They were also defying the laws of physics, and demonstrating that man underwater can push back the barriers of what science says can and cannot be done.

Neal Watson is still in the scuba business, operating a string of diving resorts franchised under his name. I travelled to Fort Lauderdale to meet him, to try to understand what drove him to attempt such a potentially suicidal dive.

Watson accepts that what he did in 1968 was dangerous, and he would never encourage anyone to set a depth record using compressed air. The hazards are well documented, and no responsible diving organization would sanction such an attempt. Today, depth records on air have become a virtual taboo subject, with anyone claiming a record drawing censure and criticism from the diving establishment, in the diving press and from the world of medicine. And yet, there is a glint in Watson's eye when he talks about the adventure of deep diving. I asked him if he had thought he might achieve fame or fortune by setting a record for compressed-air diving.

'No way,' Watson replied. 'A local paper reported the story, and eventually the *Guinness Book of Records* picked it up, but most people in the business thought it was a bad idea. At 437 feet it was cold and dark. We were like vegetables down there, because of the nitrogen in our bodies, and neither of us could remember anything about what happened when we attached our markers to the depth line. The first thing I said when we came back was that if anyone else wanted the record they could have it.'

By defying the rules, Watson and Gruener were confronting all of the most important dangers in scuba diving with compressed air. Alongside the increased risk of the bends if they miscalculated their rate of ascent, two hazards, nitrogen narcosis and oxygen poisoning, are silent killers which lure divers into irrational behaviour, or simple oblivion. When Cousteau and his team experimented with their new aqualung in the 1940s, 'rapture of the deep' was part of the learning process, a hazard which they eventually realized was potentially fatal. In those days, they had no definite scientific information on the processes causing the sensation. Now, divers commonly allude to the feeling as 'being narc'ed', a catch-all phrase which jokingly denotes any kind of unusual behaviour, above or below water.

The process of intoxication with nitrogen is related to the effect of pressure upon the nitrogen particles contained in air. At normal atmospheric pressure at sea level, nitrogen accounts for the largest proportion of the mixture of gases we call air – about 79 per cent.

At sea level, nitrogen plays no part in the normal respiration process, since at atmospheric pressure it is not absorbed into the tissues. Under pressure, i.e., as a diver goes deeper underwater, the air he breathes will be subject to the prevailing pressure at that depth. For reasons still not precisely understood, nitrogen breathed under pressure leads to sensations similar to excess alcohol in the body.

In the eighteenth century, John Dalton discovered that the total pressure in a mix of gases is equal to the sum of the individual partial pressures of the gases in the mixture. That is to say, oxygen and nitrogen will each exert part of the overall pressure within a given quantity of air. Each gas is therefore said to exert a 'partial pressure'. To calculate the partial pressure of a gas, it is necessary to determine the fraction of that gas in the breathing mixture, and multiply it by the total pressure of all the gases present. The unit of measure for breathing gases is usually expressed in terms of atmospheres (atm), with the pressure at sea level representing 1 atmosphere. Using this formula, if we know that the percentage of oxygen in surface air is 21 per cent, the partial pressure of oxygen is ·21 × 1 atmosphere = ·21 atm, and in the same way, the percentage of nitrogen is ·78 × 1 atmosphere = ·78 atm. If atmospheric pressure is doubled, then the number of oxygen and nitrogen molecules contained in a given volume of air will be twice what it would be at the surface. The percentage of oxygen in the mixed gas never changes, but the concentration of oxygen molecules in a given lungful of inhaled air will become greater.

Dalton's Law, when combined with Boyle's Law, is crucial to an understanding of diving physics. Boyle states that at a constant temperature the volume of a gas varies inversely with pressure (i.e., less pressure = more volume), while the density of a gas varies directly with pressure (more pressure = greater density). This is the reason why divers must never hold their breath as they ascend after breathing compressed air – the air bubbles will expand as pressure decreases, and if not released from the lungs in time will burst them like balloons. A third law of physics must also be taken into account. Henry's Law, formulated in the nineteenth century, states that the amount of any gas dissolved in a liquid at a given temperature is a function of the partial pressure in contact with the liquid. It follows, then, that greater pressure will lead to larger amounts of the gas being absorbed into the liquid human bloodstream, and hence into the tissues.

When a diver goes deeper underwater, these laws of physics account for an increase in the partial pressure of nitrogen and oxygen, resulting in higher concentrations of both being taken into the body as he breathes. Below about seventy-five feet of seawater, nitrogen begins to affect a diver's mental processes, in part because it interferes with the way nerves function. Below about one hundred and seventy-five feet of seawater, the oxygen in compressed air becomes poisonous. Pure oxygen alone, while vital to life, is poisonous even at the surface if breathed continuously and will eventually lead to lung damage. Under pressure, the effects of breathing pure oxygen are more dramatic, and more swiftly felt. As shallow as thirty feet underwater, it can cause seizures. Hans Hass, whose first dives were all carried out using pure oxygen, described the onset of symptoms to me as white patches appearing at the edge of his sight, with his view gradually narrowing to tunnel vision. When oxygen is mixed with nitrogen, the effects of oxygen toxicity will not be felt during recreational dives, but once beyond the two-hundred-foot depth, anyone may fall victim. Theoretically, at depths below three hundred feet, almost all divers will succumb to its effects after only a few minutes of breathing compressed air. However, most physicians argue that oxygen toxicity remains a theoretical risk, since nitrogen narcosis will cause them to succumb before it takes effect.

Watson and Gruener's depth record in 1968 is remarkable on several levels. In the first place, they knew that they had an estimated fifty–fifty chance of dying during the dive. They knew that nitrogen narcosis would affect their ability to reason under-water, and they also knew that breathing compressed air at extreme depth would expose them to the risks of oxygen poisoning.

Neal Watson, although almost sixty years old now, is as fit and strong as a man twenty years younger. He is lean, with the wiry physique of a lightweight boxer, broad chested and narrow hipped. When he speaks his voice is a deep baritone, molasses mixed with gravel. It holds the attention, and it is easy to imagine him pushing himself to the limit. He admits that he is addicted to deep diving.

'There's nothing like it, and to this day I still do deep dives. When I see a wall I have to do at least two hundred and fifty feet. I won't let others do it, but for me that's virgin territory. I'm comfortable and at peace down there.'

What about narcosis?

'At one-eighty, one-ninety feet you get that little buzz. In the Bahamas we have what we call the Tongue of the Ocean, where the walls start at forty feet and go down six thousand. The water is clear and you look up and still see the boat. I love to level off at two-twenty-five, or two-fifty feet, and just hang for a minute, then start coming back. Slowly. It's a sensation you can't get anywhere else.'

Casting his mind back to the October day in 1968 when he and Gruener went down to four hundred and thirty-seven feet (and one inch), he claims that part of their success was due to mental attitude. Having spent time in the Far East in the military, he picked up the techniques of Zen meditation. Staying calm during the deep dive was vital to survival. Any panic, any attempt to bolt for the surface would have been fatal. By meditating and focusing

completely on what they were trying to achieve, they gave themselves less to think about underwater.

Watson is keen to stress the hazards of depth. 'The best way of
explaining the deep dive is to think of getting in your car and
driving at forty miles an hour and taking a shot of whiskey. Then
go to fifty and take another shot. Then go to sixty and take another.
And then seventy, and more whiskey. So, at the same time as you
get impaired by the alcohol you put yourself in a situation where
you increase the need to be in control. You can never allow
recreational divers to get into that situation.'

In common with many experienced divers, Neal Watson believes
that he developed an increased tolerance to nitrogen narcosis. By
frequently diving deep he became acclimatized to the effects of the
gas on his body, in the same way that the brain can, over time,
become accustomed to higher and higher levels of alcohol in the
body.

Neal Watson also remembers that, mixed with the narcotic
effects of the depth, he experienced a feeling that he can only
describe as 'enlightenment'.

'It was a spiritual feeling,' he recalls. 'I went to Sunday school
as a kid and was brought up religious, but this was something
different. It was like being given the key to the universe. Suddenly
there was this pleasure, and I just understood everything. For years
I just chalked it up to narcosis, but then a few years later I read
about people who had had what we call near-death experiences
. . . drowning or whatever . . . and in retrospect, I think the
enlightenment comes from pushing yourself to the edge and coming
close to death.' Watson thinks about it for a moment, clearly
recalling the sensation, then continues, 'It's changed my attitude
to life and death. I was always annoyed when I came back to the
surface that I could remember the feeling of enlightenment, but
couldn't quite remember the secret of life, the universe and

everything that had been so clear down there! But my attitude to life and death since then has changed. I'm not scared of anything much any more . . .'

There is a confidence about Neal Watson which might be mistaken for arrogance. 'I didn't expect the deep dive to make me well known,' he claims. 'But I do like looking in the mirror in the morning and knowing that I've done something no one else has done.' By his own admission, he has an addiction to adrenaline. In 1972 he flew a gyrocopter, a miniature one-man helicopter, from Miami to the Bahamas, setting a record for distance in the machine which he says now was as dangerous as deep diving. 'I really thought I was going to die on that one.'

Watson is able to laugh at himself too. Some time after setting the depth record for diving on air, he established a record for smashing concrete blocks with his forehead. 'I don't boast about that one, but I did break ten inches of concrete, which I had set on fire for effect, and managed to set my hair alight and split my head open.'

In 1975, Neal Watson returned to scuba diving to attempt yet another record, this time for distance rather than depth. He intended to swim one hundred miles in scuba equipment, but in the event only managed sixty-six miles from Islamorada in the Florida Keys to Miami.

'I wanted to do the hundred miles, but my support team made a mistake,' Watson says with a hint of displeasure. 'After about nineteen hours in the water I signalled for them to bring me fresh water to drink and they sent down the hose-pipe containing warm seawater that I used to heat my wetsuit. The salt water made me sick, and we had to abandon the dive.'

Other problems dogged the record attempt. Safety divers travelled behind the dive boat in a shark cage, ready to provide assistance should Watson get into difficulties. The cage fouled the umbilical communications cable designed to allow Watson to talk to the boat. From then on he had to use a waterproof slate on which to write messages to signal his needs to the safety divers, who would also swim down to transfer him fresh air tanks during the dive. 'Unfortunately, when it got dark we had no lights because of the problem with the communications cable. They tied a lot of chemical glow-sticks to me so they could see me. I was like a piece of trolling bait in the sea at night, and I had to stay down at least twenty feet to keep out of the boat's wake and the surge.' Watson was able to attract public interest in the distance record since people could more easily relate to the concept than they could to the problems of a deep dive.

'As far as I know that record still stands,' Watson claims. 'But I guess there are some records that are too crazy for people to want. If someone had challenged me I would have gone after the distance record again, because it's about strength and physical stamina. I trained hard for that, getting up at dawn and swimming underwater, mile after mile after mile.'

Neal Watson still dives, and teaches people to dive for pleasure rather than to get into the record books. He values the peace and tranquillity of being underwater, and, like many businessmen, says he often has good ideas underwater. 'A lot of guys say they have all their good ideas in the shower,' he grins. 'Multiply that tenfold when you're diving.'

Deep diving continues to be a controversial topic. In 1999 a British diver, Mark Andrews, claimed a new record for diving on air to just over five hundred feet. Like Neal Watson, he claimed he was mentally prepared for the attempt, although in the event an equipment malfunction made Andrews ascend too fast, at a speed of around a hundred and fifty feet per minute. To avoid lung expansion injuries, sport divers are advised to ascend no faster than sixty feet per minute. Andrews came out of the water like a rocket, and began to feel nauseous. He had the presence of mind to return to depth and begin a two-and-a-half-hour decompression. He survived, complaining of temporary blindness before he reached maximum depth, possibly due to oxygen toxicity. Like Neal Watson, Andrews claims he survived the experience by withdrawing into his own mental space, virtually willing his body to relax and cope with the demands being placed upon it.

Many divers are excited by depth, especially male divers. 'How deep have you gone?', they enquire innocently, knowing that they must keep up the pretence that diving deep is not a sign of machismo. Of course it is.

The considered response to such enquiries is normally to explain that going 'deep' is pointless in terms of marine life, and safety. With each successive foot of depth, the diver's air consumption will increase, thereby shortening the available dive time. As you swim deeper, you enter a world where there is less light, and hence less life, and almost always less coral growth. All scuba training is designed to drum into people's heads the premise that beyond recreational limits of thirty to forty metres, diving becomes much more hazardous. In some countries there are now legal limits on recreational diving, and tour operators and dive shops must adhere to the restrictions or lose their licence. Dead tourists are bad publicity, after all.

Deep diving on air is an exercise in probability. Go deep enough for long enough and you will die. Individuals may prove that they are less susceptible to narcosis or oxygen toxicity than the norm, but eventually they will find their place on the statistical graph. The physics and physiology of deep diving is not new, yet every few years it seems as if a group of sport divers will claim that they can do something previously thought impossible.

I once dived on a deep wall in the Caribbean with a group of half a dozen divers. As we sailed over the edge of the wall, the visibility was as good as it gets, there was no breath of current and the deep blue was all around. Without a signal between us we all went down the wall as a group until we were past our planned dive depth. The oldest and least fit diver among us carried on until he was at a hundred and eighty feet on the wall, twice the recommended maximum. The desire to keep going just another few feet was strong, and I felt it myself. I looked at my depth gauge and checked my air supply. Everything was in order. I looked up at the surface, and it didn't seem far. Except that my depth gauge told me it was too far to swim if my air supply failed. I imagined the desperate swim to the air world, fighting for breath, legs kicking against the weight of water pressure, and the panic it would induce. I decided not to go deeper, not least due to the fact that I wouldn't have trusted my companions to rescue me if something went wrong.

When we returned to the boat the skipper was annoyed. He had been watching us go down, and seen the mass hysteria (what else can I call it?) that had led to a flagrant abandonment of the instructions in his dive briefing. The skipper told me that only a few weeks previously one of the crew on his boat had done the same, and simply never been seen again. Later, it emerged that the diver had just learned that he had been jilted by his girlfriend. Officially, his lonely death remains a mystery, but to many divers *in extremis*, the embrace of the depths seems like a fitting and logical end to life. Swimming further and further downwards, they eventually reach the point of no return. Like a desperate suicide who drifts off into an eternal sleep with the aid of drugs, the diver finds deep immersion the ultimate gentle release, a homecoming in an element where they have known only joy.

Farquhar Island, Southern Indian Ocean

On Farquhar, one hundred and eighty miles north of Madagascar, I found a turtle skeleton. The bones lay where the beast had died, or at least where the carcass had been dumped after the meat had been removed from its back along with its valuable shell. What I saw was the view from underneath, laid out on the ground like an x-ray image. The remains were as carefully arranged in death as some specimen in a zoological museum. A symmetrical lozenge of whitened flat plates lay on either side of the spine. These irregular four-sided plates had formed the underside of the carapace, and around them was a perimeter of bone, white spokes similar in shape to those under the flesh of a human finger. Now devoid of cartilage and muscle, meat and skin, the neat spokes in turn had formed a circular rim, on to which the outer shell would have been attached. I stared at the collection of dried bones for minutes, wondering why the mere skeletal shape of the turtle was so fascinating. White, and clean and desiccated, the bones were just the framework of a being, yet they possessed the same grace and beauty as a living turtle. Even in death, the creature mesmerized me with its compact, self-contained neatness of being. The bones lay undisturbed on a patch of coral above the tide-line beside the lagoon on the western edge of the island. This was *pavé* coral, compacted and dried, cement-like, and flattened into a solid mass by the wind and tide. The flat block stretches for a hundred square feet back from the lagoon in a rectangular patch as if it had been built by human hands. At the water's edge it drops sheer into the clear blue water, and I could see sharks in the lagoon, dark shadows moving against the pure white sand bottom. In the centre of the natural lump of grey *pavé*, man had made his mark. There, in the shade of the first casuarina trees of the shore, is a square pool, carved out by inhabitants of the atoll over a century and a half ago.

The pool was a turtle pen, where the creatures had been kept alive for use as food. Plantation workers in the early nineteenth century were settled on Farquhar, some of them African slaves freed from Arab traders by Royal Navy ships and put down on any island where they could survive. Eventually the island had become a copra farm, where coconut husks were dried and baked to produce the rich oil used all over the world for cooking or as an ingredient in soap.

When turtles came ashore to lay their eggs or entered the shallow waters of the lagoon to feed, they would be caught, placed in the pool and saved for slaughtering until fresh meat was needed.

As I walked around the pool, I saw that a long channel about three feet deep and a couple of feet wide had been dug between the pool and the edge of the pavé block where it dropped into the lagoon. Following it, I saw that the channel led directly out from the solid coral to the high-tide mark. At high tide the channel would be filled with seawater, running along to the pool to replenish and refresh the water in which the turtles were trapped.

Turtles do not cry out in pain. When sailing ships made long voyages of discovery, the turtle was a favourite dish. Once caught, it could be kept alive for weeks in a ship's hold without food or water, ready to be slaughtered as needed for fresh meat. Obligingly, a turtle will lie helplessly on its back for weeks in a shady corner of the ship's larder, waiting for the day when the cook decides to boil it up for dinner. The only precaution necessary is that a small wooden block be inserted under the turtle's head while it is upside down to act as a pillow, supporting its weight and keeping its airway straight, so that the animal does not suffocate.

The modern-day plight of the turtle is well documented. Images of hatchlings scrambling across a beach at dawn to face the assault of predacious crabs and sea birds are a staple of the wildlife documentary film. Like soldiers on a First World War battlefield, they drag themselves across the wet mud in their hundreds, while all around their brothers are pecked and dissected by beak and claw. Few survive the first days, perhaps less than 10 per cent of the original clutch so laboriously buried in the sand by the mother several weeks before.

Once at sea, the perils of the turtle include a host of other marine creatures. Fishing nets may entangle the animals and drown them, for like us they breathe air.

Even in places where turtle hunting is officially banned, the creatures are still caught and eaten. Sometimes, if a poacher finds a turtle in shallow water or on the beach in daylight, he will hide it in the bushes until dark, when he can return to carry it off unseen. To prevent the turtle dragging itself down the beach to the sea, he will chop off its front flippers and leave it, bleeding quietly in the grass.

Once I saw a female hawksbill turtle who had lost a flipper, perhaps to a shark when she was young. Under the leathery skin an inch or two of the stump would twitch in unison with that on the other side, but it gave no real propulsion. She swam well enough with just the remaining limb, and was a regular visitor to this particular reef. How would she manage to mate without being drowned, I wondered, and how would she fare when the time came to haul herself up the beach to try to dig a nesting pit for her clutch of eggs? Would she drive herself to exhaustion, and die of heart failure in the attempt?

The numbers of turtles worldwide continues to fall. They are fished, netted, even shot with rifles. They eat plastic, the blight of the sea, which floats ceaselessly around the globe. Ironically, the advent of plastic in its many forms has relieved the turtle of the need to provide man with its shell, once polished to transparency for ornament or spectacle frames. Instead, the threat now comes from floating plastic refuse, which may choke and then starve the animals as it blocks their stomach in an indigestible lump. The beaches on which they nest are often those which attract man the most: clean, wide expanses of soft sand, ideal for tourists. Bright lights from electrical installations scare away the pregnant females, or confuse and disorientate the hatchlings, who are programmed to make for the source of light when they emerge from the sand. They mistake the brightest areas for the sea, which would normally reflect the moon and stars and stand out from the darker shoreline.

Even without man, the turtle must survive a tough life at sea, with females coming to land only to lay their eggs perhaps every two years. They eat jellyfish, soft coral, fish and crabs as well as sea grass and algae. They have no teeth, chewing and grinding their food with the sharp edges of their horny jaws. Leatherback and Olive Ridley turtles are particularly rare now, and green, logger-head and hawksbill turtles are all under threat. Each year, all over the world, fewer and fewer females return to the beaches to lay. A marine biologist explained to me that it is possible that we will not know when all the turtles become extinct. For several years we may see females laying eggs, and assume that there are enough turtles out there to keep the species viable. Some species are thought to reproduce for up to thirty years, and, like tortoises on land, the turtle may keep a store of fertilized eggs within her body for laying in batches. And so the last generation able to find mates will keep on laying throughout their reproductive lifespan. However, their hatchlings will enter the sea and reach the point where the few survivors are insufficient to maintain a breeding stock. Only when the last individuals of the last successful breeding generation die will we find that there are too few turtles around to maintain the species. Then they will be gone.

The sea turtle is an old life form and a gentle one. To swim underwater with a turtle is one of the greatest privileges granted to a diver. To quietly observe the animal feeding, crunching its way into a piece of coral growth, and then see it raise its head and stare back, is an emotional experience. It will swim on, steady in purpose and uninterested in human contact. Sometimes nothing will induce the turtle to leave its feeding spot except the need to return to the surface to breathe. It will look at you as it chomps, so that you become embarrassed as if caught staring at a stranger in a restaurant. At last it will stop eating and swim up for air. From below, the sight of the graceful disc of the turtle's body rising in silhouette against the bright surface of the sea is unforgettable. The awkward flippers, which make turtles so vulnerable and clumsy on the beach, have become efficient paddles. One powerful stroke from the front flippers and the turtle is a flying thing. It will turn and glide, using the momentum of its heavy body to swoop and soar like a paper aeroplane. Water is almost a thousand times more dense than air and yet the turtle flies with the grace of angel wings.

Turtles are vulnerable and unthreatening. Many divers report that every time they see a turtle close up they feel like crying. Even in a young animal, the skin around the neck and eyes appears cracked and worn. Improbably, the turtle's eyes appear moist even underwater, coated with their own tears, and they peer at the world around them intently. If a diver grasps a turtle, as some persist in doing, it will make no attempt to bite or harm the attacker, even though the creature may drown under such attention. Once released, the turtle swims away, usually into deeper water, even though it must be in desperate need of air. At night the turtle may feed on a shallow reef, or find a protected ledge in which to wriggle out of sight and rest. Slowing down its metabolism, it will remain immobile for an hour or more. Periodically, it will surface for a brief refill of air and then glide back down to pass the night sequestered below.

To swim at a respectful distance from a turtle and match its pace without making it fearful is to fall in love, charmed by ancient eyes.

6. Flickering Images

I showed my pictures, and had the great joy of seeing they made a good impression. They were the best he had ever seen, said William Beebe; and I believe my work could not have had any finer reward.

Hans Hass, Diving to Adventure

Vienna, Austria

Flurries of swirling white particles obscured the road ahead as the airport bus pushed its way through a snowstorm, taking me towards the centre of Vienna late at night. The snow obscured any sense of the approaching city until we reached the terminus, an anonymous row of bus shelters alongside a large hotel, the streets and pavements all but deserted in the storm. I exchanged the warmth of the interior of the shuttle bus for a large Mercedes taxi to reach my small guest-house on the outskirts of town, the only accommodation available on this night, the climax of Vienna's winter-ball season. Driving past the baroque architecture of the old town I had my first glimpse of the grandeur of the former Imperial city. Outside the State Opera House, a convoy of police vehicles and armed men stood ready to prevent any interruptions to the debutantes' ball, and there was a brief glimpse of bright light from the plush-covered interior. It was a scene from another age, a romantic dreamscape of sweeping public squares and ornate buildings illuminated by floodlight reflected in the gathering snow.

The snowfall persisted overnight, and I awoke to the muted sounds of electric trams and snowploughs carving their tracks from an icing-sugar world. Joining the ranks of heavily wrapped commuters at the metro station, I found my way to the *Steffl*, the Gothic cathedral of St Stephen which dominates the pedestrianized centre of Vienna. Smart clothes shops, jewellers and antique dealers crowd together in the surrounding streets, interspersed with an essential supply of coffee shops, chocolatiers and fast-food outlets. Glass-fronted post-modern architecture mingles with the Baroque, and although much of the city centre was bombed during the Second World War, it is difficult to discern the truly ancient from the neatly reconstructed.

Sonnenfelsgasse is a narrow street a few minutes' walk from the *Steffl*. Here, in a utilitarian postwar apartment block, I had come to meet Hans Hass. To television viewers in the mid-Sixties, the work of Hass had been eclipsed by the longer running and more sophisticated films and series of Jacques Cousteau. Cousteau's pre-eminence in the popular imagination has undoubtedly over-shadowed the public memory of Hass, and yet to a whole generation of sport divers in the 1950s and 1960s, it was Hans Hass, and his expeditions to the Red Sea with a small team of marine biologists, who first created mass interest in diving for pleasure. Although Hass had enjoyed world renown in the 1950s, later he practically dropped from view, devoting his time to research in social science, and leaving most of the glare of publicity to Cousteau and the plethora of other underwater cameramen who hit the small screen in the 1970s and afterwards. Following Cousteau's death in 1997, interest in Hass was revived, and for the first time in a quarter of a century, the gentle and dignified Austrian scientist began to speak up about his own role in early diving. Jacques Cousteau perfected the aqualung in 1943 for use with compressed air, but by this time

Hass had already successfully used an oxygen-based scuba system to film coral and sharks in quality good enough for German and Austrian cinema audiences.

In *Sonnenfelsgasse*, Hans Hass opened the door to apartment thirty-nine and extended his hand in greeting. The grip was strong, and it was hard to believe that this energetic man with his trim beard and dancing eyes had just celebrated his eightieth birthday. 'Come in, come in,' he said warmly. 'Make yourself at home, and welcome to Vienna.'

The apartment was small, a simple L-shaped design with a square living-room leading off from a short corridor. From floor to ceiling there were bookshelves crammed with scientific papers, books by Hass and other marine biologists, and piles of paper and correspondence on every available surface. In one alcove an old film-editing table took pride of place. There was order in the mess, and a neat desk clear of clutter at which the man himself now sat. I explained apologetically that I wanted to talk about the early days of Hass's experiments with diving, material on which I knew he had been questioned exhaustively over the years.

'I am at your disposal,' said Hass, fixing me with a professorial stare. 'I do not mind repeating my story; it is only when I am asked questions which are somewhat, how shall we say, uninformed, that I get a little angry.'

There was enough steel in the warning to put me on my guard, but after a few minutes the atmosphere relaxed again, and Hass seemed to be enjoying himself. Sitting close to him, I was impressed by his alertness, his ability to recall clearly the events of sixty years previously, anecdotes which in no way differed from his many published accounts written at the time. He delivered his story with old-world *politesse*, an educated gentility which made no concessions to the socially inelegant levellings of the late twentieth century. Hans Hass had the ability to mingle appropriate phrases from

English, German and French with ease, names and places from a dozen scientific expeditions and as many countries flowing through his recollections without falter.

Hass told me that he was inspired to take up the new sport of skin diving after a chance encounter on the French Riviera with its chief exponent, Guy Gilpatric. According to Hass, at the age of eighteen he was on holiday at Cap d'Antibes and had been unlucky in his first attempt at love. Seeking solace in a lone vigil on the rocks of the Cap, he spotted the American swimming in the bay with a primitive harpoon. Every now and then the man would sink smoothly below the surface, only to reappear with a fish on the end of his harpoon. Hass says that he struck up conversation with Gilpatric, who told him where to obtain a harpoon from a local mechanic. In Gilpatric's *The Compleat Goggler*, he mockingly refers to an Austrian youth pestering him with questions about diving, and describes him as 'that goggling Kraut, who had come from far out to sea', having eyes that 'were the Beautiful Blue the Danube is supposed to be but isn't'.

Hass, a natural athlete, taught himself by trial and error to become a skin diver, and subsidized his time at Antibes by selling his successful catch to hotels and restaurants. When he returned to Austria, he earned further income by giving a series of lectures to sports clubs. He became a successful and popular public speaker, raising significant amounts of funding for diving expeditions. He had speared giant grouper and wrestled with octopus bare handed. At first his true stories were met with amusement and scepticism, and the disbelief from his audience inspired him to prove what he was saying about the marine world through underwater photography.

Hass designed his own waterproof housing for a camera, and had it made up by a blacksmith in Vienna. To test the housing and perfect his technique, he then organized an expedition with some student friends to the Dalmatian coast in 1938. The funds generated by subsequent illustrated lectures, and his first book, *Jagd unter Wasser mit Harpune und Kamera* (Hunting Underwater with Harpoon and Camera), allowed him to mount another more ambitious expedition the following year, this time to the Caribbean. Hass had official backing from Vienna's Natural History Museum for a fish-collecting visit to Curaçao, an adventure which was complicated by the outbreak of war.

According to Hass, who eventually returned to Vienna in 1940 along a circuitous path from the USA via Hawaii, Japan and Russia, his fame as a diver and scientist was sufficient to allow him to pursue his studies during the War. In 1941 he managed to publish his second popular diving book, *Unter Korallen und Haien* (Among Corals and Sharks), a book which even Adolf Hitler is said to have read. Excused military service due to poor circulation in his feet, he passed much of 1942 cruising the Greek Islands and studying corals for his doctoral thesis. A film of the expedition shows Hass and two friends who had been on the Curaçao expedition living a seemingly carefree existence, sailing among the Sporades and testing various prototype diving helmets. By 1943, Hass had made enough money to buy his own boat, and began to mount his own independent diving expeditions.

Hass was lucky enough to be awarded his doctorate in zoology during the War, when his thesis miraculously escaped damage during a bombing raid which destroyed much of Berlin University. The end of the War was a major setback for Hass: his boat was commandeered by invading Russian troops, the same army which disposed of many of the specimens collected by Hass's expeditions to the Mediterranean. The soldiers' interest was not zoological, they simply wanted to drink the alcohol in which the specimens had been preserved. For several years Hass was unable to travel, and he returned to Vienna to painstakingly resurrect his public-speaking career. He hired a pretty young assistant named Lotte Baierl to run his office, a girl introduced to him by mutual friends. By 1949, Hass was back in the water, mounting the first scuba expedition to the prolific waters of the Red Sea. For the first time a free-swimming diver took close-up photographs of giant manta rays, photographs syndicated to newspapers and magazines around the world. A ciné film of the dives won first prize at the Venice Biennale, assisting Hass's reputation, and his income, with international sales.

In 1952, a year before Jacques Cousteau's *The Silent World* hit the book stands, Hass's third book, *Diving to Adventure*, was already an English language bestseller. After the War, feature films for cinematic release and the first television documentaries on under-water life followed, with the hugely successful series *Diving to Adventure* screened by the BBC in 1956. It was television – moving pictures from under the sea – which would turn Hans and Lotte, whom he had now married, into the first household names in diving.

Today, the presentation style of those early black-and-white pro-grammes seems charmingly outdated. On a television stage-set of complete domestic perfection, Hans sits in a high-backed armchair in front of a fireplace. Neatly groomed in dark jacket and tie, Herr Doctor Hass stares straight at the camera, addressing it in what then was regarded as an informal manner. To his right, Lotte, in a floral-print dress, her hair in a perfect bouffant, makes scripted asides to the eminent man in her heavily accented but grammatically perfect English. In one early episode, Lotte remarks, 'Hans, in our last pic-ture we didn't show the viewers how you began to be an underwater explorer. I think they would like to know how these things start.'

Hans goes on to recount how at the age of nine he told his mother that he wanted only to become a deep-sea diver, and wanted nothing whatever to do with women, adding with deadpan delivery, 'I've changed some of my ideas since then.'

'I know,' Lotte replies, with a theatrical downward cast of the eyes.

To the first generation of underwater tourists, Hans and Lotte were matinée idols. Tanned and photogenic, they toured the seven seas on board their elegant, three-masted sloop *Xarifa*, capturing the wonders of the reef for the first time with modern photographic techniques. Accompanied by a crew of lean, tanned young men, their first films for an international audience brought exotic images of the Red Sea coast with the added attraction of sexual chemistry under the Arabian sun.

The early helmet divers were not interested in underwater scenery. They were carrying out functional tasks, working underwater but getting back out of it as soon as the job was finished. It was rare for a diver to give us any flash of lyrical description about being underwater. The naturalist William Beebe used a diving helmet to take photographs in the 1920s, and he was amongst the first to convey any sense of joy when describing his underwater experiences:

Your attention swings from wonders to marvels and back again. You begin to say things to yourself, gasps of surprise, inarticulate sounds of awe, you are troubled with a terrible sense of loss that (as the case may be) twenty, thirty, or fifty years of your life have passed, and gone without you knowing of the ease of entry into this new world.

Beebe was a prominent member of the New York Zoological Society, who abandoned shallow-water diving in a helmet for a new invention of his own conception, the bathysphere – a large steel ball with small observation windows that could be lowered from a ship by steel cable. Beebe worked out that the perfect shape for a deep diving machine was not a cylindrical tube, like a conventional submarine, but a sphere, the shape which could best withstand extreme pressures. It would have a skin made of steel over an inch thick, with three small observation windows made of quartz, the strongest material they could find that would allow them to look out of the bathysphere. An engineer, Otis Barton, built the bathysphere, and in 1930 he and Beebe tested the device, which would take them deeper into the sea than any other men had ever gone. By 1934 they were able to make a dive to over three thousand feet in the Atlantic near Bermuda. Unlike his early helmet dives, this was not the stuff to inspire underwater tourism, since Beebe's ultimate adventures took him into what he called the realm of perpetual night, the dark abyss beyond the continental shelf which he likened to deep space. Beebe's love for the sea is evident in his writing, and he predicted that diving would become a major human activity, inspiring underwater artists and even underwater gardening of anemones and coral. Beebe said that he could imagine nothing more thrilling than his glimpses of the underwater world, perhaps only a trip to Mars.

Other scientists had also seen diving as a means to an end, using the technology to achieve first-hand observation of the marine environment. In 1844 the French naturalist Henri Milne-Edwards had preceded Beebe underwater, using a surface-supplied helmet. Milne-Edwards dived along the Sicilian coast, collecting samples of sea life in shallow water, determined to see the animals in their natural environment rather than the dried specimens he was used to examining. Fifty years later, another Frenchman, Louis Boutan, a member of the Academy of Sciences and an expert on pearls, became the first scientist to take underwater photographs. They were fuzzy images in shallow water at first, but by tinkering with his camera design he eventually produced creditable results, even manufacturing an underwater arc-light of considerable power for night photography. By 1908 an Englishman, Francis Ward, had taken moving pictures of otters and birds swimming underwater, an achievement made possible by building a glass-fronted cement observation tank inside an artificial pool in which the creatures he wanted to film could be more or less controlled. It is a technique still in use today. However, such achievements did not stir the public imagination. Film-makers had to learn how to make the underwater world exciting to the general public. Entertainers, not scientists, would see the real possibilities of underwater drama – in Hollywood.

In 1913, John Ernest Williamson was working as a reporter and photographer for a small American newspaper in Virginia. To impress the paper's editor, he adapted a device which had been built by his father to salvage shipwrecks. The invention was a telescopic metal tube which dangled below a ship's hull. It was big enough for a man to climb down inside it, and had an observation chamber at the end where the salvor would sit and manipulate a set of grappling hooks. Williamson had the idea of using the new observation tube as a way of taking underwater pictures. The editor was suitably impressed, and the results were published, claimed erroneously as the first ever underwater photographs. Soon, the young journalist had backers offering him money to make an underwater moving picture. With help from his brother George, Ernest Williamson took his equipment, and the observation chamber which he called a photosphere, to the clear waters of the Bahamas, where he succeeded in filming not just colourful fish and coral, but real-life drama. Determined to capture the most exciting images possible, he held his breath and swam down with sharks close by, even stabbing one in the belly with a knife.

Williamson's early Bahamas films were turned into a document-ary, *The Williamson Submarine Expedition*, which was a commercial success. Several other short films followed, and then the Williamson brothers obtained backing from Universal Studios for a full-length feature, their 1916 version of Jules Verne's *20,000 Leagues Under the Sea*, which instantly became a box-office hit. The underwater scenes were like nothing audiences had ever seen, and the *New York Evening Sun* described the film as 'the most thrilling photodrama produced to date'. In several scenes, Captain Nemo and his companions are seen walking along the seabed wearing diving helmets and self-contained breathing apparatus. Williamson had ingeniously adapted some oxygen breathing sets designed as escape systems for submariners, and concealed them under the helmet divers' costumes, allowing them to walk upright across the sand without the complicated air hoses reaching down from the surface. Rather than actors, Navy divers hired for the purpose did the actual work.

Ernest Williamson made other underwater films, *Wet Gold* and *Mysterious Island* among them, beginning a trend for other film-makers to follow. After *20,000 Leagues Under the Sea*, cinema audiences expected anything to do with diving to involve high drama, dangerous sea creatures and a large helping of derring-do.

In the face of any calamity, my grandmother would always intone the adage, 'Worse things happen at sea', a motto which conjured up every eventuality from drowning in a shipwreck to corporal punishment at the hands of a vicious bo'sun with a cat o'nine-tails. To my impressionable mind no terrestrial disaster or personal predicament could ever compete, a belief which seems to hold true for successive generations of film-makers. However ludicrous the premise, it seems we will believe anything that the scriptwriters conjure up, as long as it comes from the depths. From B-movies like *It Came from Beneath the Sea* (1955), with its poster catch-line: 'Out of the Primordial Depths to Destroy the World', to box-office record-breakers like *Jaws* (1975), with its demonic great white shark, the studios have relied on the sheer terror inspired by an unbelievably large monster from the deep to bring in the crowds. In 1916, Ernest Williamson had his own patent for a giant mechanical octopus which he used to supplement his real shark footage, and the latest special effects continue to make virtually anything possible underwater.

As society's preoccupations change, and general knowledge about the natural world improves, the scriptwriter's portrayal of our relationship with the sea follows suit. It has moved from being the home of Moby Dick and radioactive killer squid, to being a beleaguered natural resource prey to the careless actions of mankind. In *The Abyss* (1989), aliens living in deep water come to the aid of humans who have been careless with nuclear weapons, and in *The Deep Blue Sea* (1999) – 'Bigger, Smarter, Faster, Meaner' – innocent sharks suffer at the hands of unscrupulous geneticists, who eventually reap their gruesome rewards for tampering with the size of the sharks' brains.

Fiction, as ever, takes its cue from fact, and the early underwater documentary film-makers were not averse to engineering a little extra drama from their subject matter, depicting reef sharks as potential man-eaters or giant clams with jaws like bear-traps waiting to slam shut on the unwary diver. Even Jacques Cousteau, the master of underwater film-making, was willing to sacrifice the odd marine mammal in the interests of a good photo-opportunity. And yet, and yet, the sea maintains its secrets. There really are giant squid, *Architeuthis dux* – demonized by Peter Benchley (author of *Jaws*), first in his novel *The Beast* (1991) and then in a television film of the same name. But no one has ever seen a healthy living specimen in its natural environment. In four hundred years, only a few dozen such squid, or portions of them, have been examined worldwide. Tentacles up to forty feet long, and eyes as big as a human head confirm that the creature is massive, but exactly where it lives, what it eats and how it breeds remain unknown. These are the creatures which fight with sperm whales in the deepest, darkest reaches of the cold oceans. It is a truly titanic struggle, which the whales seem to win, since their stomachs are often full of these partially digested monsters; some whales have been found to contain several thousand squid beaks, an indigestible inventory of the deep ocean larder. No man has witnessed such a battle. Modern video cameras mounted on remotely controlled submersibles can film the depths of the ocean, but we still have many thousands of new species to identify accurately, and there is insufficient scientific evidence to prove the scriptwriters wrong. I find it comforting to know of this unknowable realm, and I am content that the sea continues to guard its rarest treasures.

While Yves Le Prieur and Jacques Cousteau were refining their aqualung systems, Hans Hass was already making a career out of underwater photography. He, too, experimented with homemade underwater cameras and he, too, had learned to spear fish with a crude harpoon on the French Riviera. Hass combined the intellectualism of a scientist with the passion of a film-maker. He also combined a serious quest for knowledge as a marine biologist with the charm of a showman. Perhaps ironically for an academic, he was the first man to make diving glamorous, and with the help of his attractive diving companion, Lotte Baierl, scuba diving acquired sex appeal.

After we had been talking for a couple of hours, Hans interrupted our first interview to ask me the time. 'We will talk for three more minutes,' he announced. 'And then we must go to meet my wife. She is never late.'

The streets were treacherous that day, with compacted snow and dissolving slush on every corner, but Hass moved quickly along.

Hass led me across to a modern building at one edge of the cathedral square. Promising me a view over the spires of

St Stephen's from the top-floor restaurant, he stabbed at the lift sign on the wall with one hand, not seeing that the call button was several inches below. The lift ignored us and descended to the basement, and I reached out to press the call button once more.

'I'm sorry, I have a problem with my eyes,' he explained. 'I think I have been overworking these past few years, and now I cannot see clearly except for one small window in one eye.'

The lift returned from its downward journey and as the doors sprang open they revealed a lone woman. Bang on time. It was Lotte, the woman with whom Hass had travelled the world, researching, and diving reefs of the Pacific, the unknown islands of Nicobar and the shark-filled edges of the Red Sea.

In the smart penthouse restaurant, we weaved our way through the packed luncheon crowd and the other diners paused, in a polite way, to stare at Vienna's most famous living couple. Later, meeting the same response as we walked through the streets to their home, I asked Lotte if she enjoyed the public recognition. 'I hate it,' she said. 'If I am alone, I can go unrecognized, but with Hans, his face is too well known. When I look at him now I see the same man I married fifty years ago, but nature is not so kind to women. Just look at me.'

As a young woman, Lotte's sex appeal was crucial to the success of the *Diving to Adventure* television series, and she still has a beautiful face. Lotte Hass paused, and stared at me for a long time. 'Hans is very fit for his age, and apart from his eyesight, he is still strong. In a way I don't mind that he sees me only as a blur,' she exclaimed with a forced laugh. 'At least he can't see how I look now.'

Hans and Lotte had been married almost half a century when I met them first. Like many couples they argued, in a gentle way, about the small things in life. 'No, Lotte will not have wine with her meal,' said Hans. 'Yes, I will,' she argued, pushing his hand away from the carafe at the lunch table.

'We will take the subway staircase to reach our apartment,' said Hans afterwards, as we negotiated the icy main road. Too late. Lotte was already halfway across the busy four-lane thoroughfare. 'Her eyesight is better than mine,' said Hans as I waited for him, anxiously scanning the approaching traffic as he chased his wife across the road.

Once safely inside the rooftop apartment which the Hasses have made their Viennese base for forty years, Hans continued his reminiscences of a life of adventure. It was clear that he had been irritated by modern accounts of diving which overlooked his role in the sport's development. In his gentlemanly way, Hans Hass denied reports I had heard that he was bitter, or that he resented Cousteau's populist reputation.

'No, why should I be bitter?' he shrugged, clearly uncomfortable with the word itself. 'The sea is so big, certainly big enough for two men to experiment in. I just think, like they said about de Gaulle, "For de Gaulle there existed only France," well, for Cousteau there existed only Cousteau. He never acknowledged others, or corrected the impression that he wasn't the first in diving, or in underwater photography.'

We talked for some time about Hass's continuing research into population growth and the forces of human biology which we cannot curb. For Hass, his time as a diver was a period of intense scientific enquiry: fun while it lasted, but, after all is said and done, just one part of a lifetime devoted to the quest for knowledge.

Before the winter afternoon light faded completely from the room, I asked for permission to take Hans's photograph. 'Come, darling,' he called, putting his arm around his wife, as if fearful she would feel left out.

In fact, when she talked, it was clear that Lotte Hass was more than capable of telling her own side of their remarkable partnership. Indisputably, she had established a key role for herself in Hans's expeditions, and had produced her own successful book, *Girl on the Ocean Floor*. She told me that she felt that Hans, and other men on the early diving expeditions, had been resentful of the idea that a young girl would be seen swimming with sharks, confronting the terrors of the deep – images which might weaken the heroic impact of the male adventure. However, in the early days of 1950s television, the visual appeal to male viewers of Lotte in a swimsuit was crucial to the show's success.

In his prime, with his athletic physique and thick sun-bleached hair, Hans would have easily attracted his own share of female attention. Once, he said, he had been sitting alone in a café in London when an attractive young woman had approached him, and, with what he called typically English manners, enquired if she might ask him a question. Before Hans could continue the anecdote, Lotte tugged at my elbow and said, 'Remember, this incident happened forty, maybe *fifty* years ago.'

'Never mind, then,' Hans said gruffly. 'You tell the story.'

Lotte demurred, and Hans picked up where he had left off. 'Even if it was fifty years ago, I remember the young lady was very polite, *and extremely attractive*. Anyway, she eventually plucked up the courage to ask me her question. "Are you, perhaps, Hans and Lotte Hass?"

' "Well, I am Hans Hass," I said. "*Lotte* is actually a separate person; she is my wife." '

For those who watched their television series, and were inspired by the remarkable sight of stingrays, sharks, octopuses and manta rays, the equality and inseparability of the partnership was evident. After we had talked for another hour or so, Hans excused himself, saying he had work to do, and I was left alone with Lotte. As we talked, she showed me the artefacts that decorated their apartment, brass knick-knacks from sunken ships in the Red Sea, a lantern from a British destroyer wrecked somewhere in the Indian Ocean, each souvenir a reminder of a time when the seas had been theirs to explore. 'We didn't know how lucky we were, then,' said Lotte, wistfully. 'When you are young, you just do things.' She stared at a wooden carving from the Nicobar Islands, before continuing: 'I didn't stop and think then that I was seeing things, doing things that no other woman had the chance to do.'

Lotte's own story was remarkable. Initially she had worked for Hass as his secretary, and harboured a secret and deep-seated desire to travel. Having grown up in Vienna during the War she had never even seen the sea, and the idea that Hass was about to go abroad on his Red Sea expedition made her desperate to accompany him. One day, when Hans had been out arranging matters for the journey, Lotte borrowed one of his cameras and took it into the River Danube. Diving in a shallow tributary, she experimented with the camera and with the diving equipment she had also borrowed. Unknown to Hass, Lotte submitted the photographs to an Austrian magazine and they were published under the title 'Expedition to the Viennese Arctic'. Reluctantly, Hass had to admit that the pictures were of excellent quality, and he slowly came round to the idea that Lotte might be a useful assistant in the field.

It seemed to me that Lotte had learned to accept that her husband's first passion was still the sea, his research and his writing. Hass believes that mankind is heading for the abyss, the human population increasing out of control and using technology in the wrong way to subjugate the environment to his will. It is, he says, as if we never know when enough is enough. In a sense, the crusade to publicize his research on the subject has left Hass isolated, even unpopular in some circles. Without the glamour of underwater exploration he has struggled to find an audience for his views. In part, the doomsday implications of his many years of research have contributed to his marginalization in diving history. Diving organizations continued to want Hass to talk about his early adventures underwater, but they were less keen to hear a lecture on population control and individual responsibility in the face of mass destruction. For Hass, however, the pursuit of ideas and new research were more important than self glory, or recognition.

'Hans is not always easy to live with,' Lotte remarked. 'He has an iron will, and I cannot stop him from doing anything he puts his mind to. Even at eighty years old, and with his eyes like they are, he insists on skiing at our house in the mountains, and won't be told not to. But then, that is the man I married, and I chose him because of his energy and vitality.'

The next day, I walked through the snow to Maria-Theresien Platz, where Vienna's Natural History Museum and Art Museum face each other across an impressive formal square. I wanted to look at the zoological collections, especially the large coral specimens, many of them from the places Hass had visited on his early expeditions. Hanging in a small circular opening in the ceiling above the Natural History Museum's entrance hall there was a scale replica of the *Xarifa*, the boat that Hans and Lotte loved so much, and which had taken them around the world. The museum was virtually empty and the other visitors all seemed to be speaking English, weekend visitors driven inside by the snowstorms outside. There was no plaque or sign explaining the history of the *Xarifa*, or its connection with Hans Hass, and sitting in the museum coffee-shop I could watch the other visitors passing by, scarcely glancing at the small model yacht.

I was about to leave the museum when I spotted a display cabinet next to the entrance to the ladies' lavatory. Inside was an oil painting of a tropical coral reef and nearby a replica of an early diving bell. According to the display, a bell like this had been used underwater in Ceylon in 1865 by Eugen von Ransonnet, an Austrian diplomat and naturalist. Von Ransonnet designed the bell as an observation chamber, a box with a bench seat and a circular window through which he could make sketches of what he saw underwater, sketches that he later turned into oils. I looked at the oil painting closely, and saw that it was remarkably accurate. There were just a few fish in the scene but I could clearly identify the trailing dorsal fin of the yellow and black Moorish idol (*Zanclus cornutus*) and a blue and yellow striped surgeonfish (*Acanthurus lineatus*), as well as several slightly less distinct varieties of chromis and butterfly fish. The only perplexing thing about von Ransonnet's work was that on the sandy seabed he had painted what were clearly the remains of a human skull, and nothing in the accompanying information explained why it was there.

Von Ransonnet's oils brought the fish and coral heads to life, and are probably the first accurate depiction of tropical fish produced from observation in their natural habitat. It seemed fitting that his painting and the *Xarifa* model should be within sight of each other in the museum. Landlocked Austria's two sons, Hass and von Ransonnet, had beaten the rest of the world to it on both occasions, producing the first painted colour scene from underwater, and the first successful television films from the liquid world.

7. In the Shadow of the Fire God

It was very warm and the air was scented with the white flowers of the night. The full moon, sailing across an unclouded sky, made a pathway on the broad sea that led to the boundless realms of Forever.

W. Somerset Maugham, *The Fall of Edward Barnard*

The Bismarck Sea, Western Pacific

The western tip of New Britain is haunted by spirits. They are the troubled souls of men and mountains, and of volcanoes and war. In the waters around the island, there is some of the best diving in the world.

The eastern end of New Britain is known as the Gazelle Peninsula, and is separated from the rest of the island by impassable terrain. Its port, Simpson Harbour, is a natural deepwater anchorage, sheltered from rough seas and strong winds by a range of hills, and at certain times of year it is possible to pick up a boat there which will sail north into the Bismarck Sea to explore submerged volcanic peaks, which rise to within a few feet of the surface from the ocean floor.

A couple of hours' flying from the giant mother shape of Papua New Guinea, New Britain stretches east-north-east for four hundred miles, like a natural breakwater between the Bismarck and Solomon Seas. On the end of the island, there is a small town named Rabaul. Few foreigners seek it out, but many of those who do come for the diving, hoping to find the seas nearby as untrammelled by tourists as the land.

After a short transit stop in the capital, Port Moresby, I took an Air Niugini flight to Tokua, the closest airport to Rabaul, and the last leg in a series of a half-dozen connections across the Pacific from Los Angeles.

This was the start of the summer holidays, and hundreds of children were returning to New Guinea from schools in Australia. I found that I was virtually the only adult on the aircraft, surrounded by teenagers who were making life difficult for the single air stewardess in charge of the cabin, continually swopping places, shouting personal jokes and arcane obscurities of adolescent communication across the aisles. Just before the door was closed, two young girls and their father rushed on to the aircraft, flustered and perspiring. They were late arrivals from an international flight from Brisbane and we had been waiting on the tarmac in the heat of the day for them for almost an hour. Once on board, the trio split up, forced to sit wherever they could find an empty space on the crowded plane. Father was an overweight man, whose complexion bore the signs of a life in the tropics, and he collapsed heavily into the seat beside me. For a few minutes, he sat mopping his face and neck with a handkerchief, and muttering to himself as he fought for breath. 'Jesus Christ . . . what a run for it . . . Jeez, thought we wouldn't make it.'

Eventually, his panting subsided, and he extended a free hand, uttering words of greeting. 'Howdy mate, the name's Ivan . . .' his surname lost in the hubbub of the take-off announcements whittering through the aircraft's p.a. system. He began a monologue which ensured that the only information I gained from the in-flight announcements was that lap-top computers should not be used until we reached cruising altitude, and that the chewing of betel nut was forbidden by government regulations. I possessed neither. Ivan explained that he had journeyed to Port Moresby from New Britain earlier in the day, to await the arrival of his daughters from Australia. Realizing that the girls' flight was late, he managed to persuade the airline to hold our plane for them so that they were not forced to spend a night in the capital. 'Oh no,' he gasped, 'that's the last thing I need, a night in the Moresby with two young girls. Not bloody worth it, mate.'

Like many overcrowded cities, Port Moresby has a reputation for lawlessness, a reputation which by all accounts, including Ivan's, is well deserved. Ivan was not a comforting person to sit beside. I hardly needed to do more than nod or shake my head in response, as the man filled me in on life in the islands without further prompting. 'We're all nervous fliers, the girls and me,' he told me. 'You heard about the crash today, did you?'

In fact, I had seen the headlines in a local paper on arrival. Seventeen people had been killed when an aircraft belonging to a regional airline hit a mountainside in the New Guinea Highlands early that morning, confirming the region's reputation as a challenging place to fly. By now, we were climbing away from Port Moresby International, and heavy clouds signalling the beginning of the rainy season obscured most of the ground and high hills below. Turbulence began to rock the small jet, and even the excited schoolchildren fell quiet. In spite of Air Niugini's good reputation, and his own nervousness, Ivan chose to talk about the hazards of flying over the steep backbone of hills dividing the island below us in two. After seventeen years in New Guinea, he had much to relate about life in what he called the 'bush'. Like many residents, he described himself as an ex-Australian, and was married to a Papuan woman. 'It doesn't work the other way,' he said. 'You don't find white women with local men much.'

'And what about you?' I asked. 'Are you accepted?'

'Oh yes, no problems there. We tried living in Australia when the kids were small, but this place gets under your skin,' he explained. 'We had to come back.'

An hour later, our flight touched down at Hoskins airfield, halfway to Rabaul, and many of the passengers, including Ivan and kids, disembarked.

For the final leg of the journey, I was able to look down at the landscape below, undisturbed. A heavy mist shrouded the hills for the most part, but the plane's trajectory hugged the coast and there were occasional patches of sea visible here and there. Papua New Guinea reminded me of Madagascar, a country I knew through several extended stays in the course of reporting on successive general elections for the BBC.

It struck me that, in the case of both islands, we are aware of their shape, yet generally know little about the detail of their existence. Madagascar and New Guinea are highly visible on our television screens whenever the satellite weather map focuses on larger areas of population and commerce, respectively southern Africa or Australia. The islands sit offshore from these landmasses, but are mainly politically and economically peripheral to the interests of their bigger neighbours. They are deceptively familiar in outline, through repeated exposure to the eyes of the viewer, but the realities of life in these island nations, and the circumstances of their people, are lost on us. Even their sheer physical magnitude is rarely pondered, although Madagascar is the second largest island in the world, and New Guinea the fourth. Both countries carry a heavy weight of spirituality throughout their culture, and of their magical qualities we scarcely even dream. Perhaps that is why foreign visitors to both places are so often changed by their experience, and why they become protective of them, nurturing their connections and contacts like secret memories.

Giant islands, each with unique flora and fauna, Madagascar and New Guinea remain at the edge of the developed world, and in spite of advances in communications and transport, both countries present significant difficulties of access to the majority of modern tourists. These difficulties are attractive to some, the roughshod 'adventure travellers' who thrive on stomach upsets and brushes with erratic airline schedules, but anecdotal knowledge of such things represents a significant barrier to many visitors. Withal, the islands manage to retain a sense of mystery and allure, a reputation for savagery, insect-ridden jungles and isolation which allows them to keep a place in our imagination. A reputation for petty crime in their respective capitals, Antananarivo and Port Moresby, and a crumbling infrastructure beset by unstable government make development a permanent battle against the forces of institutionalized inefficiency, apathy and corruption. Their very hostility to mass-market travel ensures their appeal.

We circled the airfield at Tokua for several minutes before landing in a heavy rain squall. A crush of parents arriving to retrieve their children from the small baggage hall made my exit from the airport a protracted affair. The children were well dressed, and had the air of big city sophisticates returning to the provinces, while most of the parents were scruffy and mud splattered.

There were no taxis at the airport, but I managed to cadge a lift from a hotel driver sent to pick up another passenger from my flight. Like many of the slightly grizzled expatriates in the outer reaches of New Guinea, my fellow arrival was an engineer, part of the steady flow of foreign experts who help retrieve rich deposits of gold and minerals from the country's mines. As darkness fell, we hardly spoke, jolted around inside the small van which hurtled towards our destination.

At the regional capital, Kokopo, I was halfway to Rabaul. I made contact with my hotel and waited a further two hours for a car and a driver prepared to brave the final stretch of road to my destination. I was assured that the journey onwards was far too hazardous for anything but a 'four by four' vehicle and a driver who knew the road. Now that the rains had come, they told me, mudslides could shift tons of earth, and crevasses could open up without warning. Eventually, transport appeared, in the form of a large high-wheeled truck driven by an enormous man named Benjamin. He picked up my forty-pound diving-gear bag with one hand and threw it into the back of the vehicle. Benjamin's control of the truck was equally heavy handed, and we set off with a squeal of tyres through the dark and the rain. In the glow of the dashboard light I noticed that his forehead bore several deep scars.

Even at night, the sickly smell of sulphur strikes you first as you drive along the heavily potholed road, which leads along the coast from Kokopo to Rabaul. The fumes come from Tavurvur, the active volcanic crater that has turned the town into a modern-day Pompeii. Since the last violent eruption in September 1994, the eastern half of Rabaul has been buried under a moonscape of ash. It cloaked the streets and houses in fine soot, as black as gunpowder. Soaked by rainwater and baked by the sun, it has now solidified like concrete, leaving the tops of houses, cars and lorries protruding from the mix like toys in a child's sandpit.

Until the Second World War, Rabaul was known as the loveliest harbour in the Pacific, a sheltered bay surrounded by the green forested slopes of volcanic hills. Mango Avenue, the main street, was once a neat tree-lined boulevard laid out by linear thinking German colonists in the nineteenth century. Now, five years after Tavurvur's eruption, it is a muddy, treeless strip of black dust. And now, especially when the wind is from the south-east, a drizzle of fine ash falls from the sky. It sticks to everything, and when the rains come it can break free in solid chunks large enough to smother unwary travellers.

When I arrived, it was too dark to see more than a scatter of low buildings dotted along the Avenue, although Benjamin provided a tour commentary of the empty plots beside the road. 'This Barclays Bank,' he said, 'and this Air Niugini Office. Over there cinema.' In fact, there was rarely more than an occasional pile of concrete struts to peer at through the gloom of the sideward beam of our headlights. Benjamin explained that most of the town was without electricity, and had been for the past five years. Even so, I appreciated the Avenue for its straightness, and its relative flatness after the bumpy and alarming ride from Kokopo. Once installed at my final destination, the Kaivuna Hotel, I fell into bed and slept until dawn, glad at last to be stationary. I had two days to wait for the live-aboard diving boat which would take me into the Bismarck Sea.

The next morning was bright and dry. My room overlooked the hotel's small swimming pool, and a man in overalls was scooping it out with a long-handled net. The pool-man was wearing a facemask, the sort normally worn by builders to prevent them inhaling noxious fumes when sawing or clearing hazardous material. I realized then that the pool was black. Full of ash, which the wind and rain had deposited over everything during the night.

Rabaul residents are proud of the fact that their town is built entirely within the rim of an active volcano. The smoking peak of Tavurvur is one of several surrounding the town, all of them just small vents in the rim of the caldera which collapsed six thousand years ago and created the perfect natural harbour which is the reason for Rabaul's existence. Its port, Simpson Harbour, is the lifeblood of the landlocked Gazelle Peninsula.

In geological terms, Tavurvur erupts as regularly as clockwork, roughly every fifty or sixty years, most recently in 1878, 1937 and 1994. The town was hit on all three occasions, the severity of the damage depending on wind direction at the time. 'Once in your lifetime,' the local Tolai people tell their children, 'you will hear Rabalanakaia, the Fire God, speak.'

Rabaul has been flattened by man as well as by the Fire God, and the volcanic eruption of 1994 was not the worst punishment the town has ever received. In the Second World War, Rabaul was taken over by the Japanese as they advanced across the Pacific *en route* to Port Moresby, from where they hoped to base their attack on northern Australia. In January 1942, barely a month after Pearl Harbour, they secured the Gazelle Peninsula. Between 1942 and 1944, the town was repeatedly bombed by Allied planes trying to stop the Japanese reaching Australia. Meanwhile, Japanese fighter planes hopped south through Taiwan and the Philippines, one of three air corridors into the Pacific from Japan. Rabaul and Simpson Harbour became major command centres for the Empire, and 100,000 Japanese troops made their base in the hills around it. For the Allies, B-17 bombers from Port Moresby were the last line of defence, and in 1943 they successfully cut the Japanese column from Rabaul (which was trying to reach mainland New Guinea) to pieces. Later that year, the assault on Rabaul was intensified when US planes from the aircraft carriers *Saratoga* and *Princeton* hit the harbour. Over fifty Japanese ships lie on the bottom, though many of the wrecks have now been cocooned in ash.

To escape the heavy bombing, the Japanese Army dug almost four hundred miles of tunnels into the limestone cliffs around the tip of the island, hiding men and munitions underground with which to replenish their submarines operating in the Western Pacific.

The relics of war still litter the jungle around Rabaul, and I wanted to see them. After a solitary breakfast at the Kaivuna, cocooned inside an air-conditioned dining-room, I set out to explore the town. Outside, the smell of sulphur had abated slightly from the night before, the wind had dropped and the sky was clear again. It was warm and humid, reaching eighty degrees well before midday.

The Kaivuna Hotel sits in the middle of the black wasteland. The owners, Brian and Bev Martin, ex-Australians who have taken PNG citizenship, have simply refused to give up hope that Rabaul will come back to life. In 1994, as soon as it was safe to return, they ignored government warnings and dug out the building from under its cloak of ash before the weight destroyed the walls. The Martins say that if only the ash was cleared, the roads underneath would still be serviceable, but the government is loath to reinvest in infrastructure which, one day soon, may disappear under more ash. Slowly and painstakingly, the couple have cleared a road from the hotel into town, and on a Friday night the Kaivuna becomes the heart of Rabaul. Locals, miners, wealthy Taiwanese shop-keepers and the occasional visiting government minister crowd into the small hotel bar. There is nowhere else to go. In the daytime, without the laughter of pub regulars, it is a dismal, stale-smelling place, decorated with photographs taken on the September night when Tavurvur signalled its anger, sending arcs of fire through the darkness like distress flares.

I walked along the strip of ash road towards town, and for the first fifteen minutes saw no one else along the way. My shoes turned brown with the fresh ash which puffed off the road as I walked, and then became white as it dried out. I had paused to take photographs of the ash piles at the edge of the harbour when a truck, identical to the one I had ridden in the night before, stopped beside me in a cloud of choking dust. A very brown white man sat at the wheel, and beside him a Papuan with big hair and reddened stumps of teeth. He was chewing betel nut.

'G'day, mate,' said the driver. 'Where 'ya goin'?'

'Into town,' I smiled.

'What for?'

'I just want to have a look around.'

The Australian peered down the road, which was a featureless strip of ash, and shook his head. 'Look around? What at?'

'I haven't been here before, and I just want to walk around and take a look.'

'There's nothing to look at, mate, hop in the back and I'll drop you at the market.'

It was clearly going to be difficult to refuse a lift, so I climbed into the back of the pick-up, and hung on tight, as we carried on into town. The ash and grit thrown up by the truck and the occasional passing vehicle made it impossible to keep my eyes open for more than a few seconds at a time. My contact lenses couldn't take it, and when we arrived in the main street beside the local market, I was in tears.

As I jumped down, the truck pulled off with a hoot on the horn in lieu of further conversation. Once my eyes had partially recovered from their grit bath, I stumbled across the road to the market, blinking and sneezing.

Dozens of women sat knitting and chatting with their legs extended straight out in front of them, their limbs the dividing line between one another's wares. Many of the women had babies on the ground beside them, or a young child helping them to sell their produce. In one corner of the market a few simple stalls gave shade from the sun, but most of the traders sat in the open. Beside them, their goods lay on rattan mats, and occasionally the women would fan their produce clear of flies. There was little variety on offer. Yams with pink skin lay arranged on banana-leaf trays, peanuts in clusters still attached to their green roots sat in neat rows like pieces of a board game, and huge single bunches of mountain bananas, green as a parakeet's feathers, were hefted on to the ground.

In the centre of the market, a solitary man made himself heard through the cracked plastic trumpet of a battery-powered megaphone. I watched as he made an impassioned sales pitch for a series of hardware items which a team of young girls held up before the crowd. There were wooden stools with metal prongs at one edge of the seat, for de-husking coconuts, foam-rubber cushions covered in cheap fabric, and wooden bed frames and chairs on which to place them. A range of crudely made metal goods was on offer, including bread ovens and copra smelters, small stoves of black ironware which could be fuelled with wood or coconut fibre. No one seemed to be buying, although the most expensive items on sale were no more than ten or fifteen pounds.

The bark of the market hawker's megaphone followed me up the road as I walked away from the town, climbing a slight incline which I hoped might give a view over the port. A sign said 'Tunnel Hill Road', and I followed it.

After less than a mile, I came to a bend where a narrow offshoot of tarmac led more steeply up a forested track. Along one side of this road, a neat line of rectangular holes led into the hillside, the remains of some of the Japanese wartime tunnels. I clambered inside, but they were entirely empty apart from some small bats which flew out from the deepest reaches when I walked too near their resting place.

At the top of the hill the road ended in a small flat car-park, poised on a promontory. Further progress was blocked by a large white board which announced I had reached the Government Vulcanology Centre, a division, it said, of the Government's Department of Mineral Resources. A cluster of new buildings stood at the edge of the car-park, built with a bird's eye view of the town beneath the hill, the broad sweep of Simpson Harbour and the smoking top of Tavurvur to the north. From this vantage point, something of the beauty of the place was at last apparent. The hillside beneath the promontory was lush, and palm fronds framed the waters of the harbour and Blanche Bay beyond. It was a deceptive picture-postcard view of a tropical scene. Dead ahead, on the flat land beside the sea, the corrugated-tin roofs of the small town reflected shards of silver light against the network of dust and ash roads. Traversing left, the tin roofs thinned out as I looked towards the volcano, and the dark ash-covered grid lines of the road network became more dominant. There were no trees on that side of town, and from this distance not a patch of scrub or grass broke the ash. Finally, a lone patch of white cement stood out from the wasteland. It was the Kaivuna Hotel, the last building in the devastated area, and the closest to the smoking volcano.

At the Vulcanology Centre, a few children were hanging around outside one of the buildings, and they waved at me as I walked towards them. They belonged to one of the men working at the complex, and they pointed me in the direction of the duty officer's control room. Inside, I found Jonathan Kuduon, a geologist who had worked in Rabaul for over ten years. He explained that there was someone on duty at the Centre twenty-four hours a day, monitoring a bank of seismographic instruments placed near the volcano, and recording any movements in the earth around it. He invited me to drive to the old Rabaul airport with him, a site completely destroyed by the 1994 eruption.

The interior of Jonathan's car was covered in dust, and he apologized for the lack of air conditioning. 'Tavurvur,' he said by way of explanation, pointing out that everything electronic in the car had been extinguished by the dust in the atmosphere. The clock, the radio and the air conditioner were all dead.

We drove down the hill from the Vulcanology Centre and in a few minutes reached the beginning of what is officially marked on the map as the 'Area of Devastation'. We carried on down Mango Avenue past the Kaivuna, and into the wasteland of deepest ash. Close up, a few clumps of yellowing grass poked through the soot

1. In the 1900s, the rich sponge beds of the Gulf of Mexico made Tarpon Springs the centre of the trade.

2. Greek immigrants trimmed and finished the dried sponges for sale and export.

3. (*left*) Greek sponge divers, Aegean Sea, 1910.

4. (*below left*) The naked diver uses a heavy chiselled stone as an aquaplane to guide him towards the sponges.

5. (*right*) Louis de Corlieu wearing his rubber fins and hand paddles.

6. Members of the *Club des 'sous l'eau'*, including Yves Le Prieur (dark swimsuit fourth from right) and Jean Painlevé (immediately in front of him), at the Piscine Pontoise, Paris, 1935.

7. In 1942, inspired by Italian successes, the Royal Navy produced an élite band of men prepared to drive the underwater chariots.

8. British frogmen in suits made by Dunlop emerge from the sea after training, 1945.

9. Hans and Lotte Hass
in the Red Sea, 1955.

10. Dottie Frazier with
Californian lobsters,
1960.

11. Sealab 1 prior to launching from Panama City, Florida, 1964.

12. Aquanauts Manning, Anderson and Thompson enjoy dinner inside Sealab 1, 1964. Note the tin can crushed by pressure on its way down to the habitat.

13. In 1967, US Navy diver Bob Croft achieved celebrity status as the first man to free-dive below 200 feet, setting a world-record depth of 240 feet the following year.

14. Neal Watson and John Gruener after their record-breaking dive on air to 437 feet and one inch, Freeport, Bahamas, 1968.

15. Umberto Pelizzari can hold his breath for seven minutes.

16. Using a weighted sledge to carry him down, Umberto Pelizzari became the first man to descend to 150 metres without air.

here and there, but given the tropical climate it was a pitiful display. A few yards away, the roof of a family saloon car rose out of the ash. The windows were gone, so that it looked as though someone had taken a hacksaw and neatly removed the top six inches of body frame and the roof of the car, and then placed it on the ground. In fact, the body of the car was buried underground, the interior of the vehicle filled with ash, perfectly level with the surrounding area. The scrap of metal was as white as the bones of a skeleton.

Jonathan pointed at a vast flattened area ahead. Specks of silver mica glittered on the surface of the nude black expanse, and ahead the shape of Tavurvur was no more than half a mile away. A tumbled group of concrete blocks stood at one edge of the area. The old airport terminal.

Jonathan Kuduon knew everything about Tavurvur. It had killed five hundred people in 1937, but only a handful in the most recent eruption. On a satellite map, he showed me the ring of fire which stretched its perimeter through the Solomon Islands up to New Britain and round through the Ritter Islands, Karkar and Bam in the Bismarck Sea. Around Rabaul itself, there was Tavurvur, marked by a red dot on the map to indicate that it was still active. At the other side of Simpson Harbour her grey ash-heap of a son, Vulcan, had risen from the sea in 1878. Just behind the observation centre we could see the dormant Kombiu, known as the mother, and her two offspring, Turanguna (South daughter) and Toyanumbatir (North daughter).

People with an interest in volcanoes come to Rabaul. It has been suggested that the government could market the attractions of the town as a kind of modern-day Pompeii, but there is little incentive in attracting people to a region which will almost certainly suffer again at the whim of the Fire God. And there have been accidents. Mud slides, noxious fumes and unstable ground around Tavurvur have all claimed the lives of locals and tourists in recent years.

From Jonathan I learned that only a year ago, a German doctor had ignored advice not to climb the slopes of Tavurvur. He had fallen through a crevasse in front of his wife, and died. Six local villagers who had been digging for wildfowl eggs, which the birds cunningly incubate in the warm soil near the volcano, had been overcome by carbon dioxide seeping from the earth. The men were found dead the next day after relatives set out to find out why they had not returned home.

Jonathan drove me along the black expanse of hardened ash that had once been Rabaul's main airport runway. At one end, close to the sea, a pretty bay separated us from Tavurvur itself. The blue waters of the small bay were an exquisite turquoise, until near to the beach they turned milky, then poster-paint yellow, and finally orange. Hot springs were bleeding sulphur into the seawater and the sand was stained black with ash. Other minerals exuded from the earth's crust, and there was a cocktail of smells coming off the warm black sand. During the War, when Tavurvur was resting, Japanese soldiers had used the waters as a thermal bath, but now the temperature was over ninety degrees centigrade, too warm for even the grubbiest trooper.

Jonathan took me back to the Kaivuna in the late afternoon. In need of immersion after the soot-filled day, I made for the pool, which was sparkling blue again, thanks to the man with the face-mask and his scoop. The hoteliers, Brian and Bev Martin, watched me from the poolside gazebo. I hadn't met Brian before, and as I dried off he explained that he'd been feeling a bit 'crook' over the past few days. 'They thought it might be typhoid,' he said, 'so I didn't want to hang around the guests too much.'

'And?' I couldn't help asking for more information.

'Yeah, the blood tests came up negative, so it's OK.'

Brian takes life in Rabaul one day at a time, and is one of those who believe Rabaul can come back to life. 'We were unlucky to suffer so badly during the last eruption – if the wind had been different we would have got off lightly. We dug this place out from under the ash, but most of the other places were left for weeks, until the weight of the ash made the roofs fall in.'

'It can't be easy attracting visitors here – I mean the ash makes life fairly unpleasant.'

'Look, you get used to it. A lot of the time we go for several weeks without a bad fall. A lot of people would pay money to come and see this town if it was marketed a bit better.'

I asked whether they got many tourists who wanted to see the volcano?

Brian paused for a moment. 'No. I reckon there's more of them scared of it than interested in it. But we've got the war relics, and the tunnels, and the local people are great, really friendly and hard working. There's no comparison with Port Moresby. You'll always be safe here, from people at least.'

Late the next afternoon, I left the Kaivuna, finally meeting the only other occupants of the hotel. They were fellow divers, who were in fact British, not American as the receptionist had informed me. The couple, a husband and wife, had remained in their room for their entire stay in Rabaul, uninterested in the volcano, the buried town or exploring their surroundings. It made me wonder if Brian Martin's enthusiasm for the tourism potential of Rabaul had been skewed by a life in the shadow of Tavurvur.

Our diving boat, the *Star Dancer*, was a sleek motor yacht, an occasional exotic visitor to the working harbour. Tramp freighters with rust-streaked sides and battered hatches lay at anchor nearby, working boats with tough crews whom I imagined lived like characters in a story by Somerset Maugham.

As we left port I joined the other passengers who had assembled on the upper deck to watch the sunset light up the coast. We introduced ourselves, and shared our experiences of getting to Rabaul, subtly checking out each other's diving credentials with indirect questioning and making a mental note of diving destinations visited. It is a ritual that divers partake in, an assessment of who's been where and seen what, a natural process through which they discover the level of experience of the others in the group. In general, it is not the number of dives that makes a diver good, or bad, but their attitude to diving and the type of diving they have experienced. Warm-water diving is, broadly speaking, less challenging than cool-water diving, and a diver with fifty dives in murky northern European waters is likely to be more technically proficient than someone with twice as many dives in calm clear seas such as the Caribbean. There is simply less to think about when diving in warm clear water, and the safety equipment needed is less bulky and restrictive.

The anthropology of a diving group always fascinates me. Male divers, like male car drivers, are often preoccupied with the brand of diving equipment they possess, and compare buoyancy jackets and regulators just as they might discuss engine size and torque in a sports car. Ego and the relative size of a diver's disposable income are part of the equation for many men, as with all gadget-based pastimes. Female divers are often (like women drivers) less interested in the technical specifications of their equipment, just as long as it does the job for which it is designed. Women are commonly more thorough in their preparations for a dive, and less frenetic underwater. Initially more cautious about the process of learning to dive, they often become better divers than their male companions, and normally consume less air underwater due to their smaller lung capacity and relaxed attitude. Consequently they see more.

There were just six other divers on board for this voyage: three married couples, one from America, one from Spain and the British couple who had been at the Kaivuna Hotel. I like to know what my potential diving partners are interested in, and where they have been, and can usually tell in advance who will make a good buddy underwater. Most of the divers were experienced, and there was only one keen photographer. Diving with a keen photographer is not necessarily a good idea. They ignore their fellow divers and fiddle endlessly with their equipment while quite often missing interesting events underwater as they focus on a coral head. The majority of photographers are also forced to stand or lean upon some fragile piece of reef in order to get their shot. I once saw a man busying himself with his camera while his wife bolted for the surface having run out of air during a dive. The photographer was quite unaware of his wife's predicament, or so he said afterwards.

That afternoon, Tavurvur and Vulcan provided a stunning panorama in the setting sun. Along the shore, a line of palm trees formed a green skirt to catch the golden afternoon light which made the trees stand out in relief from the grey-black slopes behind. From across the water, the ash had the steely sheen of shark skin. With a wisp of white smoke on her crest, Tavurvur looked suitably menacing. On the other edge of the bay, the grey heap of Vulcan, her infant son, sat brooding, as if he might choose to slide into the water and finally seal the harbour off from the open ocean.

That night we sailed away from Rabaul and north into the Bismarck Sea, leaving the dust and the ash-choked streets far behind. For hours, I lay awake listening to the steady drone of the boat's engine and feeling the comforting cradle-rock of the waves. At around two a.m. there was a thunderstorm, and I watched the lightning flash across the water. The sea was a dark mirror unaffected by the heaven sent light.

*

Sea mounts are not really like mountains in the sea, unless one's idea of a mountain always conjures up the shape of a spindly tipped Christmas tree wedge. Sea mounts more obviously resemble gigantic stalagmites rising from the ocean floor, pinnacles of rock encrusted at their upper ends with coral. In the Pacific, the coral will cover every nook of substrate with life. The sea mounts off New Britain are bulky and substantial, and they provide a focus for life in an endless expanse of water, a volume of liquid which would dizzy us and terrify us if we were to swim in it alone. The sea mount gives the diver a reason to be within the immensity of blue.

Sometimes the stalagmite's tip has been snapped off, or possibly it never existed, and all that remains is a flat tabular area, a table top resting on the sloping shoulders of the mountain rising from the seabed. Whatever the subtleties of its shape, the sea mount is a colony of thousands of organisms, and in the Bismarck Sea you can be certain that much of what you are looking at is still unclassified by science.

Around and within the coral, the fish live out their days, feeding on the growth, the polyps and algae, those living particles which make up what we call coral. If the fish are small, they may hide within the spaces between the bone-hard shapes, or they may choose to nestle against the flesh of the soft corals. Larger fish may spend most of their time hanging about above the reef, waiting to feed on those who have made a home there. Apart from the fish, the reef and the rock are inhabited by every form of life, which crawls, slides, flickers and oozes through the days and nights of marine existence.

Of all the world's seas, those of the Indo-Pacific are the richest in coral-reef species. This vast area, which stretches from Africa to Polynesia, contains an estimated four thousand species of the fish encountered in the first six hundred feet or less of depth. The fish of the actual coral reefs, which prefer shallower water (less than two hundred feet), account for three-quarters of those species. Within the entire Indo-Pacific, the richest sub-region of all is the Western Pacific, and within that area the waters of Indonesia and Australia are the richest still. As you travel east from the Pacific into the Indian Ocean the number of species drops gradually, with only a few hundred of the Indo-Pacific reef species present by the time you reach the eastern edge of South Africa. Then the cold waters of the south Atlantic begin to affect the marine ecosystems dramatically, and the conditions for reef growth disappear. By the time you reach the islands of the Caribbean, isolated from the Pacific hub by Africa and the bulk of the Americas, the number of reef species is perhaps only a tenth of that in the Western Pacific. Papua New Guinea is close to being at the centre of all this biological diversity and to dive there had always been my dream. This corner of the Pacific promises isolation and purity, undamaged coral, and the diver's ideal: blue water and an abundance of fish.

Of the divers who make it to the Bismarck Sea, or any of the far-flung reaches of the Pacific, many are in search of an encounter with something big – a large, reputedly dangerous species of shark, or even an orca, the so-called killer whale. To non-divers, tales of encounters with sharks still strike a note of bravado, and inevitably redound in the diver's favour, establishing him or her as a very adventurous and daring person. Which of course we are. However, it is as if by spending a lot of time, effort and money to reach a part of the world where the diversity of life is so immense, many divers will only be satisfied by a sighting of something large. In a sense I understand it, in the same way I can recognize that going on an African safari and not seeing an elephant might seem disappointing. Once encountered, large animals are easy to observe, and there is something mesmerizing about being in close proximity to something which, if it wished, could inflict death upon us without too much trouble.

I saw many sharks in the Bismarck Sea, some of them large, aggressive species which chose, on occasion, to swim towards us to investigate what we were doing. Once, while making a safety stop beneath the boat, alone, I was accompanied by seven large silvertips (*Carcharhinus albimarginatus*), who circled gradually closer and closer. It is difficult not to entertain thoughts of 'what if' under such circumstances, yet logic tells you that they are most unlikely to attack, unless provoked by the possibility of food. However, the classic pattern before an attack is this circling behaviour, a cruise in which the fish brings to bear its formidable sense organs in the hope of an opportunity to feed.

In truth, the shark is a cautious creature, at least at first, wanting to make sure that the human being is in reality a safe animal to bite. As I held on to a rope suspended below the diving boat, the sharks came closer, and began to adjust their swimming pattern from slow vaguely elliptical circuits to faster, tangential passes. The reality of the situation displaced my calm self-assurances that these were misunderstood, basically timid fish. Logic also told me that a single diver is more likely to appear like a potential meal than a crowd of divers swimming together. Survivors of shark bite are often told that they owe their escape to the fact that the shark had established by taste that the human body was not his expected meal. Such information, so logical when read in a book, becomes only partially reassuring underwater. I swam to the boat's ladder.

Sharks of every variety are undeniably exciting creatures, graceful and filled with unleashed power, the most superbly athletic animals one can imagine. Novice divers usually claim that they will be happy never to see a shark, but once they have safely encountered them underwater the commonest response is utter fascination, and a desire to see more. Commonly, divers who believe they know sharks will pursue them underwater, and even grab at them, confident that it is they who have the upper hand in such meetings. Usually, this response is based on encounters with relatively small individual sharks, in daylight and in the company of other divers, most of whom will exhibit a blasé attitude, recounting numerous occasions on which they have seen bigger, more aggressive species, in more exotic locations. And so, having encountered one small specimen from one of the two hundred and fifty or more known species, the diver is reinforced in his belief that he is brave, that sharks are timid, or at least not very interested in divers. Divers sometimes need reminding that sharks are superlative biting machines, and that all sharks are capable of inflicting severe injury on the human body.

To most people, including many divers, sharks are not appealing animals, in part because of their appetite, but more, I believe, because they show no emotion. Much as we might wish to, we cannot establish a relationship with an individual shark. Its eyes do not allow us to make contact with whatever lies within, and we believe that their brains are too small to allow much in the way of reason. The eyes, on which the shark relies less than other senses for hunting, are small impenetrable specks within the torpedo-shaped bodies, whose strength and speed the swimmer can never match. And so we envy them for their grace, despise them for their stupidity, and fear them for their power. As a consequence, sharks are overfished, and slaughtered for dubious culinary reasons, their fins being prized as the main ingredient of certain oriental soups. They attract little sympathy, and they have not fared well at our hands. We tire of the notion that they are yet another animal we have wronged, and with so many more friendly-looking species to save, the shark comes a long way down the list of charitable causes. No one knows how many sharks the sea needs to maintain a healthy balance of life, but it is conservatively estimated that ten thousand sharks are slaughtered worldwide, every day. The shark is at the top of the ocean food chain, and once removed will drastically affect the balance of life in the seas.

In Seychelles it was relatively common a few years ago to see sharks at many popular dive sites, but gradually such encounters have become less and less frequent. In the course of two years of diving there, several times each week, I would see small white-tip reef sharks perhaps once a fortnight, occasional grey reef sharks and more rarely a bull shark. And yet, almost every day there would be sharks' carcasses piled up in a corner of the small fish market in town. Hammerheads, tiger sharks, other large specimens of the deep offshore waters all lay like rubber toys in a heap. The slack white bellies of hammerhead sharks would sometimes empty out a litter of perfectly formed babies on to the greasy cement floor of the covered area where the fishermen sliced up their catch. In general they were not a staple part of the Seychellois diet, and I would sometimes ask the fishermen why they caught the sharks. The reply was inevitably the same. 'Because they eat the other fish, and the Chinese will buy the fins for export.' It is unsurprising that recreational divers report fewer and fewer sightings of this fish.

If it is difficult to attract publicity to the plight of the shark, then how much more wearying to try to interest the world in the holothurian, the humble and unchampioned sea cucumber. Whilst they may look as inert as a vegetable, in French they are more accurately christened *bêche de mer*, or 'sea spade', because they turn over the sand on the seabed by passing it through their bodies. In oriental cuisine they are regarded as a delicacy, the *trepang*, but in the English language they often receive only the crudest appellation, the sea slug.

The holothurian is often a fat, marrow-shaped lump of dull-coloured tube on the seabed. It may be just a few inches or several feet long. White, black, speckled, tasselled, ribbed, horny and carbuncular, they squidge at the touch. And if touched, some species will eject a quantity of sticky strings like a party popper, in an attempt to ward off a predator. Others will employ the same technique, but instead expel their viscera, leaving them behind as a distracting snack for the attacker. For the human palate, the animal is killed by drying it in the sun, and when boiled up as an ingredient for soup its leathery skin turns to jelly.

On a sea mount near Lolobau Island, a day and a half's sailing from Rabaul, I found a large holothurian which amazed me. Surrounded by fish and a spectacularly beautiful reef, I was captivated by the sea cucumber lying inert on a small patch of sand. In shape, it closely resembled the shaft of an uncircumcised penis. As if in a nightmare, a set of feathery tentacles emerged from what would have been the urethra. The tips of the tentacles gently flicked across the sand picking up a few grains along the way, which adhered to the sticky fronds. All along the shaft of the flesh-like tube there were round, dark-brown lumps that looked exactly like dried cocoa beans. I touched it gently, and watched the outer sheath of the animal unfurl as carefully as a prepuce in the fingertips of a lover. It is sometimes difficult to share such thoughts with other divers, particularly if they are relative strangers.

Not all holothurians are as erotically shaped. Some resemble intestines; semi-transparent coils of tubing which stretch for several feet along the sand like something which has fallen on to the floor of an abattoir from a hanging carcass. Commonly, a holothurian will look merely like a fat black turd, an ironic image for an animal which is effectively scouring the sand clean of organic debris by passing it through its own mouth and gut. Certain unfortunate specimens harbour a small fish, which has developed a way of swimming backwards into the holothurian's anus. Dissection reveals that these fish are feeding on the sea cucumber's internal sexual organs, whilst at the same time finding shelter from their own predators. Room and board.

On the same reef I found a particularly large specimen of
Tholonata rubralineata. Instead of being a sleek tube, this animal has
a surface covered in spiked cones of flesh, not perhaps an unusual
ornamentation in itself in the plant and animal world. It is the
colouring of *rubralineata* which distinguishes the species, a background of white flesh upon which contour lines have been as neatly
defined as on any Ordnance Survey map sheet. They have been
drawn in fine pinstripes of crimson ink, producing the colours of
strawberry sauce and vanilla ice-cream. Between each spike the
red lines meander, around each spike they ring. I push my face as
close to the animal as possible, until the red lines threaten to go
out of focus. Just like an intricate maze, it is hard to work out
whether the lines meet up or have an end or a beginning somewhere
else on the body trunk. A whole dive can easily be spent inspecting
and following such an individual animal.

One night, with a cloudy sky shading the liquid world from the
moon, it began to rain. Shortly after I entered the water a heavy
downpour began. Pointing my torch upwards to where the sea met
the air world, I could see the pinpricks of the raindrops stippling
the watery ceiling.

The reef at night is covered in animals which in daylight are less
obvious to the human eye. With the aid of a torch, colour is
restored, and usually enhanced. I found a large thorny oyster,
Spondulus varius, with its maw open. The smooth shell was invisible,
covered with a patchwork quilt of coral growth. Pink tube corals,
tiny fleshy sacks in a clump, nestled on the lower half of the bivalve.
Violet tunicates sprang from the upper shell and wispy, stinging
hydrozoans, as effective as miniature rolls of barbed wire, sat
upright beside them. The mouth of the oyster had its own decoration, a skirt of orange flesh which rippled in the current. In
daylight, among the moving, swimming morass of fish life, such a

creature would be overlooked, its beauty surpassed by neighbouring animals and coral. It would certainly be ignored by the thrill seekers, but in the light of my torch it glowed orange, its colour as rich as an ornamental candle lit from the flame within.

Night dives in big water are always more exciting than in coastal shallows, and full of the promise of the unknown. I signalled to my buddy to switch off his torch, and together we swam to the edge of the reef plateau. Swift hand movements produced a trail of bioluminescence as effectively as a stick pulled from a bonfire sends out a shower of sparks when struck upon the ground. Invisible dinoflagellates, microscopically small animals at the root of the food chain which create their own cold chemical light, were being sent whirling through the blackness at our whim.

On top of the sea mount, even without torches, there was sufficient ambient light to make out the edge of the reef. Cautiously, we descended a few feet, and swam a little way off into the open water around the sea mount.

Entering the sea at night always requires me to muster my courage. It is not the darkness itself I fear, but the sensation of being alone, floating on the surface with the immensity of black space beneath me. As a boy, I read about a ship's waiter who fell overboard while emptying kitchen garbage over the stern rail late one night in the middle of the Pacific. He floated alone in the sea all night, and was saved from exhaustion by a large turtle which allowed him to cling to her shell for several hours. Incredibly, the crewman's disappearance was noticed and the ship turned to make a search for him, picking him up the following day. I have never found the idea of the turtle's presence bizarre – statistically rare, certainly, but quite believable. What stays in my mind is the man's self-control, his presence of mind in staying calm and not drowning during the hours spent drifting in the bottomless sea, alone and without sight of land. At any moment he might have felt the brush of a sea creature against his dangling legs, and with every second that passed the chance of something predatory investigating his suitability as a meal would have increased.

As a child I often went to the island of Penang, which had not then been developed as a fast-paced, hotel-ridden holiday destination. My parents used to put us in either the rather smart Penang Club, or else its slightly shabbier neighbour, the Runnymede Hotel. I know I preferred the Club, for its manicured croquet lawn and kidney-shaped swimming pool. It was a safe place to be, and my parents relaxed after dinner on the terrace, served gin-and-tonic by Chinese waiters in starched white jackets.

One evening, after dinner, I left the brightly lit safety of the pool below the terrace and wandered off into the grounds. There were no other children of my age at the Club that night, and I was used to playing alone.

A sea wall, which seemed impressively high to me then, but was probably no more than about four feet tall, separated the hotel from the Indian Ocean. On the seaward side of the wall there was no beach, just a sloping seaweed-encrusted foundation lapped day and night by the tides. That evening, large crabs scuttled across the exposed stone, which was worn smooth by the sea and glistened in the moonlight. I remember the reflections bouncing off the rippling water, and the silhouettes of the giant crabs as they ran across the stone. Perhaps because the moon was full, the tide had come up close to the base of the wall. There were just a few feet of bare concrete left dry, and for some reason I decided to drop down on to it to watch the crabs.

As soon as I hit the sloping stone I knew I was in trouble. My feet, clad in the standard-issue rubber flip-flops, began to slip on the greasy seaweed, and I lay back on the wet stone desperately trying to stay away from the waves. Inexorably, I began to slide slowly but surely towards the dark water. The tide was moving around the island and I knew I would be swept away once in the sea. The noise of the waves and the scratching matchstick legs of the crabs come to me now, as if it were yesterday. I called out for help, but my eight-year-old voice was no match for the water coursing against the stones. There was no way anyone would hear me, across the croquet lawns and up on the verandah of the Club.

I lay with my back on the wet stone, slowing my progress but not stopping the slide into the sea completely. If I moved, I slid faster towards the ocean. As I lay, wet and chilled with fear, I imagined what would happen when I finally went into the current. It seemed as if the racing water would drag me away and no one would ever know what had happened.

My feet and ankles were immersed and then the sea came up my shins. I heard voices. An elderly woman and her adult son were walking by on the other side of the wall. Desperately, I cried out for help. Two faces peered over the wall, amazed at the sight of me, petrified on the rocks. With some difficulty the man lowered himself over the sea wall, and with his mother holding his wrists he extended a foot for me to grasp, unable to maintain his own position on the slimy rocks in any other way. I clung to his ankle, and have never forgotten that he had podgy, fleshy toes. Once over the wall I was shaking with relief, and hardly managed to thank them for saving me. Back on the verandah, my parents were unaware of my adventure, and I never told them what had happened. The image of the whispering waves sweeping around the island in the night was imprinted on my mind, and I never climbed the sea wall again.

I do dive at night. But the fear of black water returns, at least in part, every time I do it. For some years, I avoided diving in the dark, and dismissed the reported attractions of the nocturnal reef dwellers. Whatever unseen miracles of the marine world awaited me, they were insufficient to quell my fear of the ascent to the surface. Going down and swimming in the pitch black space, I could handle. Ascending, leaving the black void beneath me, and then floating, swimming, waiting on the surface to be picked up by a boat, that was where I baulked. However many times I told myself there was nothing there in the water that was interested in me, the fear remained. Once underwater I generally feel safer; jumping into the dark sea requires will-power. Dimitri Rebikoff, an early scuba pioneer, said that when diving at night 'you must have iron nerves to avoid the feeling that there are ghosts in this strange domain'. To me, anyone who says they enjoy surface-swimming in the sea at night is simply unimaginative.

In New Guinea on that rainy night, I revelled in the embrace of the black space. I had become part of the ink. It occurred to me that this must be the experience sought by people who lie in enclosed plastic flotation tanks at a health club. The idea of hot water, piped music and a plastic tub in which other paying guests have mused has never personally appealed. The synthesized calm of the flotation tank could never compete with the real thing. Here was the Pacific Ocean, and me, and the night, and a myriad array of creatures who were not as blind or deaf or clumsy as me. They could sense me, avoid me, or investigate me and I would never know what impression I had made upon them. In the utter black-ness, even the glass faceplate of my mask became invisible without reflections from my torch. It was the kind of blackness that induces vertigo, and I felt as though I could communicate with my com-panion by thought alone. After a minute, he grew bored with this activity and annoyingly switched on his light, tapping my arm to indicate that he was returning to the reef. Evidently I had failed to transmit my wish to stay suspended in the dark for as long as possible. I hung in black space for a minute or two, glancing backwards occasionally to verify that my dive buddy was still in sight, his torch a flickering mark as he scanned the reef. Alone in the darkness, the familiar feeling of unease began to return and I headed back to the safety of the sea mount and the silent companionship of the other diver.

The danger of live-aboard diving boats is that one's company is fixed for the duration of the voyage. Travelling alone in New Guinea, I had no obvious dive buddy and usually attached myself to one or other of the couples in the group, and we were able to make a minimum of four and sometimes five dives a day. Our group did not mesh particularly well, and the Spanish couple provided us with some drama when the wife suffered a mild case of the bends. After three relatively deep dives she complained of an itching rash on her thighs which took on the appearance of bruises. We were fifteen hours' sailing from the nearest port, from where an air evacuation to Port Moresby could be arranged, and it would cost several thousand pounds. Through an international medical-insurance scheme for divers, a series of calls on the *Star Dancer*'s satellite telephone system were put through to diving physicians in Europe and Australia. The doctors advised that the diver be given pure oxygen to breathe intermittently over a period of several hours and the symptoms monitored carefully. After two hours, the itching subsided and the bruising began to disappear.

Forbidden to resume diving, her mood deteriorated as the voyage wore on, and our discussions of what we had seen underwater were curtailed in her presence so as not to depress her further. Her husband became my buddy by default after that. The American couple kept to themselves, in part because the wife had lost a front tooth prior to boarding the diving boat and didn't want to be seen at close quarters. The British couple had no medical dramas to interrupt their enjoyment of the diving holiday, although they argued intermittently about the amount of luggage crammed into their cabin. Each evening, we were treated to a succession of different outfits from the wife's wardrobe, as well as at least three changes of swimming costume during the day.

Underwater, the topside camaraderie, or lack of it, was irrelevant to me. I had places to go and fishes to meet. Goatfish and damsels, angelfish and emperors, bannerfish and spadefish, sweetlips and snappers, too many to count and too many new varieties to remember after each and every dive. If there was a current running, the fish would gather in large clouds of shimmering colour, facing into the flow at one edge of a sea mount plateau to feed on the plankton particles being swept towards them. Effortlessly, they would hover side by side, not caring which species swam beside one another, sifting through the array of nutrients wafted to their mouths. Once, a lone barracuda as long as a man lay in the water beside me, keeping his distance and watching the swarms of smaller fish, waiting his chance to seize a meal, or perhaps just keeping an eye on his territory. If I approached him he would move, so slowly that I felt sure I was getting nearer, and then just as I expended my energy in the current he would disappear from the reach of my underwater vision, perhaps believing I had become a hunter. On another dive, a school of smaller barracuda turned around the reef as I held on to an outcrop of rock to steady myself in the current. I tried to count how many barracuda there were, an impossible task in the moving mass, woven together as tightly and intricately as a nest of wire wool. They were slim, elegant fish with delicate grey chevrons marked on their silver flanks. Only their cruel mouths and prognathic lower jaws spoilt their beauty. By my reckoning, a thousand or more of these three-foot skewers were swimming together, forming a tight circle which revolved continuously as the leading edge moved forward. It was a giant twister, a whirlwind of fish whose tapering bodies formed a living vortex which circled round and around. Their progress was independent of any single fish, the school had become a single entity, thinking and moving as one. Cautiously, I swam slowly underneath the school and looked up. There, in the middle of the circular tower, was a neat hole through which I could see all the way to the surface seventy-five feet above. The barracuda formed an aureola of metallic flesh against the dark blue water, and there at the top of the column was the bright disc of sunlight catching their scales as they moved.

My memories of the Bismarck Sea are of deep water and empty horizons, spaces big enough to breathe in, and to watch the approaching weather patterns of the Pacific sky. Sky and sea were clean and bold, swathes of blue in water and heaven, feathers of white in cloud and wave tops. In these waters the coral is mostly undisturbed by man, and the number of divers who visit is still small in relation to the wealth of life on display. The sea mounts are as sacred in spirit as any pilgrim's peak on dry land, and are as close to a lost world as we can hope to find. Above and below, in air and liquid, I felt clean.

On the return voyage to Rabaul we met a large school of dolphins, more than a hundred individuals who were crossing a flat sea several miles out from the entrance to Simpson Harbour. There were two species in the group: first, the commonly encountered bottle-nosed variety (*Tursiops truncatus*), and then the spinner dolphins (*Stenella longirostris*), shyer and less confident. Our boat slowed its engines, and after a few minutes the bottle-noses came closer, curious as ever to investigate the boat and catch a ride on its bow wave. The spinners kept their distance, but they had their own game, a headlong rush through the water and then a forward twisting leap through the air, behaviour that is natural to them, and incredible to observe. For half an hour the bottle-noses took turns to ride alongside. On several occasions there would be a pair of dolphins swimming just inches apart on each side of the bow, four animals just out of reach below the wave crest, streamlining their way through the sea so smoothly it seemed they were not swimming but flying. Bright sunlight made flashing white ripples across their backs in the clear water, as if sunshine could dissipate the barrier between liquid and air. Grey forms with arching tail flukes curved like scimitars stood out against the blue light-box of the ocean. I leant out over the bowsprit rail to fill my mind with the image, and found as I watched that I had forgotten to breathe.

8. Chariots of War

They were officially (and most dully) called the Landing Craft
Obstruction Clearance Units, but the popular name of 'Frogmen' given to
them after their fame had become known is, as so often, less clumsy, more
descriptive and presumably permanent.

Sir Ronald Storrs, *Dunlop in War and Peace*

Before daybreak on 19 September 1941, several British ships lay
peacefully at anchor in Gibraltar harbour. In the shadow of the
Rock, any ships in the harbour were well protected by shore
batteries, constant harbour patrols and steel anti-submarine netting.
The Rock's great shore guns, mounted on high, covered the narrow
Straits of Gibraltar, ensuring that no ship could enter or leave the
Mediterranean out of their range.

At just after six a.m., and without warning, the peaceful morning
was shattered by a loud explosion. A ten-thousand-ton tanker, the
Denbydale, listed heavily, sinking as water began flooding into her
hull. Minutes later, two more detonations and two more supply
ships were hit, their steel plates ripped open by mines placed
underneath them. Over twenty thousand tons of shipping were
damaged in moments.

The impregnation of Gibraltar harbour was not just a military
strike; it was a blow to morale, a wound at the heart of the
dockyards which had repaired Nelson's flagship *Victory* after the

Battle of Trafalgar. In the First and Second World Wars, 'Gib' was crucial to the operations of the Allied fleets, and now her fortifications had been breached. And yet on this occasion there was no visible enemy to retaliate against.

The silent enemy had come from underwater, launched two miles offshore from Gibraltar harbour when the Italian submarine *Scire* broke the surface in the darkness before dawn. She was no ordinary submarine, carrying on her deck several large torpedoes, a new kind of weapon to be launched from the surface. The torpedoes were driven by an electric motor, and sitting astride them were Italian divers, who could steer and submerge them at will, like miniature submarines. Steered with a joystick and wire controls to the small rudder above the rear propeller, the diver in command sat behind a low metal wave-shield with just his head poking above it. Once underwater, they had to be steered by compass. In design, the torpedoes were simple, a twenty-foot metal tube with a detachable nose containing five hundred pounds of explosive. Three torpedoes had put to sea that December night, their crews dressed from head to toe in rubber suits and carrying their own oxygen supply strapped to their chests. The breathing sets were constructed on the principle of a closed circuit, allowing carbon dioxide to be chemically absorbed within the bag so that it did not escape to leave a tell-tale trail of bubbles – an obvious advantage for underwater sabotage.

Within sight of the harbour, but camouflaged by their outfits which blended in against the dark waves, the Italians emptied the torpedoes' air ballast tanks and submerged. Underwater, they knew they would face the steel anti-submarine netting, strong enough to resist everything except cutters powered by compressed air. With luck and time they might cut through the nets, but the risk of detection was great. Two torpedoes gave up their attack due to technical problems with their breathing sets and turned back towards the Spanish coast, but the third, driven by Lieutenant Lioria Visintini, was able to sneak through the netting as it was lowered to allow a British ship into the harbour. Riding the ship's wake, the tiny torpedo crept through the water, rising shallow to allow Visintini to poke his head above water and choose his target. Cautiously he submerged again and began the work of laying his deadly cargo. Half an hour later, with explosives on timing devices attached to three British ships, Visintini and his crewman escaped underwater the way they had come.

Before the Gibraltar raid, the Italians had tried using the human torpedoes on at least half a dozen occasions, including attacks on Gibraltar, but none had been successful, the machines either breaking down or being spotted and bombed by anti-submarine air patrols. As a consequence, the Royal Navy did not regard the torpedoes, which they called chariots, as a significant military threat.

The Italian torpedoes came from a special underwater warfare unit, the Tenth Light Flotilla, a pet project of Mussolini based at La Spezia on the Ligurian Sea. In December, just weeks after the attack on Gibraltar, another chariot raid was carried out, this time on British shipping in the Egyptian port of Alexandria. Once again the submarine *Scire* was the launching pad for the daring raid. On this occasion, it was not just tankers that were hit, but two battleships, the *Valiant* and the *Queen Elizabeth*. These were the last two British battleships left in the Mediterranean, and the threat of their presence had kept the majority of the Italian battle fleet in port. It was essential that the Allies keep their loss a secret to prevent an Italian assault on North Africa. Fortunately, the Italian charioteers who made the attack were all captured, meaning that news of their success did not leak out for several months. Both ships were in shallow water and, although seriously damaged, they were eventually repaired and re-floated. The battleships were resting on their bottoms with most of their superstructure above water, and during the repair operations the crews went about on deck as though the ships were undamaged, making it seem to any passing enemy reconnaissance aircraft that they were still ready for battle.

The Italian divers continued to attack Gibraltar, and for some months they launched their chariots from an ingenious base in the neutral Spanish port of Algeciras. Visintini, the man who had sunk the *Denbydale*, was the brains behind the scheme, which involved creating a false compartment inside the bows of an Italian oil tanker which had been abandoned for the duration of the war. A hinged doorway below the waterline allowed the Italian charioteers to launch their torpedoes unseen and make their way the few miles across the bay to Gibraltar. It was an ingenious and daring plan worthy of a James Bond plot. The charioteers were always vulnerable to attack; their machines were slow moving and capable of diving only to shallow depths with the oxygen breathing sets. Lt Visintini was determined to achieve success, noting in his diary that 'These actions will cause the world to realize, once and for all, what stuff we Italians are made of.' A little more than a year after his first successful raid, Visintini was killed by depth charges as he attempted another attack on Royal Navy shipping at Gibraltar.

To combat the new threat from underwater, the Royal Navy needed a suitably trained unit. Winston Churchill, shocked at the Italian successes, penned a curt note to his Chiefs of Staff Committee in January 1942, asking, 'Is there any reason why we should be incapable of the same kind of scientific aggressive action that the Italians have shown? One would have thought we should have been in the lead.'

Shortly afterwards the Admiralty Experimental Diving Unit was formed. Once again, the Siebe (now Siebe-Gorman) engineering company was called upon to work on the Navy's behalf, and the

EDU set up shop at the company's experimental wing in Surrey. The Navy also wanted their own chariots, having seen how effective they could be in the hands of the Italians. In the meantime, in Gibraltar harbour, as an emergency stopgap, two young lieutenants were told to form a naval diving unit. They were Lionel 'Buster' Crabb and 'Bill' Bailey, neither of whom were trained divers or particularly strong swimmers. Both were mine-disposal officers, and had to learn what they could about diving by using borrowed submarine-escape breathing sets. Without rubber suits, they swam in their Navy shorts and plimsolls, sometimes using equipment taken from captured or killed Italian divers.

Buster Crabb was to become the most famous diver of the War, being awarded the OBE and the George Medal for the courage of his underwater bomb-disposal efforts. Groping in the darkness underneath ships in harbour, he and his team would feel for limpet mines attached by enemy divers. When Italy capitulated in 1943, the Italian divers joined the Allies, and Crabb and his men were able to learn more detail about their former enemy's diving techniques. Joint missions against German targets were undertaken, and Crabb even adopted Italian diving equipment as his permanent costume underwater, believing it to be better than what was available to the British. In 1956, Crabb (now a Commander) hit the headlines around the world when, supposedly retired from the Navy, he undertook a secret underwater mission to spy on the *Ordzhonikidze*, a Russian cruiser which had brought the Soviet premier, Khrushchev, to England on a goodwill visit. Crabb vanished, and although the British government at first said he had been drowned, and produced a mutilated body to prove it, the affair remains as muddy as the waters of Portsmouth harbour where he disappeared. According to the British Prime Minister of the day, Sir Anthony Eden, it was 'not in the public interest to disclose the circumstances in which Commander Crabb is presumed to have met his death'. To this day, the precise details of his death, whether by misadventure underwater or at the hands of the Russians, have never been made public. In recent years there have even been claims that Crabb was captured alive and transported to Russia, where he was forced to train an elite team of Soviet divers in the same covert techniques being practised in the West. Rather like Lawrence of Arabia, Crabb was something of an outsider, a man fêted for his military achievements but whom few other men could claim to know well. Crabb's underwater exploits became legendary and, like Lawrence, there was an air of mystery surrounding his death, the true mark of a national hero, especially if the public believed that he had been in some way sacrificed for reasons of 'national security'.

It is one of the ironies of War that the oxygen breathing systems used by the Italian charioteers had been invented in England, and licensed to an Italian company for local production several years before the war broke out.

The original idea for a so-called 'oxygen-lung' was developed in the 1870s by an engineer named Henry Fleuss, who designed a system whereby a man could breathe into a bag containing caustic soda, which would absorb and neutralize the carbon dioxide which he exhaled. A fresh breathing supply was provided by a canister of oxygen attached to the bag.

In 1880, the successful design was put to dramatic test when the well-known helmet-diver, Alexander Lambert, used the 'Fleuss Lung' to crawl down a flooded shaft during the construction of the Severn Tunnel. Lambert needed to close a flood door over a thousand feet from the main pumping shaft of the new tunnel, a distance far too great to travel with a conventional diving helmet and air hose. Against all odds, and working in pitch dark, Lambert managed to close the door, saving the excavations from disaster.

Fleuss's device went into manufacture at Siebe's, the diving suppliers, and it became the basis for breathing sets designed for rescue teams in the mining industry. The Fleuss apparatus was not a pretty sight, with four breathing hoses and a canvas mask with two small round windows for the eyes, and it wrapped around the face in wrinkled folds like a gas mask, making the wearer resemble an alien.

Thirty years later, the same principle was adapted and slightly modified for use as an emergency device for sailors who might need to escape from sunken submarines. Submariners were trained to use the equipment, which they could put on, then flood the compartment they were trapped in underwater, and use to breathe as they kicked for the surface. This incarnation of the device eventually became known as the Davis Submarine Escape Apparatus, or DSEA, and it was a modified form of this type of equipment that would become the tool of the underwater saboteurs. The same principle is used today for undercover divers in most navies. One of the advantages of the oxygen system is that the diver is not breathing nitrogen, and hence there is no risk of the bends.

When the Navy formed the Experimental Diving Unit, its main task was to develop a practicable underwater suit for its own divers and charioteers, and they also needed accurate data on how deep the men could safely go with the pure-oxygen systems used in the DSEA. Paul Bert, whose pioneering study of respiration and nitrogen had accurately identified the cause of the bends, had also proved that breathing pure oxygen under pressure presented a deadly danger. Professor J. S. Haldane, who built on Bert's work to formulate the decompression tables for helmet diving, was no longer alive, but his son, J. B. S. Haldane, was ready to take up the reins of diving research. Volunteers were called for while the chariots were being designed and built, and with Haldane junior in the role of physiological adviser, an exhaustive series of diving experiments with the oxygen breathing sets was carried out. Over a thousand dives in compression chambers were undertaken, the volunteers breathing oxygen at pressure at varying depths until the tell-tale symptoms of poisoning caused their lips to twitch, and their limbs to become numb. Locked inside the claustrophobic chambers, the novice divers knew they would stay there until they passed out. One of the first divers to take part in the experiments described watching colleagues dragged unconscious from the test chamber, or 'pot' as it became known. 'His head slumps forward on to his chest. From his mouthpiece come awful bubbling noises, and his hands, limp at his sides, are a ghastly greyish-purple colour. His face is slate-grey, eyes closed, with saliva drooling from sagging, purple lips.'

Oxygen at higher than usual pressures is a lethal gas, which interferes with the neurological function of the brain, resulting in progressive and rapid symptoms, including facial twitches, sudden blackout and, finally, convulsions. At pressure greater than seven atmospheres (about two hundred feet underwater) even 20 per cent oxygen in normal compressed air tanks can lead to toxicity. Using pure (100 per cent) oxygen, the risks are much greater, and the effects felt sooner. The early underwater saboteurs knew that using a breathing system supplied with pure oxygen was safe down to depths of around thirty feet or so, but much deeper and it became dangerous. Individual divers vary in their susceptibility to the problem, as they do to nitrogen narcosis and the bends, and many of the early charioteers went deeper in the water than was thought technically possible. This is probably because a diver riding a chariot is relatively inactive and will probably survive an oxygen dive to a greater depth than a man who has to use his legs and arms to swim against a current while breathing pure oxygen, but the results of poisoning are swift, and once felt leave little or no time for escape.

Because of the need for secrecy, and because the compressed-air demand valve perfected by Cousteau and Gagnan was not made public during the War, oxygen sets were the only option. Hans Hass, diving in the Aegean in 1942, was also using an adaptation of the DSEA, his version having been produced by the German Draeger Company which manufactured similar sets for their own U-boat crews. Hass, too, knew that the device could kill him below certain depths, and on two occasions described seeing white spots before his eyes and passing out. Only the fact that he was seen by his diving companions saved him from certain death, although he persevered with the system during the War, again because he had no alternative, and also because the oxygen re-breather was silent underwater, allowing him to approach fish and film at close range. Jacques Cousteau also experimented with the same sort of system before the War, and dismissed it as too dangerous for underwater film-making, describing again, like Hass, two occasions when he passed out underwater and had to be rescued by other divers. He states phlegmatically in *The Silent World* that these incidents 'ended his interest in oxygen'. Hass is more philosophical: 'I always thought it was a very pleasant way to die,' he remembers. 'You have only the sensation of your vision narrowing for a few seconds. And then nothing. Absolutely nothing.' Like Hass, the Royal Navy divers had no practical alternative if they wanted to swim freely underwater to carry out their hazardous work. And if the British Navy was to have its own chariots, it was these oxygen systems they would have to use.

On the first Saturday night of 1943 there was a Force Six gale blowing in the waters to the north of Sicily. Rolling in the heavy swell, the British submarine *Thunderbolt* broke the surface several miles offshore, and her skipper, Captain Crouch, took her as close to the entrance to the Italian harbour as he dared. Operation

Principle, to send five armed British chariots into Palermo, had begun.

The commander of one of the chariots launched that stormy night was Lieutenant Richard Greenland, and at eighty-six he is one of the few veterans of the early diving missions still alive. One sunny autumn day, I took a train to Suffolk to meet him at a small country station near to his home. As I emerged from the station he was waiting outside, a short man dressed in a thick navy-blue sweater which was stretched across an ample tummy. Strands of white hair were finger-combed back from his forehead in a loose style as if he had spent the morning gardening. He stood in the sunshine leaning against his car door, relaxed and at ease. When he spoke it was with the clear tones of Received Pronunciation, tainted only slightly by a bronchial wheeze. Driving through the winding lanes to his neat cottage in the village of Stutton, I felt as if modern-day England had been left behind on the dirty train.

Once inside, he offered me sherry, and we began to talk about the War. Although he had retired from the Navy immediately after the War, 'Dickie' Greenland remembered clearly the build-up to the Palermo raid sixty years earlier.

Dickie Greenland slipped back into Navy wartime slang as we talked; his enemies were the Ities and the Hun, the missions were 'ops' and 'shows', and all the other men were 'chaps'. It was the language of understated heroism; the very essence of Englishness, exactly like the speech of one of the characters played by John Mills in so many morale-boosting scripts from Ealing Studios.

After being commissioned as a Lieutenant, Greenland was sent to the north of Scotland, where he carried out sea patrols around the Orkney Islands. As we talked, it became clear that Greenland's perception of his whole time as a charioteer was that he was simply doing a job, and he wouldn't accept that he had been brave or heroic, in spite of being awarded the Distinguished Service Order.

'The chariot was just another small boat to me, I suppose,' he mused. 'I've always enjoyed messing about in small boats, doing silly things. One day there was a chitty up on the noticeboard asking for volunteers for a new kind of mission, and all it said was that you had to be single, and able to swim. We only found out later that it was going to be human torpedoes, and when I heard that I had visions of Japanese chappies, you know – kamikaze jobs, and I don't think any of us liked the idea until it was explained that there was a bit more to it than that. I never liked the term human torpedo, but the press did!'

Having volunteered for the as yet undisclosed duty, Greenland was sent south for training at the Experimental Diving Unit. Then based at Portsmouth, it was time for some training in diving, where he and other volunteers were taken to a quiet area of shallow water. 'We all had to do a bit of helmet diving in basic training – that was horrible,' Greenland recalled with a shudder. 'It was such a cumbersome piece of equipment. When we eventually moved to Scotland for more advanced training we'd occasionally see a fish, or a forest of seaweed waving in the current, and that was truly beautiful. Sometimes we'd find a scallop bed and send for a bucket so we could scoop some up for dinner, and that was fascinating, being so close to nature. But I must say it never made me want to dive for pleasure, and after the War I stuck to boats again. I preferred being on the surface.'

Greenland and the rest of the men selected for the top-secret missions had never seen a 'chariot', the torpedoes they would be required to drive into enemy waters. While Admiralty boffins constructed prototype machines which were basic copies of captured Italian chariots, Greenland and a dozen other men practised their skills, sitting on logs while being towed behind a speedboat. Pieces of lead were nailed to the logs to make them sink to the required depth, and there were no controls. Most such training was carried out in the dark in preparation for operating conditions at sea.

Although they did not yet have their chariots to ride, the men were given new specially designed rubber diving suits. Known as Sladen suits, after their inventor Captain Geoffrey Sladen, the officer commanding the human-torpedo units, they were an adaptation of the heavy canvas gear made for helmet divers, but made much lighter by the use of silk and rubber. Instead of the traditional copper corselet and helmet, they had a rubber hood with a hinged glass faceplate attached. Once the faceplate was screwed down the suit was watertight, but it was also impossible to hear one another speak. An outlet valve on top of the hood allowed the charioteer to vent air from his suit to maintain negative buoyancy. 'You had to climb into those suits through a hole in the belly, and it was hard work; you needed a ''dresser'' to help you,' Greenland remembered. 'We had our breathing bags on our chests and we had to clamp the belly hole shut with a clip. It was always tricky trying to get all the air out, almost impossible, and you wanted a little bit left inside so that when the water pressure began to squeeze you the rubber didn't nip you in the wrong place!'

I wondered whether they kept the divers warm.

'We wore an enormous amount of clothing underneath. The Admiralty gave us a pair of silk combinations; I've still got a pair. Then we had woollen combinations, trousers and maybe two or three sweaters. It was up to the individual, but we trained on Loch Cairnbawn near the Outer Hebrides, which was, shall we say, chilly. Everyone had to judge their own buoyancy, and we were told to make ourselves neutrally buoyant, but I think most of us erred on the light side, rather than wanting to sink too fast. I know I did.'

At last, after weeks of training it was announced that there was a real chariot on its way to Scotland. Like most wartime apparatus, the torpedo acquired a nickname. 'We called them "jeeps", and a jeep wasn't an American car in those days, it was a silly little character in a newspaper cartoon, always getting himself in a tangle, that sort of thing. I suppose the chariots were a bit Heath Robinson in a way; we spent a lot of time messing about in them on Loch Cairnbawn, but it was a lot of fun really.'

One unsuccessful chariot mission had already been attempted on the German battleship *Tirpitz* in October 1942, when all the 'messing about' came to an end. 'We knew the chaps had gone off on a mission, but it was all very hush-hush at the time. They were with us one day and gone the next, and one simply didn't ask too many questions.'

In December 1942 it was Greenland's turn, and he and other chariot crews were taken to London for a mission briefing in the basement of a large hotel. 'It was an Army chap who gave us the talk,' Greenland mused. 'Wasn't up to much really. I asked him if I could keep my beard and he said it would be all right as the Ities were all wearing beards. Turned out to be nonsense; in their Navy they all wore little goatees and I stuck out like a sore thumb.'

Soon afterwards Greenland was aboard ship heading for the Mediterranean and his first operational mission against the enemy. Loaded into the submarine *Thunderbolt*, he was given a short briefing and told that he was to attack Palermo. His recollection of the dramatic events that night was brisk and businesslike: 'It was hell, leaving the submarine, we were supposed to do a circuit around the sub to check everything was working properly and wave ta-ta to the Captain, but we couldn't see a thing,' he told me. 'All those "ops" were hit and miss in the end, I suppose, but nothing really went according to plan. We were supposed to have a map of our target but we had been briefed to hit the Italians in Cagliari, in Sardinia, when at the last minute we were ordered to Sicily – but then those sorts of things tended to happen quite a lot . . . ha, ha.'

Dickie Greenland spoke in a matter-of-fact way about the raid on Palermo, which would turn out to be a tragic loss of men and machines. Originally, three submarines had been heading for the Gulf of Palermo, but one vessel, the *P.313*, simply disappeared *en route*, lost with all hands, including three complete chariot crews. Unaware of what had happened to the other charioteers, the *Thunderbolt* dropped Dickie Greenland and one other chariot team, while the submarine *Trooper* launched three chariots.

'It really wasn't very funny at the time, old boy,' Greenland told me in a husky voice as he topped up the sherry glasses, 'but the Italians had been very kind and left a lighthouse flashing for us, so we made for that. The weather was atrocious, so rough we just scrambled on to the machine and were washed off the *Thunderbolt* by a huge wave. How we managed I don't know, and we were so late getting to the harbour entrance that I knew we would never make it back to our rendezvous with the submarine, even if we did make it out of the harbour alive.'

In the darkness Greenland never saw any of the other men or their machines, and heading towards the light on the shore he steered to where he hoped he would find the entrance to the harbour. Unknown to Greenland and his crewman, Leading Signalman Alec Ferrier, one of the *Trooper*'s chariots had already abandoned the mission after its crew had problems with their oxygen sets. Meanwhile, close to the harbour, the other chariot launched from the *Thunderbolt* was crippled by a battery failure and began to take on water, eventually sinking in the rough seas. As it went down it dragged one of the crewmen to his death, while the surviving charioteer was able with extreme difficulty to swim for shore. That left Greenland and two other machines from *Trooper* to carry on with the attack. As they approached the Italian warships anchored in the bay, the skipper of one of these chariots became completely incapacitated by seasickness. His number two drove the machine ashore and helped the officer on to the rocks, where the man lifted the faceplate on his rubber one-piece diving suit in order to breathe fresh air, slipped from the rocks and drowned as his suit filled with water. In his weakened state, and wearing lead-soled boots as weights to keep him on the chariot, he had no chance of saving himself. The surviving crewman had no choice but to try to carry on alone, but steering the chariot single-handed was impossible in the rough sea, and he scuttled the machine in deep water, struggling back to shore alone. Without having even sighted the enemy ships, just two surviving chariots remained: Greenland and Ferrier on one, Sub-Lieutenant Dove and Leading Seaman Freel on the other.

Greenland and Ferrier battled on through the seas in complete darkness, communicating by Morse code, which they had practised in training for several months. Greenland, who sat at the front of the chariot and steered it, would reach behind him with one hand and Ferrier would grasp his thumb and forefinger. Taking it in turn, the two men would squeeze each other's fingers to tap out a message; speech was impossible as they were wearing the Sladen suits designed specifically for this sort of mission.

Dickie Greenland's memory of the events of that stormy night sixty years earlier was equally matter of fact. 'It was as black as the inside of a cow in the harbour, but eventually we saw the target, the cruiser *Ulpio Traiano*, and so I took the chariot down about ten feet below the surface. We saw a sailor on deck, and he seemed to be on guard duty, but fortunately he didn't see us, and he disappeared. Alec had a handful of magnets and when we got below the hull he stuck his hand on to the metal and "walked" us down to the centre-line. Then we got off, one each side of the chariot, and detached the front of the torpedo, the warhead. We set the fuse for two hours, and having done that it was time to say "bye-bye", and drive away. By the way, we always attached the warhead before we set the fuse, just in case we couldn't get it off the chariot!

'We backed out then and there were a couple of destroyers nearby, so we went in on the surface and Alec slipped off and stuck a twelve-pound charge on each of them. Then we spotted a small merchant ship and we had a bit of explosive left so we stuck that on it, too. I decided we'd had enough and thought we'd better clear out. I made for where I thought the submarine netting was so we could get out of the harbour, but it was still pitch black and the compass on the machine had gone to pot – must have been all those magnets we were playing around with. Anyway I carried on and then there was an almighty bang, a noise like the clappers. I'd run into something head on – don't know if it was a ship, or a buoy, but it stopped us dead. We drove on a bit and then we were in shallow water, right by a small quay, so we ditched the chariot, pointed her into the middle of the harbour and waded ashore.'

Greenland paused, and drew a deep breath before draining his sherry glass. He sat opposite me staring into the middle distance for a time, perhaps transported back to that night in Palermo. After a time he cleared his throat. 'How about a fresh one, old boy?' he enquired, peering down at the coffee table to inspect my glass. 'All this talk about the War is making me thirsty!'

I wanted to know more about what had happened after he and Ferrier walked ashore. 'It was such a long time ago,' Dickie said. 'Good God! Sixty odd years. Seems all like a dream now.'

'Were you and Ferrier friends?' I asked.

For the first time in our conversation Greenland did not have a ready answer. After some time, he finally gave a shrug. 'Do you know, I've never, ever, asked myself that question,' he replied almost in a whisper. 'Isn't that funny? Never even thought about it. We'd often have a beer ashore, I suppose. Sometimes he'd buy me one, and sometimes I'd buy him one. But no, I don't think we were friends. "Mates", I suppose, is the word. Yes, we were "mates", but we had little in common socially I suppose.'

What exactly had happened after they abandoned their chariot?

'We stripped off the Sladen suits and then Alec produced a bar of nutty chocolate, so we munched that for a while. It was just starting to get light and we started walking towards town. Just then there was a bang, which was really quite rewarding, and of course some idiot sailor opened up with anti-aircraft fire, but we carried on and walked straight out of the docks. We were a couple of miles down the road when the *carabinieri* picked us up, and we showed them our fake German passports. They took them off us, which was just as well, and we never saw them again. They'd caught the other chaps too, and we were all locked up in the police station. After ten or eleven days we were sent to Rome, to a place for "naughty boys" and all kept in solitary for a month. There was an officer there who we called Capitano Marino, and he'd been a coal importer from Cardiff before the War. Anyway, his English was very good and he used to wake us up in the middle of the night – the rotten sod – and ask seemingly innocent questions, and I suppose he pieced the whole story together eventually. But I don't think any of our chaps said anything they shouldn't. The Italians knew all about chariots; after all, they'd started the business with their raids on Gib and Alexandria, hadn't they?

'The Italians were pretty decent chaps, can't really complain about the way they treated us, and they did recognize us as sailors, not spies, which was a bit of a relief. They shipped us off to an old monastery at Padula which they used as a prison camp, and that was fine. When the Hun took over later in the War they loaded us on to trains to the Greater Reich; and that wasn't so much fun, but I don't have any hard feelings.'

*

By the Sunday morning, all but two of the ten men who had set off from the *Thunderbolt* and the *Trooper* were either dead, or prisoners of war. Greenland and Ferrier had achieved their objective in spite of the appalling weather and the very limited intelligence given to them in their mission briefing. The sinking of the *Ulpio Traiano* was their greatest success, and they had seriously damaged three other ships. The chariot driven by Lieutenant Dove and Leading Seaman Freel had also run into problems with the weather, and its crew had used up their oxygen canisters by the time they reached Palermo harbour. Unable to dive, they attached their explosives to the sternpost of a merchant ship, the eight-thousand-ton *Viminale*, and according to Dickie Greenland 'blew the back end off it'.

For the officers on the Palermo raid there would be DSOs, and for the two sailors on their crews the award of a Conspicuous Gallantry Medal. These were four of the sixty-eight bravery medals awarded to charioteers, and later to the men in the more sophisticated midget submarines known as X-Craft, which carried divers who would swim out from the forward ballast hatch of the submarine and attach a charge to the enemy target, or swim out and cut through submarine netting so that the midget could penetrate a harbour. The midget subs carried out high-risk underwater raids on targets as far apart as Norway and Saigon, Singapore and Normandy. On both chariots and midget submarines, the crews took extraordinary risks, and in all, thirty-nine of their men died in the process.

The charioteers who sat on their battery-driven torpedoes were just one product of the Admiralty's Experimental Diving Unit, and the value of having free-swimming divers who could approach targets unseen took on greater significance as the War progressed. The equipment they needed was gradually refined, and the Dunlop Rubber Company was ordered to produce suitable equipment for the underwater saboteurs. Operational requirements and the dangers of flooding inherent in the Sladen suit (dubbed 'one breath from death' by the charioteers) made it necessary to design a mask which could be easily slipped on and off in the water. Dunlop dutifully produced a rubber-rimmed facemask, and a suit made of stockinet which was then spread with a thin rubber solution to form a costume. After the War, Dunlop's official historian emphasized the value of this seemingly utilitarian development: 'Few chapters of the War have caught the imagination of the British people, and indeed of the whole world, more vividly than these exploits of the "Frogmen". It has been universally recognized that here was something new in war, something new in heroism and a British contribution towards victory of outstanding merit. The Dunlop Organization is proud to have been the designer and exclusive producer of this equipment, which appreciably reduced the cost of the War in human life.'

By using the rubber solution spread over stockinet, the suits had the advantage of flexibility without using too much natural rubber, a scarce commodity in wartime Britain. The suit had lightweight latex cuffs for the wrists and ankles and a thicker rubber neck seal that could be stretched wide enough to climb into the suit, and finally a separate latex hood which would be pulled over the head to form a seal. The original Dunlop suits were made of dark sea-green material, thought to be the best colour for camouflage in the water, although they were unflatteringly described as making the divers look like gnomes. While the charioteers had been heavily weighted to allow them to sit comfortably astride their torpedoes, the free-swimming diver needed to be mobile. All that the divers required to complete their equipment were rubber foot fins, but there were none available in Britain for most of the War.

In France, Louis de Corlieu's rubber swimming propellers had not been a runaway commercial success, in spite of his association with Yves Le Prieur. However, Owen Churchill, an American businessman, had obtained a licence to manufacture the rubber duck's foot design, and he produced a few hundred of the fins for swimmers before the War. An emergency order for a consignment of rubber fins was sent to Churchill from England before D-Day, but in the interim Dunlop had to make their own design, their only template a photograph of an American actress wearing foot fins in a publicity photograph taken beside a swimming pool in Hollywood. According to official Dunlop records, the company's own efforts were quite as good as the American imports, when they eventually arrived, and the final rubber, stockinet and latex ensemble made the British 'frogman' the best equipped in the world.

The free-swimming diver was employed not just by the British and the Italians, but to a lesser extent by the Germans, and in greater numbers by the United States Navy. Underwater assault teams and Navy swimmers equipped with rubber fins and masks became a crucial part of the American counter-invasion of the South Pacific, and were used to clear the obstructions placed in shallow water to protect Japanese-held beaches. For Owen Churchill, the formation of what became known as the Underwater Demolition Teams was good news, and by the end of the War he had received tens of thousands of orders for his improved version of the foot fins first proposed by Louis de Corlieu.

In Britain, the very existence of the underwater saboteurs was kept secret until the end of the War. As the press began to report some of the techniques employed at the Normandy landings in 1944, news of the strange-looking rubber-clad 'frogmen' was released. These were the men who had prepared the way for the landing craft carrying the Allied troops, by dismantling and demolishing the concrete obstacles sunk offshore by the German army. Frogmen became an established part of naval activities, and with the blanket of secrecy lifted they began to assume the mantle of action men. While the helmet diver in his copper helmet continued to perform essential work around the world, increasing use was made of the free-swimming divers who could perform many of the same jobs, especially in shallow water, and without the need for a large support crew. For several years after the end of the War there would be work to be done in clearing harbours of debris and mines left behind. The Under Water Working Parties were used to examine underwater fittings, and were described in an Admiralty document as 'wearing only swimming trunks, breathing apparatus and swimming glasses. Naval Ratings may volunteer for this cold job for which they will get extra pay. After two dips each man is allowed a tot of rum.'

Pictures of these new and startling creatures from the sea fired the public imagination afresh, and for many people inspired thoughts of swimming underwater for the first time. Immediately after the War, surplus Navy diving equipment found its way into private hands, and informal diving clubs sprang up, training their members in the techniques and routines first learned by the wartime frogmen. It was common to see diving instructors advertising courses in diving magazines in the Fifties which claimed to offer 'training to the naval standard of frogging', a promise that also implied that, for many novice divers, diving would mean a certain amount of combat-style rough and tumble. I have often met divers of a certain age who claim that the modern training techniques for sport divers are too easy, and that no one should dive unless they are truly competent at handling extreme physical stress under-water, the type of physical harassment underwater that military divers include in their basic training – masks knocked off or breathing hoses snatched from their mouths without warning. Such skills also assume a certain level of physical fitness, which many sport divers assume they do not need. Perhaps a military approach to diving would put many people off, but at the other extreme I

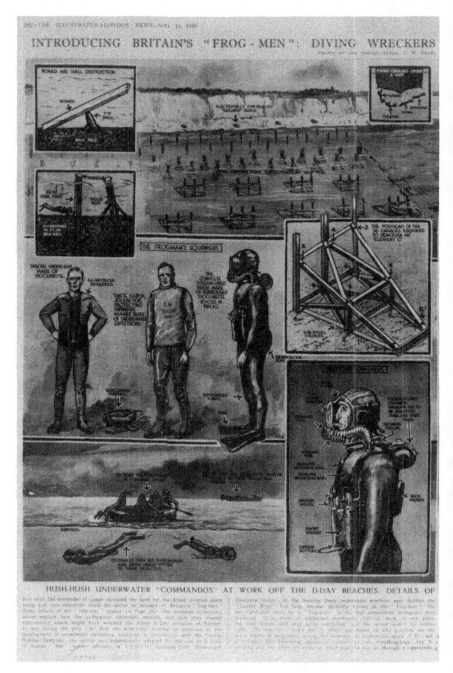

L. The exploits of Royal Navy frogmen were kept secret until the end of the War.

WHO BLASTED OPEN A PATH TO THE NORMANDY BEACHES.

WITH OFFICIAL CO-OPERATION

A MAGNIFICENT FEAT WHICH OPENED THE DOOR FOR THE ALLIED INVASION OF EUROPE

have seen obese, unfit divers who expect to be helped from the water at the end of a dive, believing that their dive leader's job is to relieve them of virtually all physical effort.

As the postwar hiatus in European leisure activities passed, there was room for the sport to grow. With divers liberated from the chill of British waters by the rubber suits perfected by Dunlop, spear-fishing and salvage diving became a passion, practised by a few hardy individuals who would soon have access to the new compressed-air Aqualungs manufactured and sold under licence by Jacques Cousteau. On the Continent and in America spear-fishing, which had been in its infancy in the 1930s, was about to return, but now it would be commercialized. Diving as a business was being born, its equipment industrially produced to create a sport with tens of thousands of devotees, especially in California.

Long Beach, California

Dottie Frazier-May was born and raised in California, and she learnt to free dive when she was six years old. Now eighty, she lives not far from the sea in Long Beach in a little house crammed with souvenirs from a lifetime of diving adventure. She was the first certified female scuba instructor in the whole of America. When I arrived at her house to talk to her about diving, and how it all began, she was in the backyard, vigorously weeding her vegetable patch. We had never met, but she showed me around as if I was a returning family member, pointing out all the changes in the garden since my last visit. 'Just look at my tomatoes,' she crowed. 'I know you call them *tom-ar-toes*, we say *tow-may-toes* of course, and just look what I've got here, artichokes, pineapples, sweetcorn and, do you know what that is? Passion fruit. I guess you don't grow that in England?'

At just over five feet tall and a hundred and ten pounds, Dottie is a dynamo, beetling about the garden and the house, swimming and playing racquet-ball every morning and generally keeping her third husband, Cyril, on his toes. Cyril was there too, a quiet man who was tinkering with a large scarlet Harley Davidson as I walked past the pumpkins and sweet peas into Dottie's neat little kitchen overlooking the yard. 'Cyril, say hello to Tim,' Dottie barked. 'He's come all the way from England.' Cyril nodded a greeting, and carried on fixing the bike, which had been polished to perfection and had calf-leather handle grips with tassels which hung down like those on the back of a cowboy jacket. 'That's our Harley,' Dottie explained. 'We take it to shows and Cyril wins prizes, but I have a dirt-bike too that I love to ride.'

Dottie made me tea and ham sandwiches as we began to talk, her conversation peppered with asides about Cyril and her first two husbands. Her first husband had died after a lengthy rehabilitation from severe wounds at the battle of Iwo-Jima during the War, leaving Dottie with two small boys to take care of. A second marriage resulted in two more sons, but it didn't last, and I realized that for Dottie the diving business had been not just a hobby, but a means of supporting her family. She confided in me that she and Cyril were actually divorced, and that they had a much better relationship now that she could choose to pack him off to his own house nearby when she tired of his company. 'We get along just fine, but sometimes I just say, ''Cyril – go home,'' and then about a week later he's back and everything is just dandy. He's a good man, but I just have to be alone sometimes.'

Dottie has lived in the same house for fifty-five years, and it is simply furnished, stacked with an assortment of marine mementoes, ship's portholes and a lamp from the *Queen Mary*. 'I didn't steal that,' she assured me. 'An elderly neighbour died and left it to me in her will. I think she worked on the ship at one time.'

Dottie also had a slightly odd collection of dead animals in glass jars. As we ate our lunch she showed me some preserved specimens, which included a dried baby octopus, some newborn anteaters and a coconut crab. She was particularly fond of a deformed abalone shell, its iridescent nacre spilling into folds and bulges, perhaps a sign that it had been irritated like a pearl oyster by a foreign body which had lodged in its flesh when it was alive. After lunch I was given a tour of Dottie's workshop, a large garage filled with every conceivable mechanical tool, neatly labelled drawers filled with thousands of nails and screws, drill-bits and hammers, trowels and files, the envy, she said, of all her male friends. Even at eighty it was easy to see that Dottie had always been something of a magnet to men, filled as she is with energy, humour and resolve, and she admitted to being flirtatious. It struck me that the dried animals and the motorbikes, and now the tool shed, all seemed like the collections of an adolescent boy rather than an elderly lady. 'You're right there,' Dottie guffawed. 'I guess I've always been a tomboy. My parents were divorced and I lived on a boat with my dad. I had my nose broken three times at school in fights with the boys, and do you know how my dad taught me to dive? I was six when he dropped our coffee pot over the side of the boat and told me to go get it!'

When she was ten a man had jumped from a diving board at the swimming pool and landed on the middle of her back, fracturing thirteen vertebrae and putting her in a body cast for eighteen months. The doctors said she would never walk again, a threat they repeated years later when she damaged one of her legs so badly that she was in plaster for another two years. She credits swimming and diving as the reason for her recovery in both cases, reminding me of Jacques Cousteau breaking dozens of bones in his body in a car crash before the War and being told he would lose an arm, then rehabilitating himself through swimming and then living to the age of eighty-seven. I mentioned this to Dottie, and told her that Philippe Tailliez, who had dived with Cousteau, was still alive and in his mid-nineties, while Hans Hass was amazingly fit and past eighty, something she did not find surprising. 'A lot of the original divers have made it to a great age,' she said casually. 'Being underwater does things to your spirit.'

Like most of the people who took up scuba diving in the early 1950s, Dottie was by then already an accomplished free-diver. She remembers being sceptical about the value of the aqualung at first. 'I thought it was for cissies,' she laughed. 'For people who couldn't hold their breath long enough to catch their dinner!' Dottie recalled entering spear-fishing contests from an early age, at first using a simple mask which her father constructed and a piece of garden hose-pipe as a snorkel. For her, diving meant free-diving, holding her breath for a couple of minutes while she stalked and then harpooned her catch. Less accomplished divers saw the newly available scuba gear as a way of collecting shellfish. Dottie simply didn't need it. 'The first time I ever saw scuba equipment was when a friend rang me and said there was an LA County instructors' course being set up, and he wanted me to go along and take the exam. I told him he was crazy, since I'd never even tried scuba, and he just said, "Come on, Dottie, with your skin-diving technique you'll be a natural."'

Before training courses were established, many early scuba divers received only the most rudimentary instruction. On first donning an aqualung, mask and flippers, they were told: 'Don't come up too fast, and don't hold your breath, it'll kill you.' For those who couldn't afford the real thing, magazines like *Popular Science* produced plans from which virtually anyone could manufacture a working scuba device. Fins, or flippers, could be made by cutting a section from a rubber car tyre and riveting it to the bottom of a plimsoll, a crude but effective means of propulsion. In California, the rich coastal waters became a burgeoning weekend destination, where men and women would collect shellfish and spear sharks, rays and game fish while experimenting with the newly available aqualungs and wetsuits.

Unbelievably, the first time Dottie put a scuba regulator into her mouth was during the instructor's practical examination in 1954, when she was required to buddy-breathe the length of the public swimming pool with her friend. Buddy-breathing is sharing one regulator between two divers, each taking their turn to take air as they swim close together, an emergency drill useful if one system fails underwater. Naturally, Dottie Frazier passed the exam and went on to become an instructor in the programme, although as the first woman in the field she met with a great deal of resistance. The first class of students Dottie was given simply rejected her because of her sex. 'They were all doctors, and they said they weren't prepared to be taught by a woman. I asked them to give me one chance, and if at the end of the evening they didn't think I was teaching them properly they could sack me. Well, boy did I work their butts off, those guys didn't know what had hit 'em.' Dottie laughed as she told the story. 'And when I wasn't sure of any of the physiological stuff I'd just ask them to explain what they understood by a certain medical term, and write down everything they said to use in my next class!'

Once established as a respected instructor, Dottie set up her own diving shop, and began manufacturing made-to-measure wetsuits which gradually replaced the bathing trunks and wool sweaters she and her friends had learned to dive with. At the height of her business she had a contract to make suits for the UDT divers based in Hawaii. When she broke her leg skiing she was out of the water for over a year, until she reasoned that unless she made herself dive again her leg would never recover. To get back into the water she designed a special wetsuit with a zip running all the way from her ankle to her chest, so that by lying down she could be rolled into it and fastened up. For a year she dragged her broken leg behind her as she dived, gradually and slowly allowing the ocean to bring it back to life.

To supplement her income, Dottie would dive for lobsters and abalone at weekends, often spear-fishing while someone else looked after her young children on the beach. 'I just got on with it,' she told me. 'In fact, one friend of mine had a flag she would wave when she needed me to come back to shore to breastfeed my youngest son. I was in that water all day if I had to be.'

One day while spearing, Dottie was knocked out by a sea lion that cannoned into her to steal the fish she had tied to her belt. The attack left her with four broken ribs, and she was pulled from the water by other divers who saw her sinking after the assault. Dottie has many such tales, and her eyes sparkled as she remembered her adventures. 'The worst experience was when I was in Mexico with about five guys and I was swimming back to the boat with a sackful of lobsters when I heard them yelling at me, "Watch out, shark!" I don't know what kind of shark it was, maybe a great white, but it was enormous, bigger than anything I'd ever seen in all my years of fishing. It circled me for about twenty minutes with me diving down again and again to face it head on so it wouldn't rush me, but I was exhausted. The guys on the boat couldn't get the anchor up to move the boat and the shark was so big they weren't coming in the water to get me. I decided I'd had enough and I swam straight for it. I just figured if this was the end I wanted it to be quick. But you know what? He just turned away. He came back again but it gave me time to get to the boat. Boy, I really thought I'd had it that day.'

In the afternoon we sat in the sitting-room drinking tea as the day slowly cooled off. We looked at Dottie's collection of old photographs, black and white snapshots with crinkle-cut borders showing her in old Bel-Aqua wetsuits which she had modelled in the Fifties, one-piece rubber affairs rather like the military Sladen suits. There were pictures of Dottie with bull lobsters, stingrays and abalone, on fishing boats and on rocky shores. She looked happy in the pictures, a woman who lived to be out of doors. The other divers with her were almost all male, big, fit-looking individuals with crew-cut hair and swimmers' bodies, holding up prize fish in the Californian sun. With hindsight she accepted that she had succeeded in a particularly male environment, and had not always been welcome, but that for a lot of women she had become something of a role model. Dottie had dived all along the California coast, and up to Alaska; she visited New Zealand, Australia, the Caribbean and Italy, diving everywhere. 'I even dived with the women shellfish divers in Japan, the ama, to see how they did it, but as far as I'm concerned nothing beats California in the old days. It's all changed now,' she added wistfully, 'all been fished out, and I guess I took my fair share of lobster and abalone and I might not have done if we'd known back then that we were killing the sea hereabouts. They say it's recovering, and maybe my grandchildren will see a time when they can find the big lobsters again. I hope so anyway.'

I left Dottie in her vegetable garden, and promised to stay in touch. I like to think of her still swimming and playing racquet-ball and even fighting with Cyril occasionally. 'What else are we gonna' do?' Dottie laughs wildly. 'Sit and watch TV all day like the other old folks? No Siree!'

*

The best way to observe fish is to become a fish. And the best way to become a fish — or a reasonable facsimile thereof — is to don an underwater-breathing device called the Aqualung.

Jacques-Yves Cousteau

Slowly but surely, the established spear-fishing and skin-diving clubs were converted to the new and exciting scuba technology. By 1948 the first Aqualungs, the Cousteau scuba brand, were being exported to America. Although initial sales were slow, they were boosted slightly by an article in *Science Illustrated* which attracted interest from the US Navy. More importantly, an article in *Life* in late 1950 focused on Cousteau and his new underwater breathing system. A large rise in the number of people wanting to spear game-fish and hunt for shellfish was the impetus needed for scuba to become big business. Picking up where Guy Gilpatric had left off, the influential *National Geographic Magazine* published a major feature article in 1949 on the San Diego Bottom Scratchers, an established spear-fishing club formed in the early 1930s. Two years later, *Skin Diver*, a magazine devoted entirely to the sport of skin diving, went on sale in California. The trickle of amateur divers became a torrent, their ranks swelled by a generation of young men who had been exposed to diver training in the armed services only a few years before. Of some thirty thousand scuba sets sold around the world by the mid 1950s, perhaps twenty-five thousand were sold on the west coast of the USA. In Europe, the same processes were at work, and the new compressed-air equipment for diving began to attract a small but passionate number of devotees.

Wherever there was an accessible coastline, people began diving with the Aqualung or any of several rival versions of the basic design perfected by Jacques Cousteau and Emile Gagnan. In France and Italy, underwater hunting became re-established in the

Mediterranean, and even in Britain there was an active spear-fishing fraternity and a growing number of divers interested in underwater prospecting for shipwrecks as well as the artefacts which had gone down with them. The British Sub Aqua Club, formed in 1953 with just a hundred members, grew tenfold in just a year, and soon had its own magazine advertising everything for the modern diver, including 'The first swim shorts designed especially for this thrilling new sport – tough cotton drill which dries quickly and won't snag.'

Just when Dottie Frazier and others were qualifying as diving instructors, there was an explosion of writing and television interest in the new sport. In 1951, Hans Hass produced *Diving to Adventure* in English, having already written four books in German. Waldron and Gleeson's *The Frogmen* became a bestseller, revealing in detail some of the first underwater sabotage missions of the War, and firmly establishing the term 'frogman' in everyday language. In 1952, it was the turn of the French pioneer Dimitri Rebikoff to translate *Free Diving* into English, the same year that the beginnings of modern marine biology were explored by Rachel Carson in *The Sea Around Us*. Hans Hass's *Red Sea Adventure* arrived at the same time, issued as *Manta* in the USA. In October 1952, a major boost to the awareness of diving as an adventure sport came with *National Geographic Magazine*'s leading article of the month, forty-two pages long and entitled 'Fish Men Explore a New World Under the Sea', by Captain Jacques-Yves Cousteau; it featured dramatic colour photographs of the Undersea Research Group diving in the Red Sea and the Atlantic. Sponges, undersea caverns, sharks and stingrays were all displayed across the pages, pictures remarkable for the time. The article was also a perfect advertisement for the newly available Cousteau equipment, and a plug for the soon-to-be-published *The Silent World*.

The following year, American zoologist and spear-fisher Eugenie Clark published the captivating *Lady with a Spear*, while Philippe

Diolé added *The Underwater Adventure* to the pile, the same year that Cousteau and Dumas' *The Silent World* came out, first in English and then in French translation. In 1954, Cousteau's colleague Philippe Tailliez produced *To Hidden Depths*, joining *Treasure Diving Holidays* by Jane and Barnet Crile, and the Italian author Folco Quilici's *Blue Continent*. Underwater hunting featured in all of these publications and was specifically addressed in *Shallow Water Diving and Spear Fishing* by Hilbert Schenk and Henry Kendall, *Modern Spearfishing* by Vane Ivanovic, *Mediterranean Hunter* (Bernard Gosky) and *Underwater Hunting* by Gilbert Doukan (all 1954). Pierre de Latil contributed *Underwater Naturalist* in the same year, by which time Hass's *Men and Sharks* was a useful trailer for his own forthcoming television series.

Apart from the books, there were increasing numbers of feature films and documentaries about the underwater world. Hass and Cousteau were enjoying limited success with short underwater films distributed for cinema release, but a mass audience had not yet been drawn in to the possibilities of the new art. *Kingdom of the Sea*, the first television series with a diving theme, was produced in America in 1954, featuring the talents of the glamorous female swimmer Zale Parry, who followed Dottie Frazier as a graduate of the Los Angeles County diving programme. Three years later, Zale Parry teamed up with the actor Lloyd Bridges for an astonishing run of over 150 episodes of the diving adventure series *Sea Hunt*. Bridges played Mike Nelson, an ex-Navy diver, and Parry did all of the underwater scenes where Nelson's female co-stars were required to dive, occasionally playing a character above water too. In 1956, Hans and Lotte Hass came to the small screen in Europe and later worldwide with the BBC's *Diving to Adventure*.

With scuba diving firmly entrenched as a modern and adventurous sport, the formalization of training schemes for divers gradually spread. The BSAC developed its own amateur club system for teaching divers the technique and skills of safe diving, while other European countries established their own similar systems. In America, regional programmes were replaced by national schemes such as those run by the YMCA. More commercial schemes were established by the National Association of Underwater Instructors (NAUI) in 1960, and the Professional Association of Diving Instructors (PADI) in 1966, who now dominate the sport-diving industry. Dozens of equipment manufacturers went into the business of making wetsuits, fins, masks, snorkels and breathing sets. Hans Hass and Jacques Cousteau endorsed and inspired a range of products, and people started looking for new ways to make a name in scuba diving. Depth records, distance records, and sleeping on a coral reef overnight were all attempted on scuba, as well as deep cave dives and explorations of hitherto unvisited submarine springs and rivers. Underwater hockey was invented in Britain as a way for scuba divers to keep fit during winter, when for most practical purposes offshore diving was prevented by the weather. Divers, comfortable with the equipment which had seemed so radical and daring only a few years before, began to look for gimmicks to promote themselves within the sport. In 1960, an American diver named Jane Baldesare, whose husband had trained with Neal Watson in Florida, travelled to England to try to become the first person to swim the Channel underwater. She failed, but a magazine article at the time began its coverage of the unsuccessful marathon dive with the question, 'Why wait for the Channel Tunnel?' In 1961 she tried again, but bad weather halted the attempt. The following year Jane's husband Fred made the attempt and reached the French coast after swimming for eighteen hours. Fred Baldesare's appetite for long-distance dives was not completely satisfied, however, and he went on to cross the Straits of Messina and Gibraltar in successive years.

Modern recreational diving is in every sense underwater tourism. The largest commercial organization running training courses for sport divers is PADI, who estimate that there are around ten million certified divers in the United States alone. This probably represents just half of the total number of sport divers worldwide. Teaching them to dive and then selling them diving equipment is big business. Perhaps equally important is the pressure that scuba divers can exert as a lobby for marine conservation, since many developing countries now recognize the need to protect their coral reefs from destruction in order to attract visiting divers. In some parts of the world a rapid over-expansion of diving, such as in the Red Sea, has led to intrusive and destructive tourism development by entrepreneurs cashing in on the numbers of people wishing to visit a region purely to dive. Slowly, the word spreads that the reefs are a complex but singularly fragile ecosystem, a source of wonder and inspiration which divers too must pledge to protect.

Sometimes, virtually the only thing divers see of a country is the diving centre from where they take their boat to the dive sites. In a superficial way, the diving operators who take visitors on underwater tours very often embody the local culture: slick and businesslike or laid back and casual, jocular or sullen. National stereotypes also seem to come out when divers gather *en masse*. When I worked as a dive leader we saw the Germans as equipment fetishists who believed that their diving computer was an infallible machine. The Italians were friendly, noisy divers, who wanted to dive in a group, hugging and kissing each other before and after each dive, and touching everything they found underwater. The French were keen on catching things which might be edible, and the Japanese wanted to be led in an orderly line of neatly paired divers who wore thin white gloves in case they accidentally touched anything underwater. The British could be equipment bores, or rough, tough deep divers who always wore a full-length wetsuit no matter what the water temperature. They would almost always want to go off and do their own thing underwater without a guide. Then there were the Russian mafiosi who appeared from the depths of a Moscow winter carrying plastic bags stuffed with dollar bills. They often had no diving qualifications, and just wanted to show that they could happily pay as much as it would take to get someone to take them diving. Diving and a tropical beach holiday were status symbols to be acquired now that they had access to hard currency. More than once I heard of them dying in the process, either from heart attacks brought on by underwater exertion, or from lung injuries caused by ignorance of proper diving procedures. In contrast, the Americans generally had lots of badges for diving courses they had completed, and they were continually surprised that our twelve-seater diving boat didn't have a lavatory or a cafeteria on board.

Large groups of divers are a nuisance, but the most profitable diving centres are the busiest. To reinforce the most basic of safety rules, the instructors warn: if you dive alone, you die alone. You rely on your diving partner as your safety back-up, and it is comforting to know that you have someone close to you in this potentially hostile environment. Equally, it can be distressing to 'buddy up' with someone who is uncommunicative or uninterested in staying close enough to help if something goes wrong. For this reason, experienced divers tend to make sure they are as self-reliant as possible underwater, adequately trained and with the right equipment for any eventuality. They call it self-rescue. To me, diving alone is sometimes a better option than diving with an unsympathetic partner, a clumsy, careless diver who is uninterested in marine life, and a negative distraction underwater. The whole point of being in the liquid world is to get away from stress and strain, and, one imagines, the annoying diver would probably be useless in an emergency in any case. There is great intimacy in diving with another human being. Diving with someone you trust as a diver is a very good idea. But diving with someone you love brings a shared joy and dependency which is a reinforcement of the closeness you feel above water. Underwater, the communication is not verbal, and a light squeeze of a hand or the brush of a shoulder is an intensified connection in a different world.

Diving companies attract staff from around the globe, young men and women who use an instructor's certificate as a passport to travel to some of the most sought-after holiday destinations available. From the Maldives to Mauritius, and from Belize to Bora Bora, they float from job to job, their limbs deeply bronzed wherever they are not covered by their wetsuits, and their hair bleached as white as salt by sea and sun. Their qualification gives them access to places they might otherwise never experience, and the diving companies capitalize on the instructor's desire to work in exotic places, paying them little and working them hard. The instructors tend to be young, lean and fit, and embody all the attributes of a carefree existence. Like skiing instructors or professional surfers, these divers are birds of passage, self-styled free spirits whose daily grind is what ordinary mortals have to scrimp and save to experience perhaps once a year.

Like many novice divers, I once fell in love with my diving instructor. Just like the agile and accomplished skiing instructor who dazzles his pupils with his prowess on the slopes, and quite often in a range of languages, the diving instructor enjoys the advantages of power. They are in control of the learning process, and eager pupils can be flattered by their attention. In any group of novitiates there is often a competitive drive to personalize the relationship with the teacher. Learning to dive involves putting extreme trust in the instructor, who quite literally has the responsibility of keeping you alive, and some instructors capitalize on that power play, chalking up sexual conquests with alarming rapidity. The professional diving organizations, especially in America, warn against such behaviour for fear of lawsuits over sexual harassment. In my case, there was definitely a certain caché to be had from hanging out with the dive team after hours, and my relationship brought with it the added advantage of free diving. In retrospect this was not such a good deal, since I spent several thousand pounds flying to and from the island where my mermaid paramour was based. Strangely, it wasn't a recipe for a successful relationship. I had confused my love for all things aquatic with my emotional needs, and above water it slowly emerged that we had little in common. We were happiest underwater, not speaking.

Peveril Ledges, Dorset

The diver's greatest danger lies within him: it is the sudden onset of fear.
                    Hans Hass, *Conquest of the Underwater World*

Returning to London from a posting abroad, I decided to sign up for a dive in British waters. After the pleasure of clear, calm seas under the equatorial sun, I wanted to experience the underwater scenery of my own country. According to the diving magazines I had read, there was a wealth of marine life to be found off the south coast of England, and innumerable shipwrecks waiting to be explored. Having found a diving club in London that made regular weekend excursions to the coast, I registered for an advanced diving course, imagining that diving with an instructor in attendance in these new conditions might be a good idea.

One Saturday in early spring found me standing on the quayside at Poole Harbour, where about a dozen people with large kit bags of diving paraphernalia were waiting for a fishing boat to take us offshore. On board, I was introduced to a slightly built middle-aged woman named Susan. She too was enrolled for an 'advanced' course and I was to dive with Susan and the instructor, with whom she had recently completed her basic diving certification. The instructor was a diminutive female in her early twenties. As I made conversation with Susan, it became clear that she had reservations about the day's diving. She smoked four cigarettes during the half-hour journey to the first dive site, and told me that she had never dived in the sea before. In common with many British divers, her training certificate had been issued after a series of dives in inland quarries, where an instructor can easily monitor and assist students without the hazards of coastal currents and excessive depth. Susan told me that she had an abiding fear that she would surface from a dive and find herself alone in the expansive Channel with no boat to retrieve her from the water. Her training in a quarry, an artificial body of water, had seemed safer, a self-contained environment no more alarming than a giant swimming pool. The open sea frightened her with its vastness, and like many divers she felt dwarfed by its scope. I assured her that in my experience the scenario of being left behind by the boat was a most unlikely prospect.

A short distance west from the entrance to Poole Harbour we prepared to make our first dive. The instructor had chosen a shallow area of seabed, no more than thirty-five feet deep, where we could practise a drift-dive, an exercise in letting the prevailing current take you along underwater to rendezvous with the diving boat after a pre-arranged time. To allow the diving boat to locate the divers easily, one of the group would hold a nylon rope-line attached to an inflatable marker buoy which would float on the surface throughout the dive.

As we put on our equipment, I struggled with the thick wetsuit which would cover all of my body. It restricted my limbs and felt tight around my chest. When I pulled on the rubber hood I found that I had difficulty rotating my neck or tilting my head downwards to look at the equipment clipped to my chest. The prospect of jumping from the fishing boat into the grey waters around us thus handicapped made me slightly apprehensive. With gloves on my hands, would I be able to operate my equipment easily? Surely this could not be fun.

Once overboard, I discovered that the wetsuit and its accoutrements worked exactly as promised. There was little sensation of cold, and the water around me liberated me from the stiffness I had felt on deck. And I could see underwater, albeit no further than twenty feet or so in any direction. As I had expected, the underwater colours were dull, yes, but there was seaweed and fish and interesting underwater rocks covered in anemones to discover. The problem was Susan. She seemed to have no control of her position in the water. One minute she would be head down, feet up; the next floating upwards towards the surface headfirst. The instructor and I would grasp her by the fins, or by her buoyancy jacket and pull her back down, and then she would roll over on to her back like a stranded tortoise. The entire forty-minute dive was spent guiding Susan through the water like a wayward torpedo. Except that a torpedo would have been hydrodynamic; she was more like a badly behaved dog on a lead.

After completing the drift-dive I decided to talk to the instructor and ask if it might be possible to join one of the other diving groups on board, so that she could give Susan some personal attention underwater. To my mind, Susan was too nervous to enjoy her dives and would be better off diving alone with her instructor at her own pace. The instructor told me that the difficulties on the morning dive had just been a case of 'teething problems', and having certified Susan as a diver in inland waters she was confident that she would handle the afternoon dive more competently. After lunch, she told me, we would attempt the next stage of our course, a so-called deep dive where we would demonstrate our ability to dive below twenty metres, a depth I had already exceeded in warm waters on several occasions. Yet again, I wondered what the underwater visibility would be like in this part of the world, but I was now at least confident that I would not be cold.

As we approached the dive site, Susan and I were told that the skipper of the fishing boat had forecast rough conditions for the area. A strong current was running, perhaps as high as four knots, and we would have to take care to stay together once we entered the water. The instructor emphasized that the current would be likely to be much stronger at the surface, and so as to avoid being separated we should be ready to jump into the sea in unison and swim straight down without lingering on the surface.

Soon afterwards, our boat drew near to a large oil barrel, a fishing buoy tethered to the seabed by a heavy metal chain. In the surging current the large barrel was being tugged below the waves, straining at the chain like a dog on a leash. Watching the barrel, I overheard the boat's skipper asking the leader of the dive club if he was sure he wanted anyone diving in the prevailing conditions. The leader seemed to think the current was only a problem at the surface, and so after a short conversation we were given the go-ahead to dive. We kitted up and stood shoulder to shoulder at the side of the boat. Other divers held on to our air cylinders from behind, steadying us against the dangerous pitching of the deck. We were poised like paratroopers waiting for the green light to hurl ourselves through the aircraft's open door. With a final OK signal from the instructor we were ready, and I took a giant stride into the dark water. To my surprise, Susan, the instructor and I all hit the water at the same time and quickly signalled that we were OK to descend. We sank beneath the violent swell and were alone in the dim water, a trio of rubber-clad shapes communicating only with our eyes and a wave of the hand. Once underwater it was clear that the current was too strong to do anything other than drift along with it. We made our gradual descent through the half-lit world of water shadows, peering below for a sign that we were reaching the seabed.

A minute later we hit bottom at around twenty-three metres and found ourselves in a submarine landscape of granite shelves. Large slabs of flattened rock like king-sized double beds lay on the seafloor. The water around us seemed to have a greenish tint, a cool illumination which dampened the emotions. Visibility was poor, and in order to collect ourselves we knelt on the bottom in the lee of the rocks, ducking down behind them to stay out of the current. As I held on to the edge of a rock next to the instructor, it was clear that Susan had a problem. Like us she was pinned against one side of a large slab by the current, not moving, but there was something unnerving about the way she looked. Susan showed no emotion or reaction to the instructor's hand signals. Behind her mask she stared straight ahead, as if in a trance. She was frozen with fear, destabilized by the knowledge that once she left her anchorage in the rocks she would be at the mercy of the current. After her performance in the morning it was clear that she felt unable to orientate herself properly in the swift flow. I imagined her rolling like a tumbleweed along the rocky ledges, propelled by the drifting water but unable to right herself and steer herself beside us in the gloom. Confronted with the deep, dark water and the impelling current, her mind refused to think about anything practical. She clung to the edge of the slab as though it was the edge of a precipice, gripped by a condition known as passive panic.

The light on the seabed was dim. Desperately, we tried to pull ourselves hand over hand across the rock slab to reach her. The current was too much for the instructor. I had almost reached Susan, fighting to keep myself out of the flow, hugging the face of the slab to minimize the amount of my body exposed to the ripping force of the tide. Just as I was within arm's length, and ready to pull Susan forcibly from where she was rooted against the rock, I felt something grasp me around the neck. Somehow, in our attempt to scramble across the rock, the instructor had allowed the rope line attached to the marker buoy to become entangled about my throat.

I could feel the tug of the nylon cord threatening to pull the regulator from my mouth. I turned to see the instructor struggling to maintain her position on the rock. Seeing my predicament, she signalled for me to release my hold on the slab. In the strong current we flew off the rock, tied together by the nylon line which was clipped to her buoyancy jacket. As I looked back, Susan was still pinned to the rock, unmoving, and seemingly unaware of what was happening. As we drifted away she was gone, a ghostly image hidden by the grey-green waters. Then the instructor and I were alone, bound together by the fouled line.

I pulled at the cord around my throat, trying to keep it away from my regulator hose, feeling the nylon biting into my fingers. I can clearly remember thinking to myself, 'This is not good', and then wondering why I was thinking in speech bubbles, like a character in a cartoon. Then I wondered why I was being so calm, and I fleetingly considered the imminent danger of drowning. It all seemed strangely academic. I was enveloped in this world of green dream water, more concerned about what might be happening to Susan than my own predicament. I was aware that she was experiencing her very worst fears come to life: abandonment underwater. She was an insignificant speck on the seabed sur-rounded by the infinite space of the ocean.

After a time I felt the noose around my throat go slack. I did not know it, but the marker buoy on the surface above had separated from the nylon line with the force of my weight pulling against it underwater. I held on to the instructor as we kicked slowly for the surface, still drifting, revolving like ornaments on a fairground merry-go-round in the current. Her eyes, as round as saucers, stared back at me from behind her mask. Slowly we kicked upwards towards the light and air. I felt a warm glow at the idea that I was leaving the green dreamworld behind.

Breaking the surface, the instructor and I maintained a hold on one another, and realized that we were drifting in the swell with nothing to signal our position. Released from its tether, the marker buoy had flown across the wave tops. Waves hit our faces at unpredictable intervals and we breathed air from our cylinders so as to avoid being swamped for as long as possible. When they ran dry we used our snorkels, kicking as best we could to maintain our breathing tubes away from the prevailing wind. We dropped our weight belts so as to lighten the load on our buoyancy jackets. Neither of us could speak except in occasional snatches of shouted instructions, but we were undoubtedly thinking the same thing. What had become of Susan? The image of her stricken face receding from my sight as we were torn from the rocks kept flashing through my head.

In dull-coloured wetsuits we were mere dots on the surface of the Channel. The swell lifted us high enough to see a panoramic view of the coastline in the distance, with several diving and fishing boats in the vicinity but all too far away to hear us call out for help. We waved at several boats and were not seen, and all the time we wondered what had happened to Susan. We barely spoke, breathing through our snorkels so as to avoid the buffeting waves which threatened to make us swallow seawater. I recalled stories I had heard about divers left adrift in cold water for hours. For about forty minutes we floated with the tide, until a charter fishing boat spotted us. The men on board were divers who had abandoned their own diving plans that afternoon due to the rough seas and strong currents. Although there were six divers and a skipper on the fishing boat, only one man had seen us waving. After we were pulled from the water we made radio contact with our own boat, which until then had no idea of our fate.

An alert was issued on the ship's VHF radio and all boats in the area began searching for Susan. The instructor and I did not speak to each other; it was clear she was responsible for the accident, and there was no point in stating the obvious. We sipped hot tea provided by our rescuers and stood apart at the ship's rail scanning the sea for signs of Susan. Forty-five minutes later we received the radio call that she had been found by another diving boat. They had to drag her from the water like a hooked fish. She sobbed uncontrollably with fear and relief.

Later that day, I spoke to Susan about what had happened. She was still shaken by her experience and brought to tears as she recounted her story. She would have to consider carefully whether she would ever dive in England again. Finding herself alone underwater after we became separated, she said she waited for us to return, somehow imagining that we would be able to find her. She felt powerless to help herself, and terrified of letting go of her niche in the rocks. After several minutes alone in the dark, she said the reality of her predicament struck her. On only her second sea dive, she had been abandoned in a strong current and in relatively deep water. She had a choice: swim to the surface alone, or die. Conquering her panic, she pulled herself from her rocky nook, mustering all her inner courage to force herself to ascend slowly to avoid decompression injury. Once on the surface safely, her nightmare was only half over. Now she was alone, and drifting in the open water, a tiny piece of flotsam in a rolling sea.

Officially, my instructor left the diving club by 'mutual agreement' the following week. As diving accidents go, our incident was quite minor, but at sea, and underwater, there is a narrow line between mishap and disaster. People die every year with great regularity diving in British waters, and now I understood why. I carried on diving with the club and soon found a regular buddy whom I trusted, but my introduction to the Channel had been a valuable lesson.

Susan did not dive again.

9. Habitats

I do not pretend to have visited the bottom of the sea . . . and it is a
great rarity in those cold parts of Europe to meet with any men at all,
that have had at once the boldness, the occasion, the opportunity, and
the skill to penetrate into those concealed and dangerous recesses of
nature, much less to make any stay there . . .

Robert Boyle, *Relations About the Bottom of the Sea*, 1671

Just after noon on a sunny June day in 1774, a small group of men
set out from Plymouth Harbour in a small barge to watch a
carpenter, named John Day, embark on an experiment. He
intended to prove that he could spend twenty-four hours underwater, and then return to the surface, with the aid of what was
termed a wooden 'diving chamber' which he had designed and
built himself. Christopher Blake, a gentleman from London, was
paying for the expedition, and three months earlier he had spent
£340 on acquiring an old sloop called the *Maria*. She had already
been towed out to a spot just north of Drake's Island in the middle
of Plymouth Sound, where the depth of water was known to be
twenty-two fathoms.

Anchored close by the *Maria*, Mr Blake and a couple of bargemen
watched as Day prepared to climb inside the 'chamber' – a wooden
box – which was fixed to the deck of the sloop by a complex system
of struts and rope ties. The old sloop was merely a platform for

Day's diving engine; she would be sunk, and after a day and a night
on the seabed, the plan was for Day to release the ties fixing him
and his chamber to the deck. Day had spent three months building
the contraption, and he had promised his backer that it would allow
him to remain underwater for at least twenty-four hours. The
carpentry and joinery skills used by Day and his workmen were
the best of the time. According to his design, when he released the
ropes the box would float to the surface and he would emerge
a rich man, having invented a survival capsule for underwater
exploration. Day's intention was merely to demonstrate that survival underwater was feasible; there was no mention of any plan
to move the box around.

Without fanfare or send-off, Day removed his coat and waistcoat,
calling out to the barge captain that he would likely be too warm
inside the box. Then, with what an observer later called 'great
composure and confident in his enterprise', he pulled down the
hatch on his wooden box and the barge eased away. The crew of
the barge then set about removing the wooden plugs which kept
the *Maria* afloat. Weighted down with stone ballast, she settled
slowly in the water. Impatient for glory, Day ordered extra stones
to be piled on to the deck to speed up the process. Then, with a
shudder, the old ship sank into the Channel, to the north of where
Drake's Island stands guard in the middle of the Sound.

Even in mid June, the waters of Plymouth Sound are rarely
clear. An offshore breeze ruffles the sea and a maze of underwater
currents and strong tides make the approaches to the harbour a test
of seamanship.

At twenty-two fathoms, or one hundred and thirty feet below
the surface, the light is muted. To the naked eye underwater, the
shades of colour are reduced to palest grey, and slabs of dark
granite tumble like giants' tombstones across the bottom. John
Day was unable to see out of his wooden cask on 20 June 1774. If

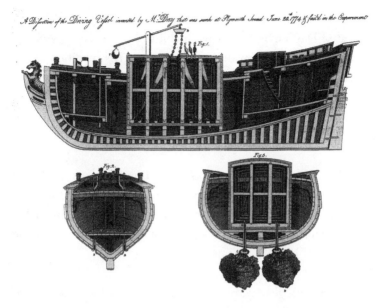

M. Mr Day's 'Diving Vessel', a wooden box fitted to the hull of the sloop
Maria, in which he intended to spend twenty-four hours underwater in
Plymouth Sound in 1774.

he had, and if he had possessed an underwater torch, the only
colour he might have glimpsed would have been the pink or orange
tentacles of the tiny jewel anemones spread across the flattened
granite. Like illuminated and hairy mushrooms, the anemones
thrive in the dull, cool underworld. Here there is no vibrant coral,
no sunlit garden of delicate growth to explore. It is a dark and
lonely place for a man about to die. Once inside the diving box,
John Day was never seen again.

A glimpse at Day's plans for his underwater box induce an
involuntary shudder. Few men can have worked so long and so
hard on constructing their own coffin, and with such conviction
that they were destined for fame and fortune.

In an effort to explain the events of that June day, an elaborate
account of Day's experiment was published a year later by N. D.
Falck, himself an underwater salvage expert. His rendition of the
events following the sinking of the *Maria* is sanguine:

She was sunk at two o'clock in the afternoon, and Mr Day descended
with her into perpetual night!

Falck makes sure in his *Philosophical Dissertation on the Diving
Vessel Projected by Mr Day, and Sunk in Plymouth Sound*, that most of
the blame falls on the hapless inventor, rather than on Mr Blake.
The social proprieties of the age are summed up neatly in the
description of Day's character:

Day's temper was gloomy, reserved and peevish; his disposition penuri-
ous; his views pecuniary; and he was remarkably obstinate in his opinion,
and jealous of his fame. But withal, he was allowed to be penetrating in
his observations, faithful to his patron and unshaken in his resolutions. If
his talents had been properly cultivated by education, they would doubt-
less have rendered him an useful member of society.

Day made little allowance for failure, but he armed himself with
three differently coloured buoys to signal his state of health to the
bargemen above. He carried with him a white buoy, which, if
released, was intended to mean that he was 'very well', and a red
one to signify that he was 'indifferent'. Even the black buoy,
signifying 'very ill', failed to appear.

Falck's final conclusion at the end of his *Philosophical Dissertation*
is as helpful as we might expect. He decides that Day must have
been 'thunderstruck with cold at the end of his rapid descent; so
as to exhaust all vilifying warmth from the automaton'.

Falck's assertion that Day would have been 'thunderstruck with cold' has at least some basis in reality. We know now that water conducts heat away from the human body at least twenty-five times faster than air. Dressed lightly, Day would have quickly chilled, even if we assume that he sank smoothly to the seabed and survived on the air contained in his diving engine. Although it was a summer day, the sea temperature at twenty-two fathoms is unlikely to have been more than twelve degrees centigrade. In a seven-millimetre wetsuit, wearing a full hood, insulated bootees and gloves, any modern diver begins to chill significantly after about thirty minutes at that temperature.

A catastrophic failure of the technology, leading to the implosion of the wooden box under water pressure, would at least have resulted in a quick death. If Day survived the descent to the seabed, and had enough air to sustain him while trapped within his engine, he would have gone through the stages of hypothermia. First, violent shivering, as his body tried to stimulate heat by contracting his muscles. As he cooled further, his muscles would have gone into spasm, becoming rigid, making his movements awkward, and effectively preventing him releasing the complicated ring bolts securing the box to the deck of the *Maria*. Then, as the cold reached his brain, he would have become passive, the blood in his veins thickening, his thoughts becoming progressively more confused. Finally, after Day lost consciousness, the final shivers, deep ripples on the surface of his heart muscle which prevented it pumping oxygen around his body, would have signalled the end. The reality of what transpired one hundred and thirty feet down in Plymouth Sound is a matter for conjecture. No trace of him, or his diving engine, was ever found. It seems most likely that John Day's diving box simply wasn't watertight. At that depth, the atmospheric pressure is five times what we experience on the surface, and any flaw, any loose seam in the wooden joints would have simply flooded the box. Even if Day had been able to get out of his chamber with his lungs full of air, swimming up from that depth without training, and without the assistance of a mask or fins to improve vision and propulsion, is no easy matter.

Underwater, Plymouth Sound may be little different today than it was in 1774. For sailors, however, the entrance to the harbour has been changed significantly by the addition of a massive breakwater which stretches like a caesarean scar across the belly of the Sound. Nuclear submarines now tie up in the lee of the breakwater, and on the shore close by there is Fort Bovisand, a grim bulwark built by Napoleonic prisoners of war in the early nineteenth century, and now a diver training centre. In June, weather permitting, yachtsmen sail along the Sound and turn around buoys beyond the breakwater, pleasure boaters oblivious to the ghost of John Day's coffin ship below.

In 1774, the great minds of the age were applying their skills to the discovery of basic scientific principles. In England, for just over a century, the Royal Society had been the main forum for men of science to exchange ideas. Learned men such as Edmund Halley, Christopher Wren and Isaac Newton had published their findings in the Society's journal, *Philosophical Transactions*. Robert Boyle, whose work with gas laws became fundamental to diving science, had also made 'pneumatical' experiments on the processes of animal respiration, and elsewhere lamented his inability to examine the seabed in person. The foundations of modern physics, chemistry and biology were being laid, but scientific method was still in its infancy.

Two hundred years after Day failed in his attempt to spend twenty-four hours underwater, such dreams have become a reality. Having perfected free swimming at reasonably shallow depth with portable breathing systems, man decided he was ready to live, work and sleep underwater. Self-contained breathing apparatus allowed him to swim freely, and scientific experiment had perfected mathematical tables to allow the calculations necessary to avoid decompression illness. Man knew about pressure, about the effects of breathing gas at depth, and how long it would take to ascend safely from depth without courting injury. The next logical step was to extend the time he could spend underwater.

Somewhere in the Sound, close to the breakwater, lie the remains of another underwater experiment less disastrous than Mr Day's diving engine. It is a metal dome on upright legs, about seven feet wide and twelve feet long. Named Glaucus, after the fisherman of Boeotia who was changed into a god of the sea by eating a magic herb, the dome is an example of one of the many designs for what we now call sub-sea habitats. Glaucus was a British project, sunken in thirty feet of water in 1965. Although it did not suffer a catastrophic failure as great as Mr Day's diving engine, Glaucus was abandoned after a short period due to bad weather. Glaucus is now a disused piece of wreckage, a curiosity for divers being trained at Fort Bovisand, and a crumbling reminder of an era when living under the sea had once again become an obsession for scientists and adventurers in more than a dozen countries around the world.

In 1954, Ed Fisher decided to use scuba to spend twenty-four hours 'living' on a coral reef in Florida. Supported by a surface boat and a team of safety divers who would take turns to watch over him, he assembled a collection of supplies which he thought would be useful for his extended underwater repose. Instead of building himself a house, Fisher took a rubber ring, which he anchored among some coral heads so that he could lie inside it without drifting away. To record his observations he carried a wax pencil and a waterproof notebook. In order to drink underwater, he carried a large syringe which he could charge from a bottle and then squirt into his mouth. By removing his regulator from his mouth he was also able to drink soup. In the same way, and in an attempt to assert his claim to subsistence underwater, he killed a small reef fish with his diving knife, and ate it raw. Fisher's night underwater was uneventful, and his greatest problem was the cold. Supplied by fresh-air cylinders whenever his supplies ran low, Fisher remained on the reef for exactly twenty-four hours, remaining at a maximum depth of thirty-three feet. Boredom and cold made him want to abandon the dive when morning came, but with encouragement from his support divers he managed to achieve his dream.

We do not need to breathe air in order to live, or at least we do not need to breathe air comprised of exactly the proportions and ingredients that are found on the surface of the earth. The air we habitually breathe is composed of approximately 79 per cent nitrogen and 20 per cent oxygen, with the remaining percentage of the total mixture made up of other gases. It is oxygen that we need to fuel our metabolism, and the waste product of the metabolic process, carbon dioxide, is what we must eliminate from our body by breathing. Nitrogen plays no part in the lungs' gas exchange mechanism and only becomes a problem as it accumulates in our tissues under pressure. Technically, our bodies can survive breathing a mixture of oxygen and gases other than nitrogen, including krypton, argon, neon, helium, hydrogen and xenon. Among these are the so-called 'noble gases', those which were originally considered to be both rare and chemically inert, and earned the honorific title because it was believed they would never absorb other elements at the atomic level.

Early in the twentieth century, an American scientist named Elihu Thompson discovered that helium could be used to replace nitrogen in a breathing mixture without harmful effects. His discovery would eventually lead to solving the problem of nitrogen narcosis at depth. In essence, helium differs from nitrogen in that it is not as soluble in the blood. It does, however, diffuse into human tissue, and quite fast, still requiring a diver who breathes helium as part of his mixture to ascend slowly. Helium does not invade fatty tissue as much as nitrogen, but, just like nitrogen, it reacts to pressure changes, and will cause bubbles to form in the blood as it comes out of solution. And, just like nitrogen, helium too can eventually induce narcosis, a pleasing feeling of drunkenness, but usually only at much greater depths. The disadvantage of helium, which is less dense, is that it conducts heat away from the human body much faster than the nitrogen in normal air. This means that divers breathing the gas will quickly become cold, and with prolonged exposure the very real danger of hypothermia sets in. Helium also carries sound faster than air, causing the human voice to sound squeaky, like a speeded-up cartoon character.

The main drawback of diving beyond the time limits of decompression tables is not the fact that inert gases like helium will be absorbed into the body, but the time it will take any of the gases to pass safely out of solution in the body tissues. Each minute spent at depth incurs a penalty, a proportionate period to be spent decompressing either at a shallower depth underwater or in a compression chamber above water. The commercial cost of employing men to sit around decompressing may be greater than the cost of the task they are employed to perform.

In the 1940s, it was suggested that once under pressure, the body would eventually become 'saturated' with whatever gases were being breathed, and that after a certain length of time there would be no concomitant increase in the resulting decompression period. So long as the diver remains at one maximum depth, his decompression time will remain constant. In other words, just as a sponge, once full of water, can get no 'wetter', no matter how long it stays in the water, the body has a limit to how much nitrogen it can absorb, and while the speed of that absorption will depend upon several factors (including ambient pressure), it too will eventually become saturated. Once saturated, the body only therefore requires one single period of decompression to remove the inert gases which have accumulated in its tissues. How much simpler, then, to send a man into the sea and keep him there until his job is done, than to keep bringing him to the surface for decompression. This is 'saturation diving'.

The military implications of being able to keep a man underwater indefinitely, or to have him working out of sight without visible surface support, are obvious; add the prospect of commercial riches, and scientific interest peaks. In commercial terms, the idea that men might stay underwater and excavate minerals, or farm the seabed, has been a dream cherished ever since Captain Nemo told Professor Arronax:

'My flocks, like those of Neptune's old shepherds, graze fearlessly in the immense prairies of the ocean. I have a vast property there, which I cultivate myself, and which is always sown by the hand of the Creator of all things.'

There is something about dealing with the sea and its resources which inspires thoughts of the Creator. It seems also to inspire a proselytizing zeal in those who work with it, and Dr George Bond was as fervent a preacher of diving science as anyone.

George Foote Bond was a family physician from the tiny community of Bat Cave, North Carolina, obsessed with the idea that the world would one day run short of food, in particular animal protein. Bond was an unusual man, a mixture of compassionate medic, maverick scientist and compulsive diarist. He saw the sea as the solution to humankind's nutritional problems, and joined the United States Navy, a move which would revolutionize the science of diving and remove Bond for ever from the world of small-town medicine. In 1957, while working for the Naval Medical Research Laboratory, he obtained permission to embark on what he named 'Project Genesis'. In common with most of his generation, Bond would have been very familiar with the biblical account of Creation in which God decrees that man will be made in His own image, and will have

dominion over the fish of the sea, and over the fowl of the air, and over the cattle, and over all the earth, and over every creeping thing that creepeth upon the earth.

George Bond began his quest to establish parameters for saturation diving, the aim being to find out how long animals, and eventually man, could breathe in an artificial atmosphere using mixed gases such as helium and oxygen, so as to minimize the risks of nitrogen narcosis at depth. Only then would 'dominion over the sea' be a possibility, since a man could remain on the seabed for as long as he had supplies of the appropriate breathing gases. Over a five-year period, the Genesis experiments would culminate in the largest sub-sea habitation exercise ever undertaken – the US Navy Sealab programme. Given that compressed air could not be used much below two hundred and fifty feet without considerable risk of nitrogen narcosis, a mixed-gas combination, which would remove nitrogen from the equation, seemed the logical answer. The dangers of using pure pressurized oxygen on its own had been established during the Second World War, with the work of Haldane in England and Steltzner in Germany, but Bond undertook further studies to determine the finite limits of oxygen as a breathing medium. First-hand accounts of the dangers of breathing oxygen alone were plentiful, and both Jacques Cousteau and Hans Hass, and a host of British charioteers had described their own terrifying encounters with its poisonous potential. Although it was known that helium might prove to be the solution to the problem, it was only in the USA that plentiful supplies of the gas were available. Until exploitable underground reserves of the gas were found, it was a famously expensive commodity, and during the War the USA jealously guarded its monopoly on helium.

For almost six years, George Bond experimented with animal subjects – rats, goats and monkeys, most of which survived the experience – until finally in 1962 he was ready to subject three men to a saturation dive, breathing a mix of oxygen, helium, and a very small amount of nitrogen for six days at a simulated depth of one hundred feet. Helium had already been tried as a breathing gas by the US Navy's Experimental Diving Unit at simulated depths greater than five hundred feet.

Within a year, Bond had men at pressures equivalent to almost two hundred feet of seawater for twelve days, using a pressure chamber with an interconnected 'wet room' where they could swim and simulate physical work underwater. However, Bond and his team were working within the labyrinth of US Navy bureaucracy and funding. To ensure safety, Bond's team would have to check and double-check all of their data before they would be allowed to test their theory in open water. Although the data collected at the naval submarine base represented the largest available body of scientific evidence on saturation diving, it would be other men who would attract public attention as the first successful residents of the sea.

While Bond and his team were finalizing the painstaking results of several years of laboratory studies, a rush of high-profile habitation experiments hit the headlines. The public race to build a sub-sea home, a viable habitat which would make prolonged diver immersion viable, was on.

On the French Riviera in August 1962, Edwin Link, a fifty-eight-year-old American inventor, made an eight-hour dive to sixty feet in a small chamber of his own design, becoming the world's first successful saturation diver. Ed Link, a former pilot and associate of Charles Lindbergh the aviator, had already made a name for himself with the invention of a highly successful aircraft cockpit simulator for the US military. For some time, Link had been interested in designing a diving chamber which would allow continuous immersion at depth. His solution was the 'Link Cylinder', a small, cramped tube just three feet wide and eleven feet long (in essence a modern diving bell), which was suspended vertically from a surface vessel and into which the single inhabitant could seal himself for immersion and recovery. Link's innovation was the construction of a chamber which a diver could emerge from underwater, carry out many hours of work, and then seal himself back into for decompression. Once sealed, the chamber could be raised by a surface vessel and carried on board to wherever the ship was going, its occupant safely contained in his own pressurized world, while his breathing mix came through umbilical lines supplied from the ship's gas cylinders.

Link, like Bond, believed the scientific theories that suggested a man might breathe a mixture of oxygen and helium at depth for extended periods and emerge without harm. No one had actually tested the theory in the sea, however, and Link took the decision to become the first human guinea-pig. He had been a regular visitor to Bond's office at the United States Navy Submarine Base in Connecticut, and was armed with data from the Genesis project to make his own calculations. Link's research programme, assisted by heavyweight political support, was named 'Man in the Sea'.

On 28 August, in Villefranche Bay, Ed Link was lowered into the Mediterranean inside his chamber, and left there for eight hours. As relief from the cramped confines of the metal tube, he made diving excursions outside lasting over an hour. The eight-hour dive then required six hours of decompression, and in order for Link to lie flat for at least some of the time the tube was hoisted on deck and laid horizontal. Just before midnight, and fourteen hours after he had first entered the cylinder, Ed Link crawled out on to the ship's deck, tired but unharmed by his experience. Within a week, the Link cylinder would be sent down to two hundred feet for a complete day and night underwater, the magical twenty-four-hour cycle which would establish a benchmark in the quest for aquatic habitation. Ed Link did not make the second dive, giving way to a younger man, a Swiss diver named Robert Stenuit.

Stenuit has been called the world's first 'aquanaut', the term loosely applied to men who have spent more than twenty-four hours living underwater. Ironically, although attention over the next decade would shift to grandiose schemes and structures aimed at building houses of various types under the sea, the very concept of Link's mobile compression chamber was to presage the end of those experiments. Eventually, it would be decided that there is limited value for commercial diving in putting men into a fixed structure on the seabed and leaving them there. How much more cost effective to send them down and bring them back in a portable structure, and move on to pastures new? In military terms, too, a fixed sub-sea structure is difficult to defend and easy to detect. Such rationales were in their infancy in 1962, and for a time the race to build an embryo city under the sea would capture government budgets and scientific brains. In terms of publicity, popular renown for building the first workable sub-sea habitat would go to Jacques Cousteau, who, only weeks after Link went down into the waters of Villefranche Bay, launched his most ambitious diving project to date: the 'Conshelf' experiment.

'Conshelf' was an abbreviation of Continental Shelf, the outward slope of the continents, an underwater ledge which extends downwards to a maximum depth of about six hundred feet of seawater. The depth, which equates rather neatly to one hundred fathoms, is also that to which sunlight effectively penetrates, giving us a ready reckoner to establish the dividing line between rich ocean and dark abyss. The continental shelf is formed largely from silt which has been carried off the land by rainwater run-off, and consequently it is full of minerals. Ninety per cent of marine life lives on or above the continental shelves, and the total global area of the shelves amounts to ten million square miles, a potentially exploitable goal comparable to the size of Africa. In 1945, the United States government laid territorial claim to the six-hundred-foot 'Drop-Off Line' in the seas around its territory, an example that caught on quickly with other nations.

Cousteau, like Link, relied heavily on George Bond's experimental findings, and indeed had met him on several occasions. Bond described Cousteau as 'the only man whose charisma is indisputable', and after his first meeting with the Frenchman wrote, 'Who was I to share scientific data with the legendary Cousteau?' George Bond maintained friendship with Cousteau throughout his life, and was a guest on board the *Calypso* in the 1960s.

In 1962, with a team from the Groupe d'Etudes et de Recherches Sous-marines, Cousteau constructed a metal underwater habitat, which they christened 'Diogenes', inspired by the Greek philosopher who, according to Seneca, lived in a wooden barrel. Cousteau's device was slightly more substantial: a steel cylinder attached to the seabed off Marseilles with cement blocks and strong chains. Diogenes was sunk in thirty feet of water, and its inhabitants would attempt to live underwater for one complete week. Instead of a hatch to the outside liquid world, Diogenes would be supplied with compressed air at a pressure slightly higher than that of the water around it, thus allowing an open space to be left in the cylinder's underside, through which the divers could simply swim in and out. By keeping water at bay by pressurized air inside Diogenes, Cousteau's team had created a liquid door. The two men chosen for the Diogenes sojourn were Albert Falco and Claude Wesley, men whom Cousteau trusted and were adjudged fit enough for the task.

The Conshelf experiment aimed to establish once and for all that men could stay underwater for seven days, with at least five hours of working time each day in the open-water environment. Cousteau described the achievement as the first 'occupation of the continental shelf', and said he envied Falco and Wesley for achieving his own dream, the reality of living in the sea. For seven days, the two 'oceanauts' (as they were dubbed) ate, worked, and slept in Diogenes, breathing compressed air fed through pipes from the surface; in effect, living in a giant aqualung. Hot water also came from the surface, allowing the oceanauts to take warm showers after a dive outside the giant horizontal barrel. Television monitors recorded their activities, and other divers (including Cousteau) paid visits to the habitat. Stringent physiological examinations revealed that there were no significant ill effects upon their bodies. Unlike Ed Link in his cramped cylinder, Falco and Wesley truly 'lived' on the seabed, even being supplied with a record player and classical music to enrich their leisure hours. When asked what he felt at the end of his week underwater, Falco famously and enigmatically remarked, 'Under the sea, everything is moral.'

Cousteau would say afterwards that the sub-sea dwellers were men of a new kind, and add ruefully that he was not one of them. And with various live specimens caught and corralled in wire pens close to the habitat, they had taken a vital step towards 'dominion over the fish of the sea'.

Conshelf led quickly to a second experiment, this time in the Red Sea, north-east of Port Sudan. Cousteau said that he chose the Red Sea 'because it is hot and far away'. His idea was that if

Conshelf II worked under more difficult field conditions, then it would prove conclusively that sub-sea habitats were a realistic option for research. This time the habitat was larger, and was romantically christened 'Starfish House' because it had four extendible 'legs' radiating outwards from the central command chamber, giving some degree of privacy for sleeping, laboratory experiments and storage. Starfish House had to become not just a house but a home to the team, a group of five men accompanied by mascots in the shape of a pair of parrots named Claude and Armand.

Cousteau's schemes for the launch in June 1963 had become more elaborate, and Starfish House, which anchored at thirty-six feet, was to have a separate annexe, a vertically mounted cylinder known as 'Deep Cabin' stationed at ninety feet. Inside the main house the inhabitants breathed compressed air, while the two men at ninety feet breathed an atmosphere of half oxygen and half helium. A small submersible vehicle with its own sub-sea 'garage' was available so that the aquanauts could travel further afield. And, unlike Diogenes or Link's chamber, Starfish House had its own cooking facilities. Two men remained in Deep Cabin for a whole week, and the Conshelf II experiment achieved continuous seabed habitation over a four-week cycle. Cousteau's team had achieved the longest running and most successful saturation dives in the open sea without injury. Years later, Cousteau's son, Jean-Michel, would say that he chose to study architecture because he wanted to build cities under the sea.

Over the next twenty-five years, most of the developed world experimented with sub-sea habitats, and more than sixty habitable dwellings were built on the seabed, from the Arctic to Australia. They ranged in size from the USSR's five-hundred-ton 'Bentos', with a crew of twenty-four, down to simple wire-and-plastic tents, like the one-man 'Robinsub' made in Italy. Bentos had the unique ability to move underwater on giant skids, like a massive sledge, at the sedate rate of just over one knot per hour, although like many Soviet inventions its true capabilities, as opposed to those claimed for it by the authorities, are a matter for debate. Even so, in a kind of proto space race, the USA and its sparring partner the USSR led the field, building half of all the habitats ever constructed. The countries of the former eastern bloc were also keen, with Czechoslovakia, Poland and East Germany all having a go. With a penchant for institutional nomenclature worthy of a script from *The Man from U.N.C.L.E.*, the habitats had names like 'Sprut', 'Sadko', 'Spid' and 'Geonur'. More prosaic contenders included the British 'Bubble', and the Czech-built 'Klobouk', which means simply 'hat'.

Scarcely half a dozen habitats remain in existence today, and the body of knowledge concerning the building and maintenance of habitats is shrinking, as the first and only generation of trained aquanauts enter old age. Due to a combination of funds, know-how and personnel, the United States led the way in aquanaut training, but deep submersible capsules have now superseded the original idea of a stationary seabed structure. The aquanauts and their adventures are in danger of becoming a forgotten piece of modern history. In part they fell victim to the diversion of cash and manpower to the space race, the headlong rush to put a man on the moon, and the prospects that space-age technology held out for industry and mankind in general. As one former aquanaut put it, 'Men found the moon's behind much more interesting than the ocean's bottom.'

In search of aquanauts I went to America.

In Panama City on the Gulf Coast of Florida, the United States maintains its Navy Diving and Salvage Training Center. It is a smart modern facility with a lobby as neat and bright as the entrance to an exclusive private clinic. The Experimental Diving Unit shares the same base as the NDSTC, and is the successor to the old 'Gun Factory' in Washington where Dr George Bond first began his experiments on the Genesis project. Smartly dressed naval officers and ratings walk purposefully around the premises and there are highly polished plaques and photographs on the brick walls commemorating ships and men in campaigns around the world. A small display of mannequins in various types of diving dress stands at attention around the lobby. Most military divers train here now, and some of them will go on to become part of the elite sea-air-land teams, the SEALs, specializing in covert operations. Originally, many of the divers training here would have been members of the Underwater Demolition Teams, a forerunner to the SEALs. The UDTs can trace their origins to 1942, when a small group of divers was formed to help clear and raise ships sunk during the raid on Pearl Harbour. Since then, their training methods and skills have been at the forefront of modern diving.

In the days of hard-hat diving, safety stops for decompression were traditionally measured in ten-foot increments, and the last stage of a dive was always the one ten feet beneath the surface. Just across the main highway which runs alongside the entrance to the diving school, there is a small bar called the 'Ten Foot Stop'. It is a serious drinking hole, where trainee divers come to relax and former Navy men swap tales of how tough things were in their day. Photographs and mementoes decorate these walls too, but they are less formal than those across the road, celebratory pictures of divers who have successfully completed tough training courses at the base.

The sounds of country and western music coming from a jukebox in the bar reminded me that in Florida, they say, the further north you go, the further south you go. In cultural terms it is true. Panama City is on the panhandle, the narrow strip of coast that faces the waters of the Gulf of Mexico and is bordered a few miles inland by Alabama. Physically and spiritually, Alabama and nearby Louisiana and Mississippi are closer than the tourist epicentres and racial melting pots of Miami or Disneyland, and, as if to emphasize the fact, the panhandle maintains a separate time zone, one hour different from the rest of the state.

The Ten Foot Stop was gloomy, the only natural light coming from the small brass porthole windows in the main swing doors. Everyone at the bar had tattooed biceps, and, apart from the jukebox, the only entertainment was a shuffleboard, an American variation on shove ha'penny. At the base of the board a sign read, 'Do not put salt on the shuffleboard, please ask management for wax.' The words were almost obscured by a dusting of salt. Inside, the atmosphere was clubby and slightly intimidating, the kind of place where a fight could break out if they didn't like your walk. But I had a friend with me who had the right kind of accent. And he was ex-Navy. With his help, discussion centred on diving. One diver, taking an interest in my obvious lack of knowledge on matters Floridian, told me that this part of America has a higher than average rate of UFO sightings. Sensing that I might not be as conversant with Unidentified Flying Objects as other residents of Panama City, he asked if I believed in 'aliens'. This bar, I reasoned, was not the kind of place to be casting public doubt on local wisdom.

'Well, yes,' I stammered, 'I'm sure there are things out there that we don't fully understand.'

I hoped this would be taken as agreement enough, but my interlocutor had not given up. He sensed doubt.

'Do you see many UFOs in England?'

'Er, not so many in London, where I live, there are too many bright lights from the city.'

'Huh . . . have you ever been to Egypt?' he enquired, conspiratorially.

'As a matter of fact I have.'

'How did you find Egyptians?'

'Friendly.' I hoped my answers were neutral enough to fall whichever way this was leading.

'Yeah, right. But don't tell me those guys got their act together to build the pyramids. Come on, you've travelled a bit, that had to be the aliens. Am I right?'

The Ten Foot Stop was not the place to delve too deeply into the merits of ancient civilizations and their origins, so I steered the conversation back towards diving. In Panama City, it is a topic on which many are expert.

The man I had come to find works a few hundred yards from the Ten Foot Stop. In a small building near to the Navy training school, the Experimental Diving Unit is the main testing facility for diving equipment and conducts physiological studies on military divers. Tucked into a small office on the ground floor, I met Bob Barth. Now almost seventy, the former Navy Quartermaster is still a big bear of a man with a grip like iron and a twinkle in his eye. 'I'm not ready to retire yet,' he told me. 'That would make too many people happy around here.'

Bob Barth is the world's most experienced aquanaut, and known to everyone who has ever worked on habitat experiments. Surrounded by files and photographs from the Sealab days, Barth now works as the EDU's public affairs officer, and organizes annual reunions of the ex-habitat divers. He also acts as the Investigator for Diving Accidents. In one corner of the jumble that was his office, a pile of scuba equipment lay on the floor. White tags like luggage labels identified where it had come from and to whom it had belonged. 'Those sets came from some cave divers killed last week,' Barth explained, adding with gallows humour, 'Yeah, cave divers are some of our best customers.'

Bob Barth's tough exterior masks an unassuming character, and

he needed some coaxing to talk about his own role in the Genesis
project. In fact, he had been in at the very beginning of Dr Bond's
experiments, as a fit young sailor who had graduated from the US
Navy Swimmers' School at Key West in 1954. Assigned to the US
Submarine Base in Connecticut, he met Bond when the doctor was
officer in charge of the submarine medical school. Barth was an
instructor working in the escape-training tank, the terrifying vertical tower, over a hundred feet tall, where submariners would
practise free-swimming ascents from depth. Bond himself was a
strong swimmer, totally at ease underwater and trained in escape
techniques. In 1959, when he was thirty-five years old, Bond
achieved the distinction of a record ascent from a submarine
without breathing gear, a distance of three hundred and twenty-two
feet.

In 1961 Barth remembers Bond 'showing up' at the base with
'a bunch of goats, which he put inside a spare recompression
chamber'. Bond told Barth that he was interested in testing theories
which would one day allow a man to live on the seabed, and Barth
was hooked. Bond had him assigned to medical school duty, and
from then on Barth helped with the decompression experiments
on laboratory animals, duties which included putting the goats on
a rope leash and running them around the submarine base for
exercise. 'You can imagine some of the comments from the guys
on the subs about what I was doing with those goats,' Barth
grins, like an embarrassed schoolboy. Laboratory experiments also
revealed that goats could be more imaginative than at first thought.

Many of the Genesis experiments involved subjecting larger
mammals such as goats and dogs to gradually increased pressure
inside a compression chamber, and observing their reactions. If an
animal exhibited signs of discomfort, then the pressure would be
decreased. In common with J. S. Haldane, the great-grandfather
of decompression research, Dr Bond discovered that the problem

with goats is that they are generally uncommunicative. During Genesis, a female goat, who remains nameless, was found to lift one of its front legs in the air whenever it felt pain, and when the scientists observed this, they would decrease pressure accordingly. A certain inconsistency began to creep into the results and the chamber operator decided to conduct a test. One day, instead of increasing pressure in the chamber, he simply opened the ventilation valves which signalled that the increased airflow was about to begin. And waited. Taking its cue from the audible click of the valves being opened, and expecting to be fed after a session in the chamber, the goat, after a respectable pause, proceeded to lift its leg.

Much of the work at the submarine base was carried out on the quiet, and it is safe to say that the US Navy probably didn't know the precise details of what Bond and his team were up to. In keeping with the finest traditions of military history, the Genesis team learned to scrounge or steal much of the equipment and supplies required for their experiments.

Bond and his small team initially fell under the auspices of the Bureau of Medicine, an offshoot of the diving research group primarily interested in the safety of submariners, who might have to work under increased atmospheric pressure or escape from a submarine at considerable depth. In April 1963, official interest in the scientific obstacles to working at extreme depth was given a crucial and sudden push. One hundred and twenty-nine men were killed when the USS *Thresher*, the most advanced nuclear submarine in the US Navy, sank with all hands. Although the submarine was located successfully, and even photographed on the seabed by a bathyscaphe, raising her proved impossible. The *Thresher* had sunk in over six thousand feet of water, probably due to a combination of ill luck and unusual water temperatures which caused a critical loss of buoyancy. Her hull, which might just have withstood the pressure at almost two thousand feet of sea water, caved in as she sank deeper, reducing the submarine to a pile of twisted metal. For the Navy, deep-recovery technology and capability was suddenly a priority.

In July 1964, Chief Quartermaster Bob Barth was chosen as one of the three men to inhabit the first US Navy habitat in open ocean. Having established his credentials by tending the goats, and then being subjected to dry 'dives' in the pressure tanks at the submarine base, it was time to put a habitat on the ocean floor. Home for the aquanauts would be a great space-rocket-shaped piece of metal, christened the Sealab. In it, Barth and three other sailors would spend eleven days at a depth of one hundred and ninety-three feet off the coast of Bermuda. Despite some technical teething problems, and a curtailing of the mission due to a hurricane warning, Sealab proved that men could live, work and function safely at depth for extended periods without harm. Unlike the major phase of the French Conshelf which used compressed air, the Sealab divers were breathing mixed gases and remaining deeper for longer than ever before. Although it was known that man could breathe helium and oxygen, it was not conclusively proven until Sealab that saturation with these gases at depth, and with the whole body under increased pressure, would not produce ill effects.

Stripped of its internal fittings after returning from Bermuda to Panama City, Sealab was left to rot before eventually being dumped in the sea. Then, almost twenty years after its historic first immersion, it was salvaged, scrubbed down and given to the Museum of Man in the Sea, a few miles down the road from Barth's office in Panama City. Sealab sits by the roadside in the museum car park, a skeleton in red marine paint ignored by the passing stream of motorists. I climbed inside, and found a warren filled with wiring tubes, metal brackets where equipment would have been originally mounted, and hard steel fold-down bunks. Almost forty years since it was shipped to Bermuda it is little more than a shell, but I imagined it full of men and equipment, and the reality of what it must have been like to be submerged in the metal tube began to dawn. Bob Barth denies that the experience was claustrophobic. 'Hell no,' he said, 'you're not stuck in your little box down there – you're free to go, you just put your diving gear on and go through the hole in the floor. Nowadays the oil guys and the military go down in a capsule, do their work and then leave. Habitats are different, they're like a motor home. You park it where you want it and you really live there.'

I asked if it wouldn't be a lot easier not to have to sink a large bulky metal habitat and tend to it from a surface ship. 'Well,' Barth grinned, 'lots of times you hear about people exploring the Grand Canyon by going down into it on the back of a jackass. Why do that? Why not go down there, put up a tent and stay there until you've seen what you wanna' see? I know which I'd rather do.'

The men who made up the early aquanaut crews put their faith in Dr Bond's scientific data, and proved him right. Like astronauts, they went into a world which would kill them unless they took their own sealed environment with them. Like astronauts, they gained a new perspective on the earth, and in many cases developed a passion for protecting and saving the environment. Scott Carpenter, an astronaut who had orbited the earth in the *Aurora 7* rocket in 1962, was selected as the team leader for Sealab II. He became the first man ever to live in outer and inner space. He claimed at the time that he had been drawn to the sub-sea research programme because colonizing the seabed would mean more for mankind in the long term than any dreams of living on another planet.

Yet, somehow, the romance of being an aquanaut did not have the same appeal to the popular imagination as being an astronaut. I asked Bob Barth if he felt that the astronauts had stolen all the glory in those days. 'Look, what NASA did with the space programme was great,' he replied. 'I'm proud of what we achieved up there. I guess I'm only sorry *we* didn't have more money. We should think about the ocean more than we do.'

Maybe being underwater is just not as glamorous as flying?

'No doubt about it: movies, TV, books, in those days the space programme and the pilots who went into the astronaut programmes were everywhere. It was new to all of us, but I was just as intrigued by astronauts as anyone else in this country.'

He admits it upset him that aquanauts didn't get much publicity, but pauses, uncomfortable with the notion of criticizing the system. 'And I guess it still bugs me, of course, especially when you're in a programme which doesn't get funding or recognition. But it's funny, there's more interest today in Sealab than there was when we were doing it. Maybe because we've been dumping so much stuff in the ocean. And now people are starting to worry about it.'

Like so many military men of his generation, Barth does not describe what he and the other aquanauts did in terms of bravery.

'Were we brave?' Barth shrugs. 'No, you didn't have to be a mental giant to understand the principles of the saturation process . . . it allows you to go down and stay on the ocean floor. To a diver, it was just like asking a pilot if he wanted to move up from propellers to jets and then on to being an astronaut. As a diver, you're gonna want to try living on the ocean floor.'

The first Sealab experiment in Bermuda led to another a year later, this time closer to home for the aquanauts: the seabed off La Jolla, California. Submerged in just over two hundred feet of water, and in conditions ideal for testing the reality of exploring the United States' own continental shelf, Sealab II was a new design, bigger and more comfortable than its predecessor. More effort this time was put into studying the physiological and psychological stresses that a prolonged saturation dive induced. Hard physical work and the high humidity of the metal habitat made the aquanauts' working day exhausting. Bond noted in his diary that the aquanauts 'moved about like shadows, and after every meal, they lay down'.

Maintaining adequate heat inside the habitat proved a significant problem. Heaters and warm diving gear were essential. Maintaining clean air, by 'scrubbing' the carbon dioxide from the habitat, was achieved by the well-tested means of Baralyme or soda lime, whose alkaline properties neutralize the acidic carbon dioxide. Such absorbents also generate heat as a by-product of the chemical process. On long saturation dives, heated air and heated floors were essential to the aquanauts' comfort. The psychology of living in such a confined space with other men proved rich grounds for research, and the Sealab II mission was scheduled to last thirty days. Three teams of ten aquanauts were to share the experience, with only one man, mission leader Scott Carpenter, completing the entire period without a break. Sealab II involved more men and a much larger budget than Sealab I, and hours of experiments had to be completed by each aquanaut every day. Afterwards, Dr Bond calculated that Sealab II resulted in four hundred and fifty 'man days' of undersea living and half a million pieces of information logged from communications, engineering and biological studies of the mission. While the French oceanauts in Conshelf II had their two parrots for company, the men in Sealab were working with a more useful aquatic companion, a trained dolphin named Tuffy. The dolphin was trained to fetch and retrieve objects from the divers, and could warn them of the presence of sharks.

In September 1965, the US Navy's second habitat was nearing the end of its mission off California, when Jacques Cousteau's third habitat went into operation six and a half thousand miles away in the Mediterranean. On one occasion, aquanauts in the two habitats made contact by telephone, although meaningful communication was difficult due to the effects of the helium on the human vocal chords. Sealab II also achieved another communications 'first', a brief exchange with astronauts orbiting the earth aboard the *Gemini V* space capsule. Scott Carpenter again takes the honours, talking to astronaut Gordon Cooper, and making the first human spoken contact between the seabed and outer space.

After the successful conclusion of the second Sealab mission, Dr Bond and his team would have to wait almost four years before mounting their most ambitious and expensive mission. They hoped to put a habitat on the edge of the US continental shelf, a structure big enough for a dozen men to inhabit at a depth of six hundred feet. In more than thirty habitat trials worldwide in the intervening period since Sealab II, no one had dared to go as deep. Ed Link's Man in the Sea project had gone further in the right direction than most, but used a small shelter known as the SPID (submerged portable inflatable dwelling). In June 1964, the SPID reached four hundred and thirty feet in the Bahamas. Sealab III would attempt to push habitation half as deep again.

The mission was to be undertaken in the waters off San Clemente Island, California. By mid February, and after a succession of delays, the Sealab II habitat had been modified and redesigned for its new task. As Bond writes in his personal journal, final checks and balances were being carried out on the morning of February the nineteenth. Aquanauts were monitored by underwater cameras stationed at strategic viewpoints around the habitat. The aquanauts had been taken down to the required depth on the shelf in a Personnel Transfer Capsule, a kind of submersible pressure chamber. Four aquanauts, including Bob Barth, now a Warrant Officer, and Berry Cannon, a civilian engineer who had worked on Sealab II, were sent down. At six hundred feet they entered a monochrome world, a twilight expanse of grey where their bodies would be subjected to an incredible two hundred and seventy pounds of pressure per square inch, almost twenty times the force our bodies feel on the surface. The following events were captured on film by an underwater camera, and George Bond, who was watching from the mission control centre aboard ship, described in his personal diary what happened:

At about 0500, the Personnel Transfer Capsule was hovering off the bottom, near the habitat. Bob Barth and Berry Cannon, wearing hot water suits which gave them warmth, entered the water and connected to their umbilicals. The word was passed to me, and I moved from control to Range Engineers Office, where we had a clear view of the divers' ladder, from another camera. Almost five minutes passed, and still no divers came into view. An inchoate web of fear began to close in on me, and I fought it back. After all, we had done it so many times at this depth at Experimental Diving Unit, I told myself. But this wasn't EDU; this was for real; and my divers were late. For perhaps the first time in my life, I was thoroughly frightened. Then Bob Barth, wearing rig #1, came swimming to the ladder, and I felt better. Alone, he climbed up and pushed on the hatch, but it would not yield. Not wasting time, he swam off camera to get a crowbar. There was still no sign of Berry, and the fear began to come back, stronger this time. I am not now certain, but I think that at this time I said, very loudly,

'God damn it! Where is Berry?'

No one answered. Within seconds we saw a tremendous boil of silt on the TV screen, and now fear became an agony of certainty. No trained diver moves so fast as to stir this type of sediment, unless there is real trouble. In a second, Bob swam pell-mell through the swirl and off camera, returning almost immediately with Berry in his arms. He tried to hold Berry's head up in the gas pocket of the skirt, but that didn't work. Immediately, he attempted to force the buddy-breather mouthpiece into Berry's mouth, but failed on three tries, stabbing against teeth locked in a final convulsion. Bob now turned quickly and began to drag Berry to the haven of the PTC.

Fourteen minutes later came the message from the PTC:

'Berry Cannon is dead.'

Somehow, time went on, and efforts at resuscitation continued for a long while. Ninety minutes later, the seal with the DDC was made, and three of my four aquanauts returned to warmth and life. Now it was day-break, or maybe full sunrise, but nobody cared very much any more.

On this occasion the Sealab prayer, penned by George Bond and spoken by him on each mission, had not been answered.

To the brave and dedicated men who have committed themselves to this project, grant Thine unending watch and safeguarding care in all the many hours of their life under the sea. Give unusual wisdom to each of us topside who might somehow control their work and safety as they perform their duties below.

Investigations would reveal that Berry Cannon died from carbon dioxide poisoning. His diving gear had simply not been re-filled with the necessary chemical absorbent to purify his breathing gas. As a result of the fatality, Sealab III was closed down, and US Navy interest in habitats declined. In spite of the obvious advantages of habitats in certain operations, particularly marine salvage work, the Sealab programme was discontinued.

For Bob Barth the events of February 1969 are as clear as if they occurred last week. The fatal accident was a personal tragedy, but not in his view sufficient cause to abandon the habitat programme. I asked him if there was more to the closure of the experiments than meets the eye.

'I'm touchy about the subject, 'cos I was the fella with Cannon when he died,' Barth says slowly. 'We took him down to six hundred feet of water, and lost him. That's traumatic. The Navy abandoned the programme and eventually went for saturation systems on board ships. I personally don't think we should have given up on habitats – after all, NASA didn't stop the space programme when they lost three astronauts. NASA had a goal, and so did we, and when you push things that far there's a good chance someone will get hurt.'

The Sealab aquanauts continue to get together once a year and talk over old times. Many of them believe interest in sub-sea habitation will one day recur, and they hope that it won't be too late to make use of the expertise of those who pioneered the technology thirty years ago. Sub-sea habitation did continue after the Sealab era, and high-profile experiments such as the Tektite programmes were carried out with the assistance of the National Aeronautics and Space Administration. US scientists working on the space programme realized that studies in underwater habitats would come close to simulating the stresses and strains experienced by astronauts on long space flights. The obvious benefits of training astronauts for zero gravity in space by putting them underwater in a tank in their space suits became central to NASA's curriculum. In the USSR, cosmonauts at the space-training centre 'Star City' would also be taken underwater.

After the closure of Sealab III, underwater habitation became the realm of marine biologists rather than military divers, and as a result the amounts of money available were considerably reduced. Occasionally, a habitat would catch the attention of the media, such as the USA's Tektite II, which in 1970 involved the first full-scale undersea mission by a team of female aquanauts. In the main, however, George Bond's dream of seabed living would not be realized. In a letter written two years after the end of the Sealab programme, he wrote: 'The in situ use of a habitat will assuredly find direct applications in the fields of marine biology, marine geology, ocean climatology, seabed mining, and undersea construction, to mention only a few of the many disciplines that could well be served by such structures.' Bond clearly believed that the US

Navy's retreat from habitat research was ill advised, and he described the decision as 'unfortunate, as at least ten major foreign nations are proceeding with habitat programmes, all utilizing the basic data supplied from our efforts and made freely available to them'.

The technology of portable deep submergence systems has replaced habitat research for the world's military powers. Today, a man can be sent down in a pressurized chamber and leave it to perform work at depths of up to two thousand feet. In dry-chamber experiments men have been compressed slightly deeper, although the logistical and physiological risks of such dives are extremely high. Much beyond that depth and a man begins to have fits. High Pressure Nervous Syndrome (HPNS) is the name given to this reaction. Refining the breathing-gas mixture to avoid this problem becomes increasingly difficult, and no two divers will react in the same way to such fine adjustments. Another problem is that the exact biological nature of the effects of extremely high pressure is still not understood. What is known is that the behaviour of gas molecules under sufficient pressure affects the very basic chemical reactions which occur in the human brain. In addition, the physical pressure exacted on tissue begins to act on the nerve fibres, causing symptoms ranging from tremors to sensory damage, problems which cannot be easily rectified.

Increasingly, such deep dangerous underwater work is being accomplished by robots. Decompressing from a dive of just one thousand feet will mean ten days in a chamber for the divers, if all goes well. Extreme-depth training continues to play a role in naval diving worldwide, however, and at the EDU in Panama City there is still a programme geared to training divers to work from deep submersible chambers which can be raised and lowered from on-board ship. However, funding and research has gone into the more practicable development of miniature submarines, research pushed forward and funded by the offshore oil and gas industry. From seabed drilling to raising relics from the *Titanic*, such vehicles can go deeper than a free-swimming man will ever go. With increasingly sophisticated telemetry and control systems, they have replaced both the skills and the risk of sending men into the deep.

Close to Bob Barth's office, I was shown a squad of trainee divers taking turns at basic diving exercises in the large white water-filled tanks known as 'pressure vessel assemblies' or PVAs. From the outside, the PVAs look like metal igloos, with thick plate-glass windows allowing staff to monitor the activity of the divers within. Wearing ultra-modern MK21 helmets attached to umbilical air supplies, young men in shorts and regulation blue T-shirts moved around inside the chambers like marionettes on strings. Outside the pressure tank I could hear the instructors passing commands to the divers through their helmet communications system. As their training progressed they would learn basic gas laws and decompression procedures, and eventually move on to the techniques of underwater salvage. As part of their naval dive training they would have read about George Bond's research, and perhaps learned a little about the Sealab experiments. However, there will be no aquanaut insignia among their badges on graduation from the Navy diving school.

The idea of sleeping underwater fascinates me. Sometimes when I am diving I feel the urge to close my eyes and drift off into dreams. At such times it seems there can be nowhere as comforting as the sea, though the practical objections to such a move are obvious and many. If it were possible to maintain position in the water, and be sufficiently supplied with air, I imagine it would be like falling asleep in the African veldt. Uncovered, unsheltered, and wrapped in nature's entirety I would be exposed to whatever the night might bring. To sleep with danger all around would awaken primitive instincts, an intensity of experience which we miss in our domestic beds. Like a small child giving up its safety to a watchful parent, I would rest, and let the current take me.

In a small lagoon in the Florida Keys there is an underwater hotel. It is the only such place in the world, and I was drawn to it by an advertisement inviting prospective aquanauts to 'Dive, Dine and Dream at Five Fathoms'.

Jules' Undersea Lodge is a free-standing structure, submerged in about twenty-five feet of water, and supplied with compressed air from the surface via a system of hoses running into the roof. The pressure of the air is slightly greater than the pressure of the surrounding water, allowing an opening in the floor to act as a liquid door into the bottom of the lagoon. As long as the air pressure is maintained, the interior remains dry. The only way to get into the lodge is to dive.

As I swam down to the hotel, its shape emerged slowly from the gloom, a ghostly white box resembling an upside-down barge more than anything else. Close up, two large circular windows, illuminated from within, shone through the murky water like the eyes of some giant marine insect.

To get inside involved diving under the hotel and between its legs to swim up and into the 'moon pool', or liquid door. Popping up to stand on a metal grille acting as a step into the habitat, I entered the air-filled environment where I could breathe normally, without scuba gear – except that I knew I was still underwater. Climbing out of the moon pool I was in the 'wet room', a central compartment where diving gear is stowed, and from which circular hatches lead off into 'bedrooms' and a combined main lounge–dining-room.

Jules' Undersea Lodge is a converted scientific habitat, transported to Florida after several years of operation in the waters off

Puerto Rico. There, in the early 1970s, it was named La Chalupa, a Spanish word for a type of small canoe. For three years, it operated as a habitat for marine biologists surveying the coral reefs of the island. Now, it has been stripped of its scientific hardware, carpeted and made comfortable enough even for honeymooners to spend their wedding night underwater. The idea appeals particularly strongly to those couples who have taken their vows underwater, although the hotel does not actually offer the service. A hot shower, microwave cooking facilities, stereo systems and a television in each of the two bedrooms make it seem more like a luxury caravan than an underwater habitat. Dinner is served by a 'mer-chef', who emerges from the moon pool with an airtight suitcase containing the ingredients for the meal. I ordered filet mignon, on the principle that underwater it seems like basic courtesy to the fish around me to eat meat.

One of the attractions of being in the Undersea Lodge is that qualified divers may slip into their scuba equipment whenever they want to explore the lagoon outside. There are no hotel staff in the habitat, they visit only when needed. Privacy is ensured, although a close-circuit television camera keeps its eye trained on the moon pool to make sure divers enter and leave the habitat safely. In the tradition of habitat protocol, and as a safety precaution, guests are instructed to radio the habitat control centre on shore and inform them when they are entering the water. The controller then logs the time for the start of the dive, and is prepared to initiate a search if the divers should fail to return.

Most divers who stay at the underwater hotel are seeking an unusual experience, a variation in the normal list of dive options to add to their logbook. For me, it was a chance to live underwater as an aquanaut, a chance to cut myself off from the air world for a whole night, with the option of diving through the moon pool whenever I felt like it.

At around midnight I slipped on my diving gear, and ducked out under the lip of the habitat. It was dark, the water was murky and the bottom silty, more reminiscent of an English quarry than a tropical lagoon. A barrier has been erected at one end of the lagoon, so that divers do not stray into the boating channel leading to the open sea, but the idea of diving alone at night made up for the comparative lack of freedom. I had a dry base to return to whenever I wished, and I was independent of any dive boat or group of divers with an itinerary in mind. At one stage as I swam around the lagoon I heard music, and discovered an underwater speaker system feeding the sounds of a cassette tape from the habitat control centre. The effect was to remove the normal feeling of isolation that creeps upon me underwater in the dark. And the darkness was intense. With my torch I found the nightlife of the lagoon going about its business. Snappers, sheepshead and parrotfish moved slowly out of my way. Crabs performed their slow-motion dance across the rocks behind the habitat, and at one point a barracuda seized a small pufferfish betrayed by the beam of my torch. I watched half of its torn body float downwards after the puncturing grasp of the predator's jaws. These creatures had no business with me, and I turned for the habitat.

From fifty feet away the light from the moon pool illuminated a cube of water underneath the hotel. It was like a lantern in the window of a farmhouse glimpsed through a winter's night, beckoning and welcoming. It drew me back to the warmth and security of my underwater lodge.

Deep night. I cannot go to sleep. The gentle hum of the air supply is transmitted through the metal superstructure of the habitat. Outside my bedroom the water in the moon pool laps gently against the edge of the dive platform. These are soothing noises. There is utter blackness inside my room and I press my face up to the large circular window which looks out into the lagoon. Nothing is visible, unless I hold a torch to the glass and surprise a fish nibbling at algae growing on the outside of the glass. I have become the goldfish in the bowl, preserved not in water but in air, while the fish look on. It is warm, and extremely humid inside the hotel. It is not this which makes me wakeful. I am simply too excited for sleep. I have a home underwater.

After breakfast, and another dive, it was time to check out of the underwater hotel. As I swam to the shore, I saw a man with only one arm walking towards the lagoon. He carried a piece of timber in his remaining hand, and sat down at the slipway to put on a pair of fins. They were the latest design, short split-bladed wedges which give maximum thrust through the water. He asked me how I had enjoyed my night underwater, and explained that he was going back into the habitat to make some repairs to the habitat lavatory. I was welcome to join him, and find out what building-maintenance work was like underwater. His name was Dr Lance Rennka, and he had been involved in the design and maintenance of La Chalupa for the past twenty-five years. No one is a more passionate advocate of underwater habitats.

We swam down to the hotel together, and I watched as he measured pieces of wood and drew plans for modifications he wanted to make to the habitat bathroom. A chemical toilet was due to be replaced with a pump-drained version, so as to avoid one of the problems of underwater sanitation. Any air space exposed to the increased air pressure inside the habitat will expand when it is taken to the surface, so that even a piece of plywood will fizz like lemonade in a bottle as it reaches the surface as air trapped in the wood fibres escapes. The chemical toilet was in essence nothing more than a plastic box, and, when uncorked at the surface, posed its own explosive hazards.

'You can write all this stuff about pressure and gas laws down,' Rennka explained, 'but until you actually build a habitat and operate it, day in, day out, you don't know what's going to happen. For example, we know we can bring a standard television down here so long as the tube isn't more than seventeen inches wide, anything bigger just implodes. The same applies to computer screens. And we're only working at twenty-five feet.'

Does that mean there are huge problems as soon as you go deeper?

'We did it; La Chalupa operated in a hundred and fifty feet of water. And we solve these problems by working on them. Turning La Chalupa into a hotel is a trivial use of a habitat, sure, but every night that people stay here is another mission accomplished successfully. We've been running almost fifteen years, and making a profit without any government subsidy, and we used old-fashioned technology. Today you could build a habitat cheaper. Underwater habitats are simple, they're like teacups turned upside down. It gives you a warm, safe, dry environment in which to sleep, rest and eat. And you have unlimited time in the environment you're studying.'

I spent the day with Lance Rennka, and learnt that he was a man driven by the possibilities of living and working under the sea. As a director of the Marine Resources Development Foundation he helps educate school children to the potential of undersea research. Did he think there was enough attention being paid to underwater research?

'Absolutely not. The public perception is that going underwater is technologically difficult. All that money that went into space research is crazy if you think about what our needs are down here. And we have the arrogance to call this blue marble we live on ''Earth''. I call that a sick way of looking at something which is 75 per cent water. All that effort and energy talking about colonizing the moon and flying to Mars. OK, we're drawn to the challenge, but let's face it – there's no water up there!'

Lance Rennka laughs a lot. Ideas pour out of him in a constant stream, and he delights in provocation. He had as many theories on life and the universe as a London cabbie. Rennka lost his arm during the launching of La Chalupa for its second mission off Puerto Rico. As the habitat was being lowered into the sea, a steel cable wrapped around his left wrist and dragged him through the air. Severely shattered, his arm might have been saved, but poor treatment led to the development of gas gangrene. Lance Rennka now says he owes his life to diving technology, since in his case the virulent decay of tissue could only be stopped by intensive oxygen therapy in a recompression chamber. The micro-organism which causes gangrene after traumatic injury thrives on low levels of oxygen, and breathing pure oxygen under pressure can sometimes halt the disease. The accident has given him the zest for life of a man born again. 'I've been there in the dark tunnel,' he laughs, 'and I've looked down on my body from above while they operated on me. Death doesn't scare me. When it comes I'll just be joining the great circle of life.'

As the day progressed, I found it increasingly difficult to formulate a response to one of Lance's theories before he set off on another tack.

'Cellular memory. That's what we need a handle on. How much do you know that you don't know you know?'

My brain played with the phrase, and I repeated it to myself like a riddle, to make sure I had understood. All I could think was, 'How much wood would a woodchuck chuck if a woodchuck could chuck wood.' But Lance was on a roll.

'Your tissues and cells are made up of organic matter that was once something or someone else. Maybe those cells can transmit what we call thoughts, can hold something in them that we think of as memory. What is "instinct"? Couldn't it be knowledge passed on from past existence? We're all part of the circle of life, recycling the same material over and over again. Maybe there are things going on in the cells of our bodies that we simply can't explain.'

And perhaps we don't need to know. It occurred to me that perhaps it is only scientists who would be amazed by such an idea. With their microscopic approach to delineating, deciphering and categorizing the fibre of human life, they might be amazed that something abstract could remain beyond the reach of their instruments. To many people, perhaps most people throughout history (uneducated in cellular atomic construction), the notion of a 'mind' or 'spirit' existing within and without our physical forms *simultaneously* would hold no surprise. After all, how many tribal cultures believe in absorbing the strength of your enemy by consuming part of his body, or assert that a proportion of what they have killed must be returned to the earth?

Like so many divers I have encountered, Lance Rennka believes that going underwater on a regular basis is virtually an elixir of youth. I made the point that many of the pioneers of diving seem to have maintained an active lifestyle well into their eighties, men like Cousteau and Hass, women like Dottie Frazier, and others. To Rennka, such a proposition is self-evident.

'Of course. If our bodies are in balance, we don't get sick. Being "in balance" means keeping our tissues supplied with the right trace minerals, and, surprise, surprise, where are those minerals all found? In the sea! I believe that immersion in sea water will allow you to absorb through the skin the trace minerals that will keep your body in balance.'

As the day wore on, we moved from the underwater habitat to a local bar, and Lance Rennka still had fresh wisdom to impart. He was worried that the number of new divers who were interested in truly pushing forward the technology of sub-sea living was insignificant. 'We've made it too easy,' he told me. 'But the number of divers continues to grow, worldwide, doesn't it?'

'Yeah. But what kind of divers are they? They do it for fun, on vacation. Most of them don't push the barriers of undersea exploration. In the fifties and sixties, diving was the male sport *par excellence*. Learning to dive was a rite of passage, but now if you tell a young guy that "anyone can learn to dive", and then he sees his granny doing it, where's the challenge? He's gonna want to join a gang, get into body piercing and who knows what else . . .'

That evening, after several hours of animated discussion, Lance Rennka drove off into the red glow of a Key Largo sunset, leaving me with a head full of questions. I couldn't quite imagine learning to dive being marketed as a rite of passage in Western society, but I agreed that teaching people to dive might eventually lead to a groundswell of opinion against the destruction of the marine environment. According to Rennka, the funding for the launch of a single space satellite would have paid for all the marine-science projects worldwide in the last ten years. It is the kind of statistic that befuddles the mind with its sweep.

I had been reading since the 1960s that the next great step for mankind would be life on the seabed. All the great marine scientists (and fiction writers from Verne onwards) had expressed that hope, but still the challenge defeats us. Habitats are expensive to build and maintain, and require large amounts of surface support. Whatever our physical affinity with the sea, our shared ancestry with the primordial ooze, we have moved on in evolutionary terms and cannot return. Even if we could live on the continental shelf, things would have to be very bad on earth to make it an attractive option. However many times we are told that the environment is in danger, we continue to abuse it on a grand scale. Underwater, divers see at first hand the massive deterioration in the coral reefs of the tropical seas, over-warmed, over-fished and poisoned by man. Unseen by the majority of the world's population they are withering. It seems far more likely to me that it will be the deteriorating health of the seas which will finally compel man to do something about the health of the planet. The sea is showing signs of sickness: if it dies then so will we.

Conception Arena, Seychelles

My wife Jessica worked for a time in a government department in Seychelles. One day, sitting in her office, she heard the unmistakable and heart-stopping sound of screeching brakes and rubber on tar combined with the thud of something being hit by a car. She ran down from her office and as she reached the road saw a car speeding off. In the road lay a small dog, its head gashed open and its body bruised and soiled. As Jessica bent down over the motionless animal it opened its eyes and stirred its head. Its hind legs were useless. On the pavement people passed by, unconcerned. Dogs have a miserable existence on most tropical islands and few people cared whether it lived or died. Jessica picked the animal up and took it to the only available veterinary surgeon, not expecting it to live. It did, and although we had nowhere to keep it at our home, she obtained permission for the animal to be kept at the office as an official guard dog.

The dog gradually recovered and when it could walk properly it bounded to greet Jessica every morning, its whole body shaking in concert with its tail. She would take it food each day, including at weekends when the offices were closed. The dog, who was named Fleuri, prospered. It was a happy animal, always anxious to please, and devoted to Jessica. One or two of the security guards at the building took an interest in the dog, particularly those on night duty who enjoyed her company when they had to patrol the premises after dark. Occasionally we would take the dog to the beach for a run, and we hoped that when we moved to a bigger house with a garden we would take her home to live with us permanently.

One day as I was preparing for a dive the telephone rang. It was Jessica calling from her office. She was crying, almost too upset to talk. I knew that things at work had generally been going badly and that she felt she was being frustrated by petty office politics, and jealousy on the part of some of her colleagues. I also knew that she was thinking about resigning, but now there was anguish in her voice, and anger. As I listened she told me what had happened. When Jessica had arrived at work Fleuri had not been there to greet her. She asked around and someone said she knew where the dog was. Jessica followed and was shown the back legs of the dog hanging from a rubbish bin. She was dead. Deliberately poisoned.

I told Jessica to leave her work and drive to the diving centre. We would wait for her. She had to get out of the office. She arrived and I arranged for her to borrow a set of diving equipment. She had not been diving for very long and was still slightly apprehensive about the whole process. We were going to a place which none of the diving centres visited very often. It was a deep site, and subject to strong currents and heavy seas at that time of year. I urged Jessica to dive, feeling it was better for her than to stay at work, or go home and feel miserable until I could get there several hours later.

On the long boat ride to the dive site Jessica was too upset to talk to anyone. She sat beside me on the boat, holding my hand and crying silently. The dog's death was a personal loss to her, but it was more serious than that, a symptom of the negative environment in which she had been working. Most foreigners who worked in Seychelles encountered the same sort of thing, a wall of resentment and suspicion from the islanders which made the daily routine of life tedious in the extreme.

The other divers busied themselves with their kit, and took in the scenery as our small boat passed the beautiful coastline of north-west Mahé. Thick forests of palm grew on the rocky tip of the island and the waves washed against the smooth golden-brown flanks of its granite shore. We passed the broad sweep of Baie Ternay and headed onwards to Cap Matoopa, a jumble of boulders spilling from an uninhabited headland. The twin engines of the diving boat thrummed loudly as we left the lee of the shore, the waves becoming bigger and drenching us with spray. Ahead lay the open sea with just the small bulge of Conception Island a mile offshore. We were heading for a patch of water on the seaward side of Conception, an unmarked spot where a collection of large rocks lay at about thirty-five metres below the surface. The exposed offshore location of the site and its depth meant it could only be dived when the weather was good. Because of the depth we would have a relatively short dive, a total time of thirty minutes underwater and a maximum of ten minutes at the deepest parts of the site.

Jessica and I formed a buddy team. We slipped into the water and waited on the surface for the other divers. A strong swell ran behind the boat and we submerged just a few feet to get out of it. Holding on to the boat's anchor rope we looked down and saw the dim shapes of the rocks below us. They seemed a long way down and surrounded by dark deep water. Moments later everyone was in the water and we headed down the rope, kicking steadily for the shapes below. A group of large barracuda, perhaps ten in all, hovered beneath us, moving out of the way as we passed. Twenty metres below the surface the rocks came into view more clearly. They looked like a city shrouded in fog, glimpsed from the air through a break in the clouds.

The dive site was called the Arena. At one edge of the submerged rock group there was a large arch and all around it a bulbous plateau of boulders, with channels and fissures running across the top of the rocks like the streets on a city grid. The arch stood up proud of the other rocks, a cathedral to their office blocks and thoroughfares. As we swam towards the giant arch the visibility improved, but because of the depth everything appeared a uniform shade of blue-grey. Moving along a few feet above the rocks there were fish everywhere. In the crevasses of the boulders there were huge spiny lobsters, their fragile antennae twitching slowly in front of them like a samurai performing a ritual display with his sword. Beneath the boulders there were small caverns and overhangs, too narrow for a man to enter but perfect resting places for small reef sharks who turned circles in their dens as we peered inside. In another granite interstice there was a pair of green moray eels, writhing and turning around one another so that it was impossible to tell which head belonged to which body. We swam across a flat bed of exposed rock and swam for the 'cathedral' arch. From the deeper water at the edge of our vision, first two, then three grey reef sharks swam towards us, agitated that we had disturbed their hunting ground. They were shy of us. Another diver attempted to photograph them and at the sound of the high-pitched whine of his flashgun they were off, tails twitching as if electrified by the device. I checked on Jessica. She gave me a confident OK, and signalled that she was enthralled by the beauty of the underwater landscape. We left the other divers behind and made for the arch, swimming beneath the overhang, a shadowy chamber where a congregation of yellow stripe snappers (*Lutjanus kasmira*) hung head down as if mesmerized by something on the seafloor. We swam past them gently, skirting them as though they were a group of old women kneeling in prayer.

By the time we exited the chamber it was time to start upwards, using the cathedral pinnacle as our focus and ascending to shallower depth so as to avoid having to make a decompression stop. The top of the rock arch was illuminated by sunlight while everything below was blanketed in the steel shade of the deep. A spray of blue darts cleared away from the rock wall beside us, blue and gold fusiliers, their electric-blue bodies tipped with a scissor tail of sun yellow, dozens of them moving in a vibrating cloud. The rock wall stretched up towards the light, its upper reaches covered in stumpy fingers of the hard coral *Pocillopora*. In the lighter upper layers there were the smaller, brighter fish, the threadfin anthias (*Nemanthias carberryi*), bright orange slivers with erect dorsal fins, hovering in the current headfirst to pluck food from its stream and darting between the coral fingers for shelter when their courage failed. A sea fan stood out from a small cleft in the rock face, a maze of purple branches spreading from the root in smaller and smaller bifurcations as fine as a cross-section from a human lung. We reached the top of the pinnacle and looked upwards. Another ten metres to go to the surface.

We swam through the sea on a horizontal path, aiming for the anchor rope of the diving boat. When we reached it we held on, making a safety stop for three minutes as an added precaution for having dived below the thirty-metre zone, albeit briefly. Down below us the rock city had become a ghostly mirage again, its shape and life another world, busy and vibrant, unaltered by our fleeting visit. It would be weeks, if not months, before divers visited here again.

Back on the boat, we talked about the dive. Jessica said it was the most beautiful place she had yet seen underwater. As the boat turned into the wind to begin the journey back to Mahé she squeezed my hand. A tear ran down her cheek, and I knew that she had been deeply moved. That night Jessica told me that the dive had been a revelation to her. 'Seeing that place has put things into perspective,' she said. 'I'm giving up my job.'

The adventure of diving had worked its spell, freeing her mind of clutter.

10. Hell's Teeth

The Bahamas, Western Atlantic

There should be a colour called Bahamas Blue. It is pure. It is as calming as music and as seductive as the inner light in a polished gemstone. In the folding Atlantic waves there are white sand flats which sear the blue like a brand.

The Bahamas are low islands, limestone shelves laid down in perfect layers, which in some places are six miles thick. They span the western edge of the ocean in a broken line stretching offshore from Florida to just north of Haiti. Here Columbus made his first landfalls, and William Phips found his treasure. The calm, clear seas attracted the Williamson brothers with their photosphere to film *20,000 Leagues Under the Sea*. Neal Watson and John Gruener made their record depth on air in these clear waters. Flipper and James Bond fought their sharks here and Cousteau came to dive in the deep Blue Holes – vertical caves which sink down through the limestone into the unknown.

At the close of the century I arrived in Nassau six hours before Hurricane Floyd hit the Bahamas hard, the first time the main island, New Providence, had been touched in fifty years. The airport was deserted and my international flight left straight away for safer shores. Hotels and houses were boarded up and people scurried for shelter as the winds grew stronger and stronger. Floyd moved slowly, wavering in its path and raising hope that it might veer northwards into the Atlantic. No one knew what to expect and the whole island was glued to the satellite weather pictures beamed from American television stations tracking the storm. By midnight the electricity and water had been cut off in most of the capital, and by three a.m. everyone was bunkered down in the strongest buildings they could find. The local radio station kept broadcasting updates on the progress of the Eye as it crept up the chain of islands towards Nassau. Until the lines went down, Bahamians with working telephones called the station to report what they could see: fallen trees, toppled electricity pylons, smashed cars and flooded streets. The outer islands were cut off, lying directly in the path of the storm front estimated to be eight hundred miles wide. The rest of the world watched and waited, concentrating on whether Floyd would hit Florida. That was what mattered. That was where there were millions of homes and properties at risk. But on this occasion it was the Bahamas that took the brunt of the storm. A handful of people lost their lives, and the damage ran into tens of millions of dollars in a small country with limited funds.

Mostly I remember the noise, the constant flapping of roof slates and downed cables strumming in the wind. I was staying at the Orange Hill Inn, a small hotel on the north coast of New Providence. The hotel was built on a rise and the owner, Danny Lowe, reckoned it was the safest place on the island. A team of American builders who were staying at the hotel while they worked on a nearby construction site helped shore up the windows and doors with battens and sheets of timber. Danny had hurricane lamps, which for once served as illumination in a hurricane, and he had built the hotel dining-room as a concrete blockhouse for just this eventuality. Inside, a dozen marooned holiday-makers and local residents whose homes were closer to the shore huddled together to wait for Floyd to blow over. Buckets of water from the swimming pool were used to flush the single accessible toilet and gas stoves provided heat for cooking. All night we sat listening to the wind beating up the buildings and trees outside. At around five-thirty in the morning it grew light, a dull grey shade of day which scarcely brightened as the morning wore on. The hurricane rain clouds were so thick they blotted out the sun as if we were in an eclipse. The wind seemed to be dropping a little, and I wanted to see the furious sea. Covering my head with my arms against the flying debris, I scurried from the shelter to the front of the hotel and crouched behind a wall to peek out and down to the beach a hundred feet below. A mile offshore, a reef was breaking the force of the thirty-foot waves. The air was just rain and spray and the blue sea had become brown.

When communications were restored and the airport was reopened, I flew south in an attempt to find some clear-water diving away from the worst-hit areas in the north of the territory. I landed in Long Island, a thin strip of rocky potholed heat with good fishing offshore and a strange collection of expatriate settlers, mostly German. For the Long Islanders, New Providence is the mainland, and they spoke of it fearfully, dismissive of its mingled pockets of poverty and retailing glitz. For them, Nassau was the big bad city, where the main preoccupation was catering to the constant influx of short-term visitors from the giant cruise ships which steam in from Florida and the Caribbean.

A small band of regular visitors come every year to Long Island, flying their own little aeroplanes to the tiny airport at one end of the island. They know each other and have formed a seasonal community, a sort of club for themselves. Ordinarily the island only has about three thousand permanent inhabitants, fishermen and farmers and their families, but because of its shape it has two airports, one at the end and one in the middle.

There is not much to Long Island, but the Tropic of Cancer runs across its middle and there is a settlement called Deadman's Cay which has some appeal as a place to sit and write a postcard. Those who love the place say it is a sliver of calm, pretty much untouched by the tourist development of the larger islands further north.

In the aftermath of the hurricane, the potholes were full of stagnant rainwater and the island was suffering from a mosquito plague. These monsters resisted sprays, ointments and poisonous smoke coils. They bit the tourists and the locals with equal vigour and they were impervious to air conditioning unless it was turned up to levels that strained the local electricity generators to their limit. Everyone on the island looked as though they had a combination of chickenpox and St Vitus Dance as they scratched and slapped, twitched and hopped, incapable of finishing a sentence as they broke off to smite the biting menace. Everyone was in a bad mood. The only way to escape was to dive.

Offshore the shallow sea had been churned like cake mix by Hurricane Floyd's one hundred and fifty mile an hour winds. The white sand that shimmers around the limestone bones of the Cays was suspended in the water, cloaking the bright coral like talcum powder. There was another option: an inland Blue Hole, one of the famous sinkholes, which the locals said was deeper than any other in all of the islands, and perhaps one of the largest underwater caves in the world.

The Queen's Highway runs straight up and down the sixty-mile length of Long Island, which at its widest point is barely four miles across. You meet everyone on the Queen's Highway sooner or later. The settlements along it have crude names – Burnt Ground, Simms and Clarence Town – like places in the old West. South of Clarence Town we took a dirt track leading off into the scrub at the side of the road. The road petered out at the end of the track and the scrub suddenly disappeared, cut clean by one of the most

beautiful stretches of pure white sand I had ever seen. Anywhere.
The beach led into a small lagoon filled with water so shallow it
was heated up to the temperature of a tepid bath. At one edge of
the curving sand there was a low limestone cliff, a natural sea wall
which enclosed almost all of a perfect circle of deep blue water. A
small section of the circle's edge met the main lagoon like a
plughole at the edge of a sink, instead of in the middle. As I
watched, lapping waves swept a small stream of the perfect white
sand over the edge of the hole, where it fell like a white curtain of
trickling salt. This was the Blue Hole, said to be over six hundred
feet deep, but its surface diameter was no more than fifty yards.
Before donning my diving gear I sat on the edge of this blue eye,
dangling my feet over the side and peering into its iris. The colour
had every tincture from bice to zaffre, as subtle as a swathe of
tropic evening sky reaching into night above a crimson sunset.
Strong midday light reflected back off the smooth surface, making
the depths impenetrable.

I put my mask on and slipped carefully into the water to swim
out into the pool a little way. It was like looking down a mineshaft,
the blue deepening to pitch and the walls sloping away out of sight.
I had read that rainwater collecting in a natural hollow gradually
forms an acidic solution which eats its way through the limestone.
As it erodes it collects more freshwater and the process accelerates,
eroding more and more rock until the mixture eats through to the
seawater underneath. The salt and acid waters mingle, dissolving
the edges of the hole even more rapidly, eating it away to nothing.
Here was the meeting point of Bahamas Blue and Black Hole.

There were a couple of other divers with me, and a local guide
who warned us all not to panic as we swam down into the hole.
He said there were sometimes sharks in the depths, which might
appear suddenly, and large tarpon, the white game fish with pale
flesh which could reach six feet in length. He also warned us to be

careful to monitor our depth as our only orientation would be the limestone walls, which formed an encrusted pipe which undercut and fell away from the perfect circular lip we could see at the surface.

With scuba gear we sank beneath the surface and I saw that at one edge of the aquamarine eye the trickle of sand seeping from the lagoon was a steady stream. Underwater the walls of the sink-hole were uneven and covered in algae, sponges and small crusting growths. To the naked eye it was a sterile place. The water was cooler as we descended and we lost sight of the blue eye above us as we followed the shelving walls down. And down. The proximity of the wall, its colours reduced to grey by the depth and the shadow of the overhang, gave me the impression of sliding, slipping under the folds of withered limestone. The slope became more oblique, so that swimming vertically upwards meant bumping on the wall above. We had slipped through the lens of the eye into its socket. A cave. To swim away from the wall was to be lost in the middle of the ever-enlarging orbit of the cave with the yawning pit stretching below and above. Without sight of the wall I was completely disorientated. We swam in a circular direction watching the wall and peering at its crevices whenever anything caught the glare of the torches we carried.

As we went deeper the walls and the divers pressed near. The visibility grew worse, the divers just silhouettes behind their twitching torches. Someone bumped into me and I swam deeper to get away from them. I imagined the Blue Hole as an immense tin can which had been warped and twisted by a giant foot crushing the clean lines of its walls. The lid of the can was open and its rim was the circular limestone hole a hundred and twenty feet above us. Below us the base of the can had been ripped off and lay perhaps another five hundred feet deeper, while the sides of the rolled tube to which it had once been attached splayed out like a burst pipe. The cave was oppressive, and I understood why we had been warned not to panic if something startled us. Logic told me that the bubbles I exhaled would lead me to the surface if I followed them but I headed back to the wall again, a fixture in the gloom, preferring to follow it around as I made my ascent. The divers kept close to one another, afraid of being left alone in the dark maw.

The next afternoon one of the German businessmen, who had a house on the island, offered to take me on a trip in his little aeroplane. It was a tiny four-seater, the sort of thing that falls out of the sky at the hands of private pilots quite regularly. Heinz assured me that he was an excellent flier, and only when we were airborne did I ponder the wisdom of accepting his word. We flew south to Deadman's Cay, and he suggested a pit stop at the little bar at the airport. The bar doubled as the airport information centre and as we sipped our cold drinks the large Bahamian publican asked us where we were staying the night. The airport was closing shortly, he said. It seemed Heinz had miscalculated the time of sunset hereabouts. Hurriedly, he threw some cash on to the bar and rushed me back to the aeroplane. Heinz was clearly flustered as we roared down the runway, and he explained that night flights were impossible here as the runways were unlit. We just had time to fly on and over the Blue Hole, he said, but he was clearly nervous about the approaching dusk. When we reached it he banked steeply, turning for home. For a few seconds from the air I looked down on its perfect orbit staring up at us and I imagined how black its pit would be now.

Heinz did not speak as we flew northwards and he seemed to have cranked up the power on the tiny aeroplane. Occasionally he would mutter something into the radio handset on the dashboard, making sure the hotel knew we were *en route* for the unmanned and unlit airstrip. At least they would know what had happened to us. We made it back to the northern airport with minutes to spare, bouncing on the concrete strip in the gathering gloom. Airborne, I had forgotten about the mosquitoes. They got back to work as we opened the doors and I decided to return to Nassau the next day.

On the south side of New Providence there is good diving. One day, after a deep wall dive, I returned to the diving boat and climbed up to the flying bridge where I could talk to the skipper as we headed back towards the diving centre. As we chatted he pointed at the shore. 'That's where Arthur Hailey has his house,' he confided with a proud smile. 'And Sean Connery lives over there, near the golf course.' Such people become national assets on small islands. In the Cayman Islands a boat skipper had pointed out the houses of Dick Francis and an American pizza billionaire, which faced the sea. In Seychelles, the novelist Wilbur Smith was the local celebrity resident and he was often to be seen out diving. I recalled that Marlon Brando became obsessed with owning an atoll in Tahiti after he made *Mutiny on the Bounty*. Blockbuster novelists and film stars, the super rich, seem to have a thing about islands. For me, living on an island where I could dive often became an obsession. For several years I hatched a scheme which would allow me to work in Seychelles, so that I could be underwater as often as possible. Eventually the scheme worked. My dream became reality. It became hell. The diving was wonderful but living on a small island with limited access to books, conversation and a regular supply of fresh vegetables became tedious. Going underwater became a salvation from the island fever making people mad all around me.

I have met other people who nurture the same ambition. It seems to be a male thing. Women rarely want to shut themselves away on an island. Perhaps men think they can protect themselves by being on a neat parcel of land surrounded by the sea with the simple pleasures of sun, sand and sea to fill their days. Sometimes they are simply seeking a haven from tax collectors, but it occurred to me that the vision of an island fastness was a primitive and essentially male dream.

A cloud of blood poured over the sea. Now the other shark appeared from below and both fish, in a frenzy, tore and tore again at the still moving hulk whose nervous system refused to die.

Ian Fleming, *Thunderball*

Thunderball, the most successful James Bond film of all time, was released worldwide in cinemas in 1965. It is the production in which 007 establishes his credentials as a scuba diver and more than twenty-five minutes of the entire film take place underwater. The plot involves the hijacking of a NATO aeroplane and its cargo of atomic bombs, which the evil SPECTRE organization then attempts to ransom from the British and American governments for a hundred million pounds. Once hijacked, the Vulcan bomber lands in shallow water in the Bahamas, conveniently close to where the SPECTRE agent Emilio Largo has a luxury villa and a large yacht with which to transport the bombs and conceal them in a secret underwater cavern. A special underwater scooter is used to carry the bombs and an escort of black-suited divers armed with spearguns is required to protect them. Bond needs be an accomplished diver to discover the location of the bombs, to spy on the yacht and to survive immersion in Largo's swimming pool filled with the 'notorious Golden Grotto sharks', a fictitious species supposed to inhabit the reef where the NATO plane has been ditched. Bond also rescues the bikini-clad heroine, Domino Derval, from entanglement in the coral reef while skin diving. The climax of the film is an elaborately choreographed underwater battle between the bad guys in black wetsuits and the good guys wearing red wetsuits. The opposing teams unleash an underwater bloodfest as harpoons penetrate diving masks or skewer divers through the chest. Large knives plunge into flesh sending billows of scarlet into the water. Breathing hoses are slashed and underwater scooters careen wildly out of control as their occupants are killed.

For the 150 million people who went to see *Thunderball* at the cinema, the glamour and excitement of Nassau with its casinos and carnival would be forever linked with the shark-filled waters where divers battled with spears and knives and rode on underwater scooters.

The clear waters off New Providence make an ideal setting for *Thunderball*'s diving spectacular. Almost forty years later, the superstructure of the Vulcan bomber used in *Thunderball* still rests on the seabed off the island's south-west coast. Like most film props it is an imitation, just a mass of scaffolding which resembles an aeroplane only in outline, its wheels and undercarriage the only discernible clue to its original appearance. The galvanized-steel scaffolding has survived remarkably well, however, and is now held together by an encrustation of sea fans, gorgonians and sponges. It has become an artificial reef. Close by on the white sands there is another relic from the Bond era, a small boat used in the 1983 film *Never Say Never Again*, a remake of *Thunderball* with Sean Connery reprising his role as Bond even though Roger Moore had officially filled the character's shoes. Fiction and film fantasy are interwoven in underwater Bahamas. It is a strange experience to swim around these relics and impossible not to run through recollected images from the films as one dives.

Ian Fleming was a diver, and his friendship with Jacques Cousteau left a legacy of diving images in his novels. Fleming's spy took the adventure of diving to new heights. When the first films of his books were issued in the 1960s, diving was already established as a necessary pursuit for any man of action. Toys like Action Man and GI Joe had diving suits. Barbie and Ken had skin-diving outfits, and by 1967 even Elvis Presley had portrayed a frogman in *Easy Come, Easy Go*. But James Bond added a new level of gadgetry and sophistication to the adventure. When Ursula Andress strode up the beach in a white bikini with a diving mask tipped back on her head and a knife strapped against her thigh in *Dr No* (the first Bond adventure to be filmed), the image of diving was as sexy as it could get. *Thunderball* combined diving with the ultimate in boys' toys: sleek scooters, miniature breathing devices, underwater weaponry and chunky diving watches. In the eponymous novel, Bond is asked about underwater hand signals as he briefs the US Navy divers for their assault on the SPECTRE team: 'Thumbs down for any kind of emergency. Arms held straight out for a big fish. Thumbs up means "I understand" or "I'm coming to help you". That's all you'll need.' Bond smiled. 'If the feet go up, that's the signal that you've had it.'

Bond is rarely far from a scuba set. In *Live and Let Die*, the waters of Jamaica were the setting for more undersea adventure:

The great pack of barracudas seemed to have gone mad. They were whirling and snapping in the water like hysterical dogs. Three sharks that had joined them were charging through the water with a clumsier frenzy. The water was boiling with the dreadful fish and Bond was slammed in the face and buffeted again and again within a few yards. At any moment he knew his rubber skin would be torn with the flesh below it and then the pack would be on him.

Perhaps inspired by Bond, divers go to Nassau in search of sharks. South-west of New Providence, the deep Atlantic drop-off they call the Tongue of the Ocean curves around the end of the island. The sharks are there. Tigers, hammerheads, makos and silkies.

There are lemon sharks and blues too, but it is the Caribbean reef sharks, *Carcharhinus perezi*, that the dive centres feed, bringing them in to the reef flats where they congregate, dozens at a time, for a handout of fish heads. Shark feeds, sometimes called shark rodeos, are a daily ritual designed to thrill and titillate the sport diver. At selected spots on the reef adjoining the drop-off the divers are arranged in a semi-circle, kneeling in pairs on the sandy bottom while the feeder, a diving instructor, sits in the middle of the crescent producing attractive morsels from a crate with a long skewer. He proffers the food one piece at a time, so that the shark behaviour can be controlled. If an individual shark becomes aggressive the feeder withholds the food, making them take turns at the bait box. Occasionally the sharks will mouth his arm as they lunge for the fish, but they will not bite down on his flesh, which is protected by a chain-mail glove; they know what they are after. Even if you have encountered sharks underwater before, it is impossible not to be excited at the sight of their sleek torpedo forms jostling and snapping a few feet away, brushing against your head as they circle and pass, timing their arrival at the bait box to coincide with an emerging piece of offal.

The reef sharks are large fish, sometimes eight or ten feet long. They are powerful creatures and they inspire respect. The larger specimens have great tub bodies and high dorsal fins. Serious sharks. They associate divers with the possibility of food and at various dive sites they will congregate in large numbers, cruising by, waiting for the signal to feed. If you kneel in the sand, as the spectators at the shark-feed dives do, the sharks cruise closer, within reach, impassive but hopeful that you will produce some dead fish for them.

Getting into the water at one of the shark-feeding grounds is wonderful. Looking down into the clear water, the dark shadows of the sharks snake across the background of white sand with steady swishing tails. Sometimes they will swim up to the stern of the boat, their dorsal fins emerging in true cartoon-shark style from the surface of the sea. As you sink below the surface they cruise in silently from every direction and your head swivels furiously trying to count them. There are sometimes a dozen or more of them making their own circuits of the feeding ground waiting for the signal to dine. People in the diving business argue about the merits of the shark-feeding business. Does it encourage the fish to associate man with food? Is it an accident waiting to happen? Those behind the idea say they have been perfecting shark-feeding dives for over a decade, and that no one has been seriously injured in all that time. And, they say, the sharks show no interest in free-swimming divers when they are not being fed. The fact is that in many places the sharks' best hope for survival is the prospect of divers paying to see them.

After attending a shark feed one day, I found a queen conch walking across the sand. There were sharks patrolling the reef nearby and the other divers had all headed back to the boat. I knelt on the sand, forgetting the sharks which cast their shadows across me now and then. The conch is a large marine snail, *Strombus gigas*, an important protein meal for the islanders of the Caribbean and now a staple item on restaurant menus across the region. In the 1820s, the queen conch was favoured by Italian and French jewellers, who carved the delicate pink shell to make cameo brooches. As a food it has been credited with aphrodisiac properties, especially when made into a thick soup or chowder. The snails are so tasty and so easy to procure that their populations are declining. The meat is firm and white, not like snail at all, more like chicken with a hint of prawn. Tourist brochures offer recipes for conch, a taste of its flesh as essential to any visitor's Bahamian experience as a visit to the beach, the casinos or the straw market in Nassau. Grilling it is simple. Take two tomatoes, an onion and a sweet pepper. Mix together with a dash of salt and then cut your conch meat into bite-sized chunks. Put the vegetables and the meat together and wrap the mix in silver foil. Place on a hot grill for about twenty minutes, or until the meat is tender. Allow one conch per person. Enjoy. Apart from man, the conch is prey to eagle rays and turtles, crabs and lobsters, although as it grows to adulthood it becomes less easy to attack, and may with luck live for twenty years.

The conch leaves a trail of wiggly lines across the sand as it walks, hopping along with a single muscular foot. The conch in front of me was on a mission. Resolutely it moved across the sand, exposed against the white seabed, protected only by its shell. It was a large adult specimen, about ten inches long. By kneeling and putting my face on the sand I could look up and peer inside the opening at the front of its shell. Two rubbery stalks poked out and at the tip of each was a tiny iris, a yellow circle just visible against the black flesh. The conch has eyes, although it is unclear what exactly it can see, perhaps just shade and light. As long as I didn't move it carried on hopping along. Between hops it would pass the tip of its feeding tube, a small snout between the eye stalks, across the surface of the sand. Like an elephant's trunk, soft and strong, it was feeling or perhaps tasting for specks of plankton or algae. After several minutes I looked around. The last divers were back on the dive boat but the sharks were still all around. I had forgotten them while admiring the conch. Now I could enjoy them for a few minutes on my own.

11. Diving Free

My heartbeat slows to eight pulses a minute, and I forget my body.
At extreme depth, I am conscious only of my soul.

Umberto Pelizzari

Santa Teresa di Gallura, Sardinia

At Capo Testa, on the very northern tip of Sardinia, five men float
face-down upon a darkening sea. Behind the small inflatable boat
which has carried me offshore, the late-afternoon light is beginning
to turn the rough cliffs to gold. With each minute that passes the
rocks of the headland appear to stand out more sharply from the
shadowy waters beneath them. On the top of the cliffs above, only
the sloping roof tiles of the small town of Santa Teresa di Gallura
are visible from sea level, and they have been burnished into pink
and orange swatches of terracotta by the light.

In this fashionable resort it is the calmest time of day, the interval
between beach days and piazza nights. Inside the buildings there
are local residents and holidaymakers, all resting or getting ready
to turn out for the evening's entertainment, which mainly consists
of the after-dinner promenade, the *passeggiata*. The progress of
suntans is ritually compared and admired, as the ultra-violet junkies

pamper and moisturize their burns and display them in the company of fine clothing and jewels.

Santa Teresa sits on top of the promontory of Capo Testa, its narrow streets leading uphill from the small port to the core of the village, the main square. The summer visitors mill around the flat space, circulating and eyeing one other, purchasing *gelati* by the score, and using their *telefono cellulare* to report back the progress of their holiday to family and friends in Rome or Milan. It is a time for seeing and being seen, the chatter of privileged families from the mainland turning Santa Teresa into a desirable resort instead of a fishing village.

Half a mile offshore, where the seabed slopes away from the jutting rocks which give the coast its dramatic appeal, the diving boat has discharged its cargo into the water. At the end of the Mediterranean summer, the sea has been warmed by the sun over a stretch of many dry months. The September mistral is blowing through the narrow straits of Bonifacio which separate Sardinia from Corsica. Just a few miles away, the French cousin displays her bright white cliffs, which rise from the waters like a pallid décolletage above a rich blue dress. The mistral brings a low swell from the east, and although the sea is as warm as it ever gets, the men in the water are in full wetsuits. Unlike scuba divers, they are unencumbered by buoyancy jackets, or air cylinders and hoses. They call themselves free divers, men who swim down into the depths with only the air they can store in their lungs, divers who have taken the ancient art of naked diving to a new level. To me their sport, which they sometimes call *apnoea* (from the Greek 'without breath'), is both the beginning and the end of the story of diving for pleasure.

Each piece of the apnoeists' equipment is the same shade of black, camouflaging them perfectly against the waves which are now backlit by the setting sun. The tight-fitting neoprene is made to measure, and wraps them from ankle to head, with an integral hood encircling the face. Their disguise is completed by a face mask. The mask is smaller in volume than that worn by a normal diver, and looks more like a pair of old-fashioned goggles than the large clear plate of a scuba mask. The reason for this is simple: as one swims deeper, water pressure will squeeze the air space between the mask and the face, pressing the mask tight against the skin, eventually causing discomfort, and then severe pain. To relieve this discomfort, a diver has simply to exhale through the nose, thereby pressuring the mask space from within, against the external force. By reducing the size of the air pocket inside the mask the free diver minimizes the amount of air necessary to achieve this. At the depths to which these men dive, every scrap of air in their abdomen must be preserved, not wasted inside a mask.

Around the Perspex face mask, a silicone-rubber skirt leaves only a small area of skin on the forehead and a patch of cheek on either edge of the lower mask exposed to the water. Instead of a rigid canvas weight belt, the free diver's is made of soft rubber, like a bicycle inner tube, so that it can be drawn tight and yet expand when the belly is filled with air. These men have retrained themselves to breathe like small babies, using the abdomen and the lower recesses of their lungs too, and not just the upper portion of the chest, to inhale. Finally, the foot fins they use are made not of rubber but of carbon fibre, and are much longer than scuba divers', extending three feet from the end of their toes, like some circus clown's stunt shoes.

Everything matches. Black hood, black mask, black suit, black fins, black snorkels. Although they are no more than fifty yards away from me, the men become indistinguishable from one another, mere shadows in the sea.

Before they entered the water I watched the divers laughing and joking in Italian, strewing the floor of the small rubber inflatable dinghy with items of diving equipment. They are relaxed and at ease with each other, united in their purpose to leave the flurry of Santa Teresa in peak season behind them. They will discover another world; an aspect of diving which they believe is the purest expression of the sport, and of man's relationship with the sea.

Once they are at a safe distance from the boat, each man floats in the water, bending at the waist, hanging all four limbs beneath the surface as loose as a corpse. They make no attempt to swim or even move. The men float together in a pack, a few feet apart. Nearby, they have placed a small inflatable marker buoy, like a child's beachball on a string. From it, there is suspended a white nylon rope which is weighted with lead at one end, so that it drops vertically into the deep. The line is their vertical reference point underwater, and it also serves as a guide to alert them to any currents running beneath them. A shout from the water tells the boat skipper that there is no current tonight, and we know that conditions are right for the free-diving training session to go ahead. We will stay on the boat and wait, enjoying the sunset and watching out for the divers in case they need assistance.

For some minutes, perhaps seven or eight, the men remain motionless, and then there is a chorus of whistles from the sea. The boat skipper nods in the direction of the swimmers and I see that they have become whales, black backs arched high above the water as they fill their chests and abdomens with air in a series of rapid hyperventilations. The whistle emanates from their snorkels, as a giant inhalation is sucked into their chests with throats expanded to take up as much air as possible.

From the elevation of the boat the effect is extraordinary, as the smooth rubber suits accentuate the rounded form of their torsos, stretched by the intake of breath needed to carry them down on a free dive. They pluck the snorkels from their mouths and slide beneath the waves, arms outstretched with wrists together, holding the small plastic tube in front of them like a weapon. One by one they disappear from sight until only one man, the safety diver, remains at the surface. For a minute and a half the others are gone, and then they reappear. For a moment their faces are upturned and they emit a sharp sucking sound, stretching their mouths wide to replenish their lungs with air. The gasp and the grimace are as intense as a sexual climax, a violent affirmation which signals their return to the air world. It is as if they are being reborn, emerging from their mute, liquid, internal world and drawing air into their lungs with the vigour of an infant giving the first yelp of greeting to life outside the womb.

For half an hour I watch the divers slip into the deep, and with each disappearance they remain below a little longer, until on their last dive they are out of sight for almost four minutes. I am not a trained free diver, and on this occasion do not have the special equipment necessary to follow the group, but I am impatient to see them at work. I slip into the water, taking a pair of spare fins and a mask from the bottom of the dinghy, and swim cautiously towards the divers. I swim slowly, face down, hovering on the edge of their circle, not wishing to disturb their concentration.

As in any pack of marine mammals, this group has a natural leader. His name is Umberto Pelizzari, and I have come to Sardinia with the sole purpose of seeing him dive. Among free divers worldwide he is a legend, a multiple world-record holder in competitive free diving.

Once in the water, I am close enough to pick him out from the other men. In spite of their identical uniforms of black rubber, Umberto is easily distinguishable, in part because he is taller than the others, but more precisely because none of them has his grace or elegance underwater. With long legs made even longer by the addition of specially designed fins, Umberto extends his arms ahead of him, and with slow gentle kicks he seems to fall rather than propel himself downwards into the deep. No movement is wasted, no spare energy dissipated from the black form. He has become something other than a man in a wetsuit. Free divers are often compared to dolphins, but this man is somehow less distinct than those curving joyous shapes, his form too lean and projectile. I follow him downwards for a little way, not wanting to lose sight of him as he passes the knots in the white line which mark each five metres of depth. In my borrowed equipment I make it to the second knot and stop, but he is now at the fifth, then the sixth and still going. In the evening light I can see no deeper, and I return to the surface. Other free divers had told me that Umberto was the best, somehow special, and I had seen films of his world-record attempts at breath-hold dives. Now I had seen Pelizzari at first hand, and I understood why free divers held him in awe. I was hooked, and determined to dive with him again.

Umberto Pelizzari can hold his breath for just over seven minutes. To achieve this feat, he has learned to relax so completely, and to so extend his tolerance to the state of not breathing, that he can totally ignore the visual and auditory stimuli of the world around him. Once embarked on a series of breath-hold exercises he finds an inner peace best compared to a mystic trance, like an Eastern yogi.

In 1993, off the island of Elba, Pelizzari set his first record in what is called 'no limits' free diving. Standing on a specially made sledge (a wedge-shaped bucket attached to a steel cable), he took one last deep breath and gave the signal for the pin attaching the device to the cable to be pulled. One minute and thirteen seconds later, the sledge had pulled him down to a new world-record depth of one hundred and twenty-three metres (four hundred and three feet) beneath the surface. Down there, in the virtual dark, the combined pressure of water and gravity on his body was thirteen times what we feel above. His lungs, which ordinarily have a capacity of seven and a half litres of air, as opposed to an average man's four and a half litres, had been squeezed to the size of apples. Umberto recalls staring into the eyes of Steffano May, the safety diver who was waiting for him at the foot of the cable:

My sense of well being was astounding, and I had an overwhelming feeling of victory. My heart beat faster. At last, I was 'the deepest man in the world'. I shook Steffano's hand and then grabbed the balloon that would pull me back up. One by one, as it sped through the water with me hanging on, I heard every safety diver screaming at me with joy. It was the happiest moment of my life and I never wanted the journey upwards to end. As I broke the surface I cried out, as if every ounce of bottled-up energy was bursting from inside me. Ten months of training for a total time underwater of two minutes and twenty-seven seconds, and a lot of sacrifices for a few moments of the most intense pleasure imaginable.

Since then, Pelizzari, and other men, have extended that depth record. Such dives are a high-profile enterprise, and extremely expensive. Each record attempt requires commercial sponsorship to equip a boat, medical teams, a diving bell for diver support, and a horde of highly trained safety divers, who must be in place at intervals along the cable to assist the free diver if something goes wrong. Because they are breathing compressed air, or other mixed gases, these men must then endure several hours of decompression stops before they can safely ascend from the same depths. If all goes well, they will see the record-breaking free diver for just a few seconds as he descends and then for a brief moment again as he ascends.

The idea of sending a breath-hold diver to these depths divides the sport. It also arouses medical fears that it is only a matter of time before they reach the absolute limit of stress that the chest and circulatory system can take.

Willingly depriving oneself of air, the fuel of life, is less uncommon than might at first be supposed. Small children sometimes hold their breath until they pass out, and in extreme cases they will suffer a 'fit', induced by the lack of oxygen reaching their brain. Usually, such behaviour is a means of exerting independence, a power play against parents when the child's ability to communicate emotions is frustrated. By contrast, older children and adults who hold their breath are compelled to breathe after a short time by a series of unpleasant sensations, both physiological and psychological. Free divers, and other apnoeic individuals, learn to resist the urge to breathe, and with practice an adult can so accustom his mind to the idea of breath holding that he too will pass out. The likelihood of such a lapse into unconsciousness is increased if the apnoeist takes a series of rapid breaths, or hyperventilations, before the breath hold. These rapid breaths will lower the level of carbon dioxide in the blood, and therefore delay the urge to breathe, by which time the oxygen levels in the blood will be so low as to provoke unconsciousness. Once unconscious, the automatic breathing mechanisms resume, and consciousness returns.

Free divers are aware of the dangers of such extremes of concentration, and of the set of phenomena which lead to what they call 'shallow-water blackout'. For the apnoeist it is the last few seconds of the dive which are the most hazardous. Here, just as the diver is almost at the surface of the water, his levels of oxygen are at their lowest. This coincides with the moments when the lung volume is expanding with the reduction in pressure caused by the ascent. The remaining oxygen is, in layman's terms, spread more thinly over a greater lung space, and may be insufficient to keep the diver awake. Death by drowning easily follows, and has done so on many occasions, particularly in the world of spearfishing. In such cases a diver, anxious to pursue a wounded fish or a prize specimen, will over-exert himself at depth, and then pass out just a few feet below the surface.

In competition it is common to see free divers emerge safely from the water after a deep dive. Then, even as they give a victory cry, they will seem to shimmy in the water, their head will loll to one side and their hands will grasp ineffectually for a rope or a hand to cling on to. This they affectionately call the 'samba', after the Latin American dance with its loose-limbed rhythm. A diver who experiences a samba is automatically disqualified from the competition, and is all too often oblivious to the near blackout, arguing afterwards with the judges that he never lost consciousness.

Free divers claim that under proper supervision such blackouts are of minimal danger, and no trained diver would practise breath holding in water, however shallow, without a safety diver monitoring their state of consciousness. They compare the blackouts, and sambas, to the possibility of injury in other sports, such as skiing, where lasting physical damage is more common.

At least one diving physician has unflatteringly compared the physical elation which free divers sometimes report to the dangerous sexual aberration of auto-erotic asphyxia. The practice of inducing asphyxia through strangulation for sexual pleasure is well documented. Commonly, though not exclusively, some men have heightened their sexual pleasure, usually while masturbating, by restricting their oxygen intake, through attaching some form of ligature about the neck, or even by inserting their head into a plastic bag. This habit is said, not unexpectedly, to produce light-headedness, followed by exhilaration, reinforcing the degree of sexual gratification. Self-strangulation, of whatever type, commonly leads to accidental death, perhaps through inducing a weakened ability to exercise self-control and judgement. In effect, the auto-eroticist is provoking cerebral hypoxia, the same condition that apnoeists are assumed to reproduce underwater. It may explain why some free divers have reported such a feeling of happiness at great depth, a joy so intense that they say they consider remaining below, eternally. Hypoxia among free divers has not been proved, however, and there has been no conclusive evidence of brain damage caused by breath holding. Even without hypoxia, the effects of nitrogen narcosis on deep divers will certainly induce euphoria, a more likely cause of underwater Epiphany.

Put quite simply, a breath-holding diver is moving underwater, his body continuing to use oxygen and to produce carbon dioxide without replenishing its supply. Eventually, the oxygen level in the bloodstream will be so reduced as to cause a blackout. Interestingly, however, it is now known that trained free divers exhibit physiological adaptations to low oxygen levels, and more importantly to the dramatic effects of increasing pressure on their bodies.

A remarkable number of adults never hold their breath for pleasure, sexual or otherwise, and are unaware of those sensations. If you inhale a lungful of fresh air and hold it, you feel an initial tightness in the chest and throat and then a gradual, but quite rapid feeling of unease, an urge to breathe out. If you take several deep rapid breaths prior to a breath hold you will be able to stave off the unpleasant sensations for a little longer, because you are loading your bloodstream with oxygen, and reducing the amount of carbon dioxide – the chemical trigger which compels you to breathe. For most people, unless they have been trained, the urge to breathe will become too strong to resist after less than a minute. Free divers have developed a range of techniques and several different training methods by which to overcome these seemingly primal physical limitations.

The physical barrier to depth swimming is the pressure exerted on the diver's body by the water around him. With each thirty-three feet of depth, hydrostatic pressure increases by 14.7 pounds per square inch. The physical consequence of this pressure on most of the body is minimal, since the tissues and bones are being squeezed by an even amount of pressure from all sides. However, those areas of our bodies which contain air, or air spaces, will be constricted and squeezed, until in the case of the lungs they have shrunk to a fraction of their size at the surface. Anyone who swims down below a few feet into a swimming pool feels those pressures, usually first in the ears, then the nose and sinuses, pressures which must be equalized, usually by holding the nose and mouth closed and blowing out gently so that air is forced into the Eustachian tubes to pressurize the ear drum from within.

It has been observed for many years that any human being whose face is immersed in cold water experiences a drop in heart rate. Periodically, the media will feature remarkable true-life tales of children, and more rarely adults, who are 'brought back to life' after having fallen into an icy lake and seemingly drowned. Survival in such cases is rare, and by no means the norm, but where it does occur, it is partially attributable to the human body exhibiting what is now called the 'diving reflex', a primitive response which shuts down those areas of our body's circulation not vital to maintaining life.

The diving reflex seems to be an evolutionary adaptation which we share with other diving mammals, such as whales and seals, and perhaps less flatteringly with ducks. In these species, cold water – in fact immersion in water in general – stimulates the facial nerve which in turn triggers a series of physical reactions in other parts of the body; these include a lowering of the heart rate, and a reduction of blood flow to muscles, skin and viscera. Blood flow to the brain and heart is, however, maintained.

Free diving at extreme depths begins to bring additional strains to bear on our bodies. As we swim deeper, pure physiology would suggest that a diver's lungs will be compressed to the point where they are as small as their alveoli can be squashed. Initially, it was assumed that external pressure could be tolerated only until the lungs had shrunk to their residual volume – the size at which all remaining air has been expelled.

In fact, once sufficient pressure is felt, other factors come into play which mediate the effects of the small volume of the lungs. Other organs, the spleen, the heart and the major blood vessels are all affected by the increasing pressure. The spleen may shrink by a fifth, a process which releases extra red blood cells into the bloodstream, the cells which carry oxygen. As the heart slows down, its own vessels dilate, thus using what oxygen is available more efficiently. As the blood vessels in the skin contract, they too require less blood flow, and relaxed muscles impose less burden on the oxygen remaining in the blood supply. Some of these physiological changes take some time to occur, and may explain why free divers extend their breath-hold duration with each successive dive, as if their physiology is in effect limbering up to reach maximum efficiency, just as a track athlete will only achieve full potential after a series of stretching exercises.

Unfortunately, the diving reflex is poorly developed in human beings, and immersion in cold water also often induces undesirable side effects, such as an irregular heart beat, and pressure itself will eventually have negative consequences on the major organs of the chest. Free divers often proudly proclaim that one of the observable phenomena of their sport is an adaptation to blood pooling in the chest cavity, thus maintaining heart and lungs in working order at depth, and helping to offset the squeeze induced by hydrostatic pressure. This effect, the so-called 'blood shift', certainly occurs, and leads many free divers to believe that they can emulate their mammalian cousins, the whales. They forget, or do not appreciate, that man's lungs are proportionately much larger in relation to overall body size than those of the marine mammals.

Medical science cannot confidently predict the ultimate depth

to which a free-swimming man may descend. With training, practice and the right mental attitude, the limits have been extended far
beyond what doctors thought possible a generation ago. Umberto
Pelizzari is a rare physical specimen, and has pushed those limits
further than almost any other man.

Competitive breath holding is one of the most controversial
areas in modern diving. The only way to understand it, say the free
divers, is to do it. For most free divers, the aim of training, and of
extending their ability to go without breathing, is simply to enjoy
the underwater environment without the encumbrance of a breathing device. Instead of investing in scuba training and equipment,
they arm themselves with the minimum gear – the basic mask, fins
and snorkel – and swim around underwater without the fear of
decompression illness, narcosis or equipment failure.

For a small but fast-growing number of men and women around
the world, the sport has become something more. They invest it
with a poetic quality, the mystique of a secret world, which might
be labelled the Zen of diving. It has gone beyond the simple art of
taking a gulp of air and jumping into the sea to pluck a sponge from
the bottom or to prise a pearl oyster from its bed. It has even gone
beyond the desire to take a modern speargun and go hunting fish
for sport. Free diving has entered a new dimension, competitive
apnoea, which claims to be the fastest-growing watersport in the
world.

Competitive free divers have devised a series of underwater
disciplines which test their tolerance to apnoea. In its simplest
form, 'static apnoea', men and women simply hold their breath
while floating face-down in a swimming pool, under close supervision. A free diver once explained to me that, while the idea of
grown men floating in a pool and holding their breath for as long
as possible might seem an odd way of spending an evening, the real
purpose of static apnoea is to instil in the mind a kind of memory.

This memory will get the brain and the body used to prolonging its resistance to the urge to breathe. Again to draw a parallel with athletics, the free diver becomes inured to the pain of not breathing in the same way that a long-distance runner must break through the fatigue in his legs, as lactic acid builds in his muscles.

In 'dynamic apnoea', the competitors' aim is to achieve the greatest horizontal distance underwater, just as children will often experiment with seeing how far they can swim across a pool without surfacing. A top apnoeist can cover six lengths of the average twenty-five-metre public pool without once coming up for air. Training for the discipline involves underwater press-ups, even walking around the supermarket whilst holding one's breath, anything which will accustom the body to the state of not breathing.

The most prized apnoeic achievements are those which require diving in open water, usually a warm sea or a lake. Using only the diver's own power, and with only a mask, fins and weight belt, the 'constant ballast dive' is the toughest physical challenge in the sport. The diver has to swim down beside a marked line, usually a rope, and pluck a depth marker from the furthest point he or she can reach, then return to the surface without touching anyone or anything on the way back. In other words, the weight of the diver as he descends is the same as on his return to the surface. Going down is the easiest part, since it is the upward ascent, under pressure and against gravity, that requires 80 per cent of the physical effort.

A variation of this discipline, the 'variable ballast dive', allows the diver to use a weighted sledge with a maximum weight of thirty kilograms to descend the line. He then abandons the sledge, and can return to the surface by pulling himself hand over hand up the marker line. Such records and competitions require athleticism, stamina and immense concentration, as well as a high tolerance to the sensations of breath holding.

Even more dramatic, in terms of distances achieved, are the

so-called 'no limits' free-diving competitions. Here, a diver is allowed to use a sledge of his own choosing. Pelizzari, for example, dives with over fifty kilograms of ballast, and uses a gas-filled balloon to drag himself back to the surface. The limiting factor is not how heavy the diver makes his sledge, but how quickly he can equalize the pressure on his eardrums as he descends. With around fifty-four kilos of ballast, Pelizzari's ears have to cope with a descent rate of over four metres per second.

To a television audience, or to an uninitiated public, the drama of someone hurtling down a steel line into the deep blue sea to reach a depth approaching five hundred feet is a saleable commodity. It provides a spectacle, a true-life drama with the greatest possible cost payable by the participant. Death. Diving-equipment manufacturers thrive on the publicity such feats attract. The dives themselves are as much about circus and showbiz as sporting achievement, but for many people there is no stronger evocation of man's confrontation with the deep.

In France and Italy, where the largest numbers of competitive apnoeists are found, the competitive art of free diving developed as a natural progression from spear-fishing and underwater hunting. The Mediterranean Sea has spawned as many natural divers as any body of water in the world. Anecdotal evidence suggests that a Greek sponge diver, Stotti Georghios, made a successful breath-hold dive in 1913 to a depth of approximately two hundred feet. He had been hired by the Italian Navy to attach a line to a lost anchor from the battleship *Regina Margharita*. Georghios used the ancient sponging technique of diving with a weighted stone to carry him down into the water, and according to naval accounts he went down feet-first, using the same technique that modern 'no limits' divers employ. However, he had no safety divers at hand to save him, nor, for posterity's sake, were there any cameras to record his success. Interestingly, an examination by an Italian doctor revealed that both of Georghios' eardrums were perforated, ruptured permanently by his deep diving, although he still had some hearing in one ear. The injuries were chronic rather than a result of the record dive, indicating that the Greek diver had sacrificed his hearing to the need to penetrate the depths on a regular basis.

In 1949, Raimondo Bucher, a Hungarian who became a naturalized Italian, made a bet of 50,000 lire that he could swim down thirty metres (ninety-eight feet) into the rather murky sea near Naples. He would prove it by taking a sealed parchment bearing a selection of judges' signatures down to a scuba diver waiting at the prescribed depth. Competitive free diving was born.

Bucher's exploits were a spur for others. Ennio Falco and Alberto Novelli began setting new records, adhering to the same rules by wearing only a mask and fins. In the 1960s, Frenchmen like Jacques Mayol and Italians like Enzo Maiorca became interested in pushing the depths to which they could descend without breathing apparatus. The technology for manufacturing fins, masks and wetsuits improved, making their immersion marginally less physically uncomfortable. Gradually, records were pushed beyond the fifty-metre mark, in the waters off Rio de Janeiro, the Bahamas, Capri and Florida. Before long, there was a succession of tit-for-tat dives, each a few feet deeper than the last, with men reaching depths that confounded medical experts' opinion on how deep the human body could descend without suffering catastrophic pressure damage to the lungs or heart.

With scientific opinion divided on how deep a man might go, it was left to the United States Navy to make an intensive physiological study of free diving, research which would be relevant to the development of survival training for submariners. The man chosen to test all the theories was Robert Croft, an instructor at the Submarine Training School in Connecticut.

Bob Croft was thirty-three when he volunteered for diving experiments under the supervision of one of the Navy physiologists, Dr Karl Schaeffer, a man who had originally fought against the US Navy, whilst serving in the German submarine corps. After the War, like many top scientists, Schaeffer was offered the opportunity to work for the American government, and his expertise in submarine medicine was highly valued. Using the decompression chambers at the Navy submarine school, Schaeffer devised a set of scientific experiments to test the physiology of a man swimming at increasing depth.

Bob Croft was chosen as the official guinea-pig on the basis that he alone of all the swimming instructors at the submarine school could happily descend to the bottom of the training tank while holding his breath, a depth of just over one hundred feet. In 1967, under Dr Schaeffer's supervision, Croft gained worldwide recognition when he became the first man to achieve a verifiable swimming descent below two hundred feet. A primitive weight attached to a cable, with a homemade brake designed from a pair of calliper handles, was used to pull him down the line. In the first dive, Croft achieved two hundred and seventeen feet, and successive dives the following year eventually took him to two hundred and forty feet. He was without doubt the deepest-ever American free diver, and the records were established on home territory off the Florida coast, near Fort Lauderdale. Public interest was aroused, and Croft's dives were verified by film star and Olympic swimming champion Johnny Weissmuller on behalf of the Swimming Hall of Fame in Florida. In America, Croft achieved celebrity status, albeit short-lived. And when he broke the world record, his story was featured in *Life* magazine and the *Wall Street Journal*. His achievements led to appearances on chat shows with David Frost and even on the massively popular *Today Show*.

Since then, Croft's record depth has been more than doubled, but at the time it was believed that anyone swimming much below one hundred feet would be killed by the pressure on their chest. More remarkably, Bob Croft dived in just a pair of bathing trunks, with no fins on his feet, and with a mask which by today's standards looks prehistoric. He eschewed wearing rubber fins, as they would have simply increased drag through the water on the descent, while for the ascent he would pull himself back up the rope. Modern free divers owe a debt to Croft, who pushed the limits of experiment to new levels.

Bob Croft has recently retired from a career in industry in New York State; his connections with free diving ended when he left the Navy. He is a cheerful, robust character, modest in his assessment of what he achieved. When I asked if he considered his diving records as evidence of bravery, he was matter of fact. 'In the Navy we had something we called the "can-do spirit", and that's how we achieved things. I don't think it was a question of bravery.'

In physical terms, Croft's record-breaking dives were extremely strenuous. He told me that whenever he dived he would experience difficulties with equalizing the pressure on his ears, a problem he was told was due to having very narrow Eustachian tubes. In order to make the deep record attempts he consulted an ear, nose and throat specialist who suggested stretching the tubes surgically. The doctor explained that this was an experimental procedure, and with Croft's agreement proceeded to insert a heated wire into his Eustachian tubes via his throat, without anaesthetic. After this unpleasant experience Croft recalls that equalizing was marginally easier, although medical opinion now would caution against the operation, as burning out the delicate tissue inside the Eustachian tubes is likely to cause scarring, and eventually a further narrowing of the airway.

Bob Croft acknowledges that there was also a psychological

aspect to his training, but puts his survival down to sheer physical fitness, and his complete confidence in Dr Schaeffer's assessment of how deep he could dive without injury. Jacques Mayol, the French free diver who would achieve fame through record attempts over the following decade, visited Croft in Florida, and insisted on witnessing the record attempts in person, while wearing scuba. 'Mayol was into yoga, standing on his head and such,' Croft remembers. 'I didn't pay much attention to that. I trained by running regularly, and going to the gym.'

In fact, in many ways, Croft's claim to amateurism rings untrue. Mayol, and others, studied his technique and training very carefully. The fact that Croft had been able to push the limits of what was thought safe inspired them to emulate his dives, and eventually surpass his records. On closer questioning, Croft says that Dr Schaeffer's intensive physiological studies had revealed that he had an extraordinarily large lung capacity, despite having shown little athletic promise when he was a boy. 'It's funny, I definitely wasn't a strong child, in fact I was born with rickets,' Croft laughs. 'And I had pneumonia twice as an infant. I guess I grew out of those things.'

Bob Croft dropped out of the business of setting records, once he had established himself as the world's deepest-swimming diver. 'I decided the scientific value of doing deeper dives was kinda pointless,' he says now. 'And I guess I was scared that what I did would be seen as a stunt, in some way.'

Photographs taken of Croft as he swam back to the surface from his deepest dives revealed for the first time how the skin on his back and torso had fallen into loose folds due to the extreme pressures he had experienced. To escape the problem of mask squeeze, he became one of the first men to experiment with underwater contact lenses. Initially conceived as something which might benefit Navy swimmers in covert assault raids, the lenses were designed to replace a face mask, which might be dislodged if the raiders had to drop from a fast-moving boat into the sea. Croft was given a pair of experimental lenses which contained their own air space, so that vision underwater would be possible. He remembers trying them in the base swimming pool and finding himself in agony as the lenses trapped chlorinated water against his eyes. Similarly, in seawater, the lenses trapped salt against his cornea and were too painful to wear. A wetting solution was provided which would allegedly neutralize the salt water, but when Croft tried to use it his eyes reacted badly, and he had to jump overboard in the hope that seawater would neutralize whatever was in the solution. Instead, the pain became worse, and he had to be dragged from the sea and have his eyes prised open to remove the lenses. Ingeniously, he worked out that the only way to get the lenses on to his eyes without pain was to fill a bowl with saline, immerse his face to insert the lenses, and then wear a mask over the lenses which trapped saline and lenses together. 'The lenses were quite comfortable once I figured out how to use the saline as a barrier to stop the salt water seeping in behind them and burning my eyes,' Croft recalls. 'They were about the size of a quarter coin, and had two layers of plastic moulded together with an air space in the middle. I had to put saline water into the mask so that it didn't become a dead air space when I dived. The pressure on the mask would have damaged my eyes, even pulled them out of their sockets.'

Such experiments, and analyses of gas exchange and blood samples taken from Croft before and after his dives, were carefully recorded, greatly expanding the slim body of scientific knowledge about free diving. Bob Croft gave up free diving before it attracted lucrative sponsorship, and indeed funded many of his early diving records at great personal expense.

Jacques Mayol, meanwhile, went on to find other sparring

partners, and to establish a reputation as the founding father of competitive free diving. As public attention focused on the dare-devil record-breaking business, he found a new rival, the Italian Enzo Maiorca. Between 1974 and 1988, the two men jockeyed for supremacy, swapping places almost annually as holder of the 'no limits' title, Mayol finally achieving the magical goal of a 100-metre (328 feet) descent in 1976, off the island of Elba. The legacy of that head-to-head rivalry has been at the very roots of the growth in interest in breath holding.

In 1988, the duel between Jacques Mayol and Enzo Maiorca became loosely fictionalized in the French feature film *Le Grand Bleu* (The Big Blue). Based upon a storyline by the French cinema-tographer Luc Besson, who also directed the feature, it aimed to give viewers the sensation of free diving. On film, Mayol's rival became a man called Enzo Molinari, but it was clear upon whom the character had been based. *Le Grand Bleu* set box-office records when it was released, and drew a cult following around the world, a following which continues to grow, prompting re-releases in the cinema and several video versions of differing lengths.

For a mass commercial audience, and for many mainstream critics, the film's departure into mysticism was too much. How-ever, free divers worldwide agree that Besson's stunning under-water photography portrays their obsession with the 'Blue' as a visual poem. As one publicity blurb put it, 'No coral, no tropical fish, no white sand, just Blue, immense Blue.'

In the film, the two characters, Enzo and Jacques, have a close friendship, but they vie for ascendancy in free-diving competitions. While Enzo is a *bon viveur*, an exuberant Italian with a tight-knit family background, Jacques is a loner, an orphan who saw his own father drown while diving for sponges. The story follows the two men's exploits from innocent childhood in the Mediterranean to a final and fatal adult confrontation. Much of the action takes place in the clear blue waters off the Sicilian town of Taormina, where Enzo Molinari eventually pushes himself too deep in an attempt to beat his younger rival. Above and beyond the story of the two male rivals, *The Big Blue* is a love story. The character of Jacques (played enigmatically by Jean-Marc Barr) is torn between his love for a woman and his love of the water. Part of Jacques's attraction to the viewer, and to his female lover, is his utter calm and self-control. Jacques is impervious to materialism, his love for the sea overrides all emotion, all ambition and ultimately all human relationships. It is clear that the responsibilities of the air world are a trivial distraction from his spiritual home, the sea. His centre is the liquid world.

Within *The Big Blue*, there is a series of encounters between Jacques and dolphins. At one point, he releases captive, ailing dolphins from an aquarium, and their plight is clearly a metaphor for the poverty of spirit induced by the limits imposed on us in our own world. Wild dolphins symbolize everything that is good, pure, loving and free, and Besson uses them as a totem, a shamanistic embodiment of hope and happiness. Jacques Mayol's own book about man and the underwater world, *Homo Delphinus*, makes a further symbolic connection, tying human spirituality with our evolutionary links to the marine mammals.

Since its release, *The Big Blue* has become compulsory viewing for breath holders, its plot and images revered as the only way to explain the sport to the uninitiated. The climax of the film shows Jacques swimming off into the blue depths with a dolphin, choosing never to return to the air world with its problems and complications. In Jacques's case, these complications include a pregnant girlfriend, and, given her characterization, following the dolphin seems like a better option.

Umberto Pelizzari has a small dolphin tattoo on his right shoulder-blade, and in the real world of competitive free diving the animal holds a special place, revered as a symbol of strength and intelligence combined with purity of spirit.

There are no dolphins in the waters off Capo Testa this night, at least there are none visible from where I sit. The sun is an orange sliver at the edge of the sea and it is time to return to port, time for Pelizzari to return to Club Mediterranée where he makes his summer base in Santa Teresa. Standing at the wheel of the speeding boat, Pelizzari is relaxed and happy, refreshed by his hour in the water. He is physically imposing, and although well over six feet tall, he weighs little more than thirteen stone. With salt blond hair, and his entire body the same shade of boat-boy tan, he attracts commercial sponsorship as much for his looks as his skill. Lean and bronzed, with the chiselled features of a catwalk model, he represents an ideal of athleticism and is an idol for his followers. I wonder what it is that makes him risk his life in search of communion with the sea.

'I don't care why anyone else dives,' he smiles. 'For me, the sea is life itself. When I go down I am not trying to be a dolphin, or a fish. No, I try to become water.'

If I had not seen him dive I might have dismissed such pronouncements as poetic hyperbole, but he spoke with such conviction that I seemed to understand what he meant.

Umberto tells me that the summer has been 'crazy', a busy season at his diving centre, and that he needs a holiday, some peace before his next project, a documentary film about his next world-record attempt. We agree to meet up again at his diving school the following day for an interview and some more diving, if the weather is right.

Pelizzari, like Jacques Mayol before him, accepts that he will see his records broken and one day be succeeded by a new generation of record breakers whose equipment will be gradually refined and improved. Becoming a world champion has enabled Pelizzari to open a diving centre in Sardinia, but not to become wealthy, or permanently financially secure.

But in Santa Teresa di Gallura, he is in every sense a local hero. Over the course of several days in Santa Teresa, I watched Pelizzari run his business, go diving, eat with his family and friends, and fend off requests for more interviews, photo shoots and publicity duties for his sponsors.

'Umbe!', the locals call out as he walks to the docks to go diving, and a salute of cheery waves from shopkeepers marks his passage as he straddles a moped to run an errand in town. With mirror sunglasses pushed back on his head and a seemingly endless selection of swimming shorts, he evinces beach style *par excellence*. I am introduced to a succession of his friends, some of them divers, some not. Giancarlo, Ludovicco, Maximilliano, Pier Paolo. All agree that, in spite of his fame, Umberto shows no sign of arrogance.

'I am not like a footballer, or a tennis player,' he told me. 'Yes, in the world of free diving I am a name right now, but that is still a small world. For me, the aim is to leave the record attempts and establish my name as a teacher of the sport, to show people the beauty of swimming freely, watching the marine environment and developing their techniques.'

Each day something would disrupt his training schedule. One day it would be a problem with his boat, the next a logistical problem with the scuba divers or one of his staff. It seemed to me that this was not an environment conducive to contemplation, or mysticism of any variety.

Sitting in a small café at the port of Santa Teresa, Umberto admitted that he was in no fit state to think about any new free-diving records. In a matter of weeks, he said, he would go to Greece on holiday with a few close friends, and perhaps do some spear-fishing, but further than that he couldn't plan. I asked him if he would really be content to let another winter season slip by without regaining his constant-weight title. After all, only days before, another Italian diver had set a new record, beating Pelizzari's most recent depth record by six metres. 'Records are not why I dive,' he said. 'I like to be "Number One", sure, but when I set a record I get publicity, and people will come here to train with me when they know I am the best.'

The training required for a world-record attempt on the constant-ballast record is as gruelling as for a marathon race. 'I need ten months to prepare. I need to get away from all this.' Umberto nodded at the crowds and the activity around the diving boats.

Only a few weeks later, Pelizzari went on holiday, and made what he calls a few pleasure dives. Remarkably, he found that he felt physically strong, and mentally ready for a new record attempt. Perhaps the enforced physical activity of the summer season at Santa Teresa had been its own kind of relaxation and training. In any event, Pelizzari returned to Italy and immediately established a new constant-weight record of eighty metres – four metres more than the previous maximum depth. Once again, he had astounded the experts, setting a new record when, by his own admission, he had not been training for it. A few days later, he became the first man to reach the one hundred and fifty metre depth on a 'no-limits' dive.

When I rang Pelizzari to congratulate him on his new record, he sounded tired, but content. 'When I got down to the one-fifty mark I came out in goose bumps,' he told me. 'I stayed there for about half a minute, telling myself that now I really was the first to get there. And now, whatever other records are set, history will show that Enzo Maiorca was first to fifty, Jacques Mayol was first to one hundred, and I was the one who broke the one-fifty barrier.'

The reaction from other free divers to Pelizzari's achievement was mixed. Some even felt he had been unsporting to smash the record so convincingly. Until then, free divers had had an unspoken agreement to increase the maximum depth by a metre at a time, thus allowing more divers to attract sponsorship and publicity during the season. Very few would now be able even to claim an attempt on a new record and be believed. Pelizzari's dives, both constant-weight and no-limits, attracted fresh scientific debate, but his pre-eminence as the greatest free diver of all time was confirmed.

It has been said that free diving appeals to the spirit of the age, a new sport for the new century. It is non-invasive, and more about internal pleasure than public recognition. The joy of the free diver is internalized, and carried within as a lasting tranquillity. The symbolism of rebirth, the re-entry to the air world after a brief sojourn in the maternal element of seawater, strikes a chord with many. At Pelizzari's diving centre I met a woman who had travelled from Paris to Sardinia twice that summer, to improve her free-diving technique. She told me how she had discovered the sport during a visit to Martinique, where she had gone to distract herself from the misery of a broken love affair. 'I was at rock bottom,' she said. 'I couldn't sleep, couldn't eat. I didn't want to talk to anyone about anything. I'd tried counselling, aromatherapy, drink – you name it. And then, after three days of apnoea, I had forgotten what I was running away from.'

On my last day in Sardinia I met Pelizzari at the diving centre in the hope of a final dive. He said he was going south to the Bay of Marmorata, a wide expanse of sand sheltered by groups of granite boulders which protect it from the wind. The only complication was that he had promised to allow a photographer and a publicist from one of his sponsors to accompany him. They needed pictures of him steering his boat, which they had adorned with stickers advertising their product. At the dockside, Pelizzari was not happy. The group was two hours late, and now someone had telephoned saying she was a friend of the managing director of yet another of his sponsoring companies, and she wanted him to take her daughter diving. He had already cancelled his morning dive to accommodate the photographer, and it was almost lunch-time. In two hours' time he was due to take a large group of apnoeists from Club Mediterranée on a dive, and he couldn't be late.

Finally, the photographer, a stylist and a representative from the sponsor arrived. We scrambled into Pelizzari's boat and were about to set off when a large motor yacht hooted its horn nearby. A sunburnt matron in an inappropriate bikini waved a flabby arm, festooned with gold, at Pelizzari. It was the mother of the aspiring diver. We returned to the dockside to pick up another instructor and scuba cylinders, and Pelizzari transferred the man and the equipment to the motor yacht, telling the wealthy matron that, sadly, he was too busy to dive himself.

En route to Marmorata, the photographer decided that the light was now too harsh to take good pictures. Would Pelizzari mind rescheduling for the afternoon? He would do it, but only after he had fulfilled his obligations to the group booking that afternoon. When we reached the dive site the photographer changed his mind, since the granite boulders offshore were indeed photogenic. A few minutes were spent snapping pictures. As Pelizzari began to don his wetsuit the photographer's stylist said she wanted to return to shore. 'I thought you wanted photographs of me in the water?' Pelizzari enquired.

'Yes, but we are starving. We must have lunch first.'

'I'm diving.'

Again, I see Pelizzari make the subtle transformation into merman. Dressed in the familiar wetsuit, mask and fins, he hangs face-down in the clear sea, and the breathing ritual begins.

Once in the water, it is as if Pelizzari purges himself of all earthly tribulations. Cleansing abdominal breaths fill his chest and stomach, and in his mind a sequence of relaxing thoughts prepares him for what he must do. Not only are these thoughts calming, and therefore beneficial in slowing one's pulse and metabolism down so as to reduce oxygen consumption, but they also form a pattern in the mind. If conditions are right, and the mind is prepared, the discomfort of breath holding will be minimized by concentrating on these positive images.

Every free diver has a selection of imaginary scenes which they can run through their head, like a film projected on a screen. In a sense it is irrelevant what these images are; they are as individual as any personal recollection. To extend my own apnoea endurance I have learnt to recapture a memory of my young daughter playing at home. At first, I am standing alone, in a familiar corridor listening to the sounds of Ilona laughing and dancing in an adjoining room. As the memory sequence progresses, I hear her laughter getting louder, and then the stomp of small feet running along the carpet. Soon, she appears around the corner, her skirt flying and her face upturned with a smile of greeting as she runs as fast as she can to grasp me around the knees. This simple sequence can be broken down into individual frames, each one accompanied by different sounds and movements. For me, the images are ones I associate with deep happiness and contentment. There is sufficient detail in the sequence for me to 'zoom in' on anything I choose at any stage in the scenario. Sometimes I will visualize the pattern on my daughter's dress, at other times I will examine the pictures on the corridor wall, familiar scenes painted by my wife. There is easily enough detail in the recollected images to account for a minute of breath-holding time. If I wait to initiate the thought sequence until, say, two minutes of breath holding have passed, then the journey to the third minute, which I always find hardest, is made easy. If all is well, the sequence of relaxation techniques allows me to forget about breathing, but more importantly to forget about the need to breathe. Concentration is intensified, and the sensations of immersion become more real. There is no fear, no thought wasted on what might go wrong underwater or how long I can spend there. All of existence, all sensory information is relevant to this time alone. Life is compressed into the moment.

Off Marmorata Bay, I joined Pelizzari in the water for the last time, and looked down into the ultramarine landscape. Bright sunshine had turned the sea palest blue, and straight beams of light bounced back from the seabed as incisive as spotlights cutting through a night sky. Sixty feet below the surface, a jumble of grey steel plates were laid out in the shape of a ship. We were anchored above the wreck of the *Angelica*. She had been a merchantman, run aground on the granite headland in a storm. Twenty-five years later her superstructure is still recognizable: a tapered bow, some handrails and a bridge rising from the mass of tumbled steel plates that were once her cargo hold.

The *Angelica* is a popular site for scuba divers, her metal warren a hiding place for octopuses, grouper and countless other marine animals who are turning the ship into an artificial reef.

Five minutes of preparation time pass, and then Pelizzari is ready to begin diving. At first, he contents himself with finning down to the deck of the wreck and resting for a moment, then swimming back slowly to the surface, or sometimes pulling himself hand over hand along the anchor line.

After several shallow sorties, the warm-up phase, I follow him down, and reach the deck of the *Angelica*, where a convenient handrail allows me to hold on and rest at sixty feet. Below me, Pelizzari has already reached the lower deck, and he lies motionless, face-down on a sloping metal plate, oblivious to anything or anyone in the sea. He could be asleep.

I time him; after a full minute he stirs, but does not look up. He slides feet-foremost down the sloping plate, and then slithers around to enter the bowels of the wreck headfirst. After three minutes, I make my way to the surface, pausing on the line to scan the bottom for his reappearance. Breathing through my snorkel, I look down at the wreck. Another minute passes, and then he emerges from a different part of the *Angelica*, like a rabbit from a maze of tunnels in a sand dune. By my calculations, Pelizzari has been down for almost four minutes. When I think he is finally heading upward, he pauses. He bends at the waist and begins to twist his body like a corkscrew, his arms a violent pair of scythes cleaving the water. Pelizzari is as flexible as a gymnast, but his actions will not be interrupted by any jarring arrest on a rubber mat. His cushion is the sea.

Umberto Pelizzari has become fluid as water, in water. He is merely a shape, the details of the man masked by the neoprene wetsuit. Now, I am watching an outline of muscle, legs tapering from the cinched waist, long fins flexible as flesh. No detail of skin tone, no strand of hair emerges from the rubber to take the eye away from the simple form of the man. Finally, seeking the air world, he kicks with both feet together in unison, fins melded into a dolphin tail, pelvis undulating and thigh muscles straining, torso and stomach flexing, as loose and strong as latex.

Smoothly, and without a splash, Pelizzari's head emerges from the sea, and he re-inflates his lungs with a deep breath. The inhalation is vigorous and life-affirming but there is no desperation in his movement. Pelizzari's face is illuminated with pleasure, and he is at peace with his world. I swim back to the boat, enthralled by the grace and beauty of the man, grateful to have shared the sea with him.

12. Meeting of Minds

Many suspended together, forever apart,
Each one alone with the waters, upon one wave with the rest.

A magnetism in the water between them only.

D.H. Lawrence, 'Fish'

There is something about a dolphin's smile. Smooth skin around their large, flirtatious eyes wrinkles about the edges just as ours does when we laugh. The streamlined elegance of their sleek bodies is immensely pleasing to us. Unlike sharks, they show us nothing angular or menacing. A dolphin's snout has a rounded tip, and the teeth inside its mouth are small and regular. With their blow-holes they make a *thrirp thrirp claak claak* sound which closely resembles the giggle we produce on laughing gas. They make us feel at ease.

As a child in Malaya, I watched every episode of *Flipper* on television, enchanted by the series about Sandy Ricks, a young boy living an idyllic life in a sunny climate with minimal adult interference and a dolphin for company. Flipper was the aquatic equivalent of Skippy the kangaroo (though arguably more intelligent), and would alert the boy to danger. Flipper was adept at leading Sandy (and his father, who was a park ranger) to the site of local marine emergencies, or to track down crooks at work in

Florida's offshore waters. The boy lived in a little wooden house with mangrove forests and bush all around, he had his own small boat and he had his friend the dolphin waiting at the end of the jetty just yards from his front door. Every detail of his life, even the weathered planking on the wooden jetty, was perfect.

The original inspiration for the series was a real dolphin named Mitzy caught by accident in a Florida fisherman's net in 1958. The fisherman was named Milton Santini and he became a pioneer of dolphin husbandry, nursing Mitzy back to health and starting a sanctuary for dolphins in trouble. Today, some of Mitzy's descendants remain at the location where the original television series was made. Mitzy and her two movie stand-ins, Mr Gipper and Little Bit, formed the nucleus of a breeding programme which is now called the Dolphin Research Center (DRC), at Grassy Key in Florida. Having nurtured a fantasy image of Flipper and the simple moral world that he inhabited for over thirty years, I could not resist the desire to visit the place where Santini first trained the dolphin. I knew that I might be endangering a precious memory.

Two and a half hours out of Miami on US Highway 1, the DRC is one of several establishments advertising the possibility of what they like to call 'dolphin encounters'. The highway is virtually a strip mall dotted with fast-food restaurants, all-night grocery stores and motels catering for the endless flow of visitors driving in search of Hemingway fantasies in the Florida Keys. Like almost every other business along the route, the DRC has been unable to resist the erection of a large marine sculpture outside its door. The huge fibreglass dolphin is perhaps more forgivable than some of the other oceanic kitsch which despoils the atmosphere of the Keys. Someone there has made a fortune selling letterboxes in the shape of upright manatees, and motel signs which rest in the upturned claws of giant plastic lobsters.

The DRC is a charitable organization specializing in rehabilitating captive dolphins and educating the public about marine mammal welfare. At Grassy Key, trainers lead groups of tourists and schoolchildren around a series of enclosed lagoons, where about twenty bottle-nose dolphins (*Tursiops truncatus*) perform antics to amuse and educate the visiting humans. The trainers are mostly young women, who seem to invest all their emotional energy in the dolphins; the tours and lectures combine girlish enthusiasm and passion for the individual dolphins with a religious fervour for the plight of the species. The final ingredient in the mix is a degree of hard-nosed commercialism. Young trainers in polo-shirts and shorts put the dolphins through various routines at the wave of a hand or the peep of a whistle, including an unintentionally surreal session of dolphin painting, where one of the animals lifts its head from the water to wield a paintbrush in its mouth and daub a T-shirt in haphazard fashion. Walking around the dolphin pens among the squealing schoolchildren and gawping tourists, it is difficult not to feel uneasy about the combination of 'research' and 'entertainment' that has dolphins turning somersaults in return for fish-snack rewards.

I signed up for the Encounter Programme (advance booking essential), and having followed the guided tour around the dolphin pens was told to report for a briefing in the classroom with one of the senior trainers, Peggy Sloan. First, a video presentation alerted us to the problems faced by dolphins in the wild. Over-fishing, pollution, long-line fishing, excessive noise, and now the latest danger – the burgeoning trade in boats offering dolphin-watching tours all around the Florida coast. Thanks to this trade, we were told, wild dolphins are in some areas becoming dependent on nutritionally unsuitable handouts, and losing the ability to fend for themselves. Flipper is addicted to junk food.

Staff at the DRC point out that the health of dolphins in the wild is an indicator of the health of our oceans. Just like us, dolphins and the other cetaceans, whales and orcas, are at the top of the food chain. Research at the DRC shows that for the first time these magnificent animals are starting to display cancerous tumours and infections with new viruses, for which there is no cure. It is highly likely that these are being caused by pollution, and is another sign that we need to do more than just worry about our future on this water planet.

At the DRC, a maximum of twelve people are allowed to swim with selected dolphins each day, although the staff say it is the dolphins who choose whether or not to participate. As a precaution, no dolphin is allowed to swim with the public for more than two hours each week, to avoid fatigue and boredom. Our small group included four young children, and at least half of the people present had visited the DRC before.

As if we were in some kind of group therapy session, Peggy asked each of us to introduce ourselves and relate our reasons for signing up for the encounter. We should also confess to any previous personal interaction with the species. Perhaps unsurprisingly, it is soon clear that anyone who signs up for the DRC experience is already in love with marine mammals. This is just as well, as Peggy's briefing begins to take on the atmosphere of an ante-natal class. A plastic model dolphin is produced from a cradle and we are to tell Peggy where we think it might be 'appropriate to touch a dolphin'. Naturally, the belly and sexual organs are taboo. Peggy then talks us through the carefully staged process which will begin when we enter the lagoon to swim with the dolphins. At all times, we must obey the trainer, and we are warned that if the dolphins take a dislike to any of us the session will end. It is difficult not to feel that the animals may sense anyone giving off negative vibes, and one will be forever marked as a pariah if the dolphins don't approve.

The moment of truth comes when I slip into the water in the dolphin pen and place one hand palm down on the surface. Holding on to the jetty, and under the watchful eye of the trainer who is armed with a whistle and a bucketful of fish pieces, I tread water and wait to see if a dolphin will allow me to rub its back in greeting. For a moment nothing happens, and I begin to fear that I am that essentially bad person whose negative energy is keeping the dolphins at bay. The water is not clear, more like a goldfish pond in need of a new filter system than a tropical lagoon. I cannot see my knees. Then, a grey shadow emerges from the murk and coasts gently beneath my hand. A second later a smaller dolphin follows suit, and I have been given the all-clear to interact with a mother and daughter pair, named Merina and Pandora.

The dolphins perform a selection of exercises. I am told to swim out into the lagoon as if I have lost my way, and I hear the trainer telling the dolphins to bring me back. Like sheep dogs they appear on either side of me, edging closer until I am able to hold on to both dorsal fins. With no effort, Pandora and Merina pull me back to the jetty. As I lie flat on my back with my ankles tight together, they place their snouts, or more correctly *rostrums*, against the soles of my feet and push me fast through the water in a prone style of surfing. The sheer power of the dolphins, even in a juvenile like Pandora, is impressive. In another exercise, I am asked to perform a movement that the mother dolphin will mimic. I twirl in circles and Merina copies me, afterwards standing high in the water to allow me to 'shake hands' by gently rubbing her outstretched pectoral fins.

It was a privilege to be allowed to meet the dolphins, but I felt uneasy that there was a crowd of onlookers clapping while we played. The children in our group were ecstatic after their swim with the dolphins, and I then felt guilty for not being overjoyed.

Had I become totally cynical? Or had I simply been spoiled by earlier unplanned encounters with wild dolphins?

On a couple of occasions I have met dolphins underwater while scuba diving. Such encounters are extremely rare, and leave me bewitched by the briefest of connections with these wondrous animals. Normally, wild dolphins are wary of human contact, and although they will hitch a ride on the bow wave of a fast boat, as soon as a human being enters the water they will disappear. Attempting to swim after them I have been tantalized by the faint whistles and squeaks that we know to be their language.

In legend and imagination we humanize the dolphin. In Herodotus, this is the animal that rescued Arion of Methyma, the musician thrown overboard by thieves while sailing from Taenarum to Corinth. Singing from the prow of the ship before he fell, Arion is said to have been heard by a group of dolphins following the boat, who then saved him and towed him ashore.

In recent years the species has been held up as a potent healing force, capable of transcending the barriers of inter-species communication. These sensitive, intelligent animals nurture their young in social groups, and, according to several psychologists, may hold a key to unlock our capacity for surrender and trust, love and serenity. The DRC has its own store of miracle tales, occasions when handicapped and emotionally closed-off children and adults have broken out of their physical and mental cages by swimming with the dolphins. In the 1950s, John Lilly, an American biophysicist, predicted that man would learn to talk to other species and he chose the cetaceans, especially dolphins, as the most likely animals with whom we might converse. He proposed that dolphins transmitted their culture from generation to generation through their complex language, in the same way that primitive tribes used oral storytelling in place of the written word. Years later, having retired to Hawaii, Lilly advocated recognizing the 'Cetacean

Nation', and bestowing specific rights on these higher mammals, whom he believes rival us in intelligence. Other scientists took up his work, further embedding the notion that this species was special. Stories that the Americans and Russians used dolphins to carry weapons, find mines and even attack enemy frogmen reinforced the notion that someone somewhere had the secret to communicating with these highly intelligent and apparently willing human allies.

Ricou Browning, the creator of the original concept of the *Flipper* television series, is less romantic about the dolphin's latent talents. A veteran director of underwater television series and films, he told me that he thought we had barely scratched the surface of the possibilities of contact with dolphins, but that after working with them for many years he was convinced they were no more psychic or emotionally receptive than any other domestic pet. He compared them to cats rather than dogs, trainable certainly, and friendly when they wanted to be, but also fiercely independent. In Browning's view the dolphin only collaborates with people when it can see a positive benefit to itself.

Dana Carnegie is a senior trainer at the DRC and has worked at Grassy Key for more than a decade. 'I am privileged to live among this family,' she told me, 'and when Merina gave birth to Pandora it was just as exciting for me as when my human niece was born.'

All the staff at the DRC are equally committed. Dana agreed that there is a fine line between exploiting the captive dolphins and engaging the public in the whole issue of marine mammal welfare. She points out that a simple lecture tour and the chance to watch dolphins in an aquarium setting would not bring in the same numbers of visitors. Was she at all uneasy about the way the public expected the dolphins to do tricks? 'Living with these dolphins every day, I believe they are happy,' Dana replied. 'The tricks they do are adaptations of natural behaviour, which we have turned into a show – not the other way around. If they don't feel like playing then nothing we can do will make them join in. These animals have a sense of humour, they are sociable and they show us and each other love. And do you know what? I am in awe of the way they live their lives.'

Brissare Rocks, Seychelles

A few miles offshore from the north-east point of Mahé Island, a series of small rock pinnacles break the surface. When the Indian Ocean surges around the submerged rocks they cast white spray into the air and stand out clearly against the surrounding sea. On calm days they are a brown smudge almost invisible from the shore. Underwater the pinnacles form a sunken island, a cluster of boulders which seem to have fallen down in a heap like the remnants of some child's castle made of building blocks.

Currents play around the rocks, which are connected underwater to another series of smaller submerged boulders, sharper and more sinister, christened the Dragon's Teeth. A natural raised causeway of fire coral links the two groups of rocks, and on either side of the path the seabed slopes gently away into darker, deeper water. One bright morning I decided to visit the rocks with Jessica and some other divers. The weather had been wet and windy for several weeks and we had been restricted to diving at sites close inshore, but now the seas around Mahé were taking their rest before the start of the south-east monsoon. The two and a half mile journey was a pleasant excursion and allowed us a rare chance to look back at the mountain slopes of the big island from a distance. The sky was painfully blue and bright, and white tropicbirds skimmed across the sea, trailing their long tail feathers behind them like streamers as they hunted for flying fish or squid that strayed too near the surface.

The sea was flat and clear when we reached Brissare, but as soon as we dropped anchor we saw that a strong current was running around the outcrop, too strong to allow us to swim easily between the rocks and the Dragon's Teeth. We would have to stick to one or the other. There were half a dozen other divers on the boat that morning, and another dive leader who wanted to take everyone in one large group around the rocks. Usually, he and I would share the task, each taking half the group, but as it pleased him to take complete control, Jessica and I decided to dive alone around the boulders in the opposite direction. Before the others were ready we slipped into the water quickly and quietly, relishing the chance to dive together without the responsibility of guiding a gang of divers. The sea was clear as we submerged, an invisible plate-glass wall through which we passed without effort. The current had cleared the water of loose particles and it was one of those days when everything sparkled underwater. In every direction our vision was unrestricted so that objects up to two hundred feet away could still be seen.

To avoid meeting the larger group of divers coming the other way around the circular rock formation, we decided to swim through a natural tunnel hidden in the middle of the outcrop, where there was often a large nurse shark to be found resting during the day. There was no shark in the tunnel that day, and we began to feel a heavier current as we battled our way through the opening. Under a ledge I found a cowrie, a shining leopard-spotted bauble as big as a fist, with its soft inner mantle like a black petticoat curling from the open lips of its shell. A baby green turtle passed through the tunnel ahead of us, eyes disproportionately large in its juvenile head, its shell plates perfectly smooth and unscarred. A large and normally secretive moray eel swam free of its lair, a dark-green ribbon of stealth across the rocks. As we emerged from the tunnel we paused for a moment to catch our breath in the lee of the rocks, where we could look far out into the blue space beyond. It was a moment of utter peace in clear water, out of the clutch of the wearisome current. Thirty feet above our heads there were white bursts of bubbling water where the waves were breaking against the sharpened rock pinnacles, and schools of jacks hung below the bubbles like stars, their flanks flashing mirrors in the sunlight. Suddenly, from the deeper waters around us, a large school of mackerel appeared. As the dense silver wall of bait-fish flashed by it seemed they were driven by the communal urgency that only desperate prey can know. Jessica and I were both seized by a simultaneous premonition that something significant was about to happen. Instinctively we held hands and knelt on the clean white sand, staring into the blue, transfixed, apprehensive at what might be chasing the fish. After a moment the hunters came out of the shimmering space, a cohort of steel-grey shapes, powerful, determined and confident that they would soon be feasting on the hapless mackerel. We each counted fifteen dolphins in the pod, one a mother with a young calf swimming close against her side, synchronizing its movements to hers as if they were bound together by a magnetic field.

Jessica and I knelt awe-struck by the spectacle, afraid to move lest we disturbed the pod. The dolphins swam to within twenty feet and turned parallel to us, diverted from their chase for a moment by the sight of our strange, noisy, bubbling dive gear. They were calm. One by one, the dolphins turned their heads to study us as they passed. A large male at the front of the pod then swam back to the rear of his group to take another look at us. He froze for a second in the water, sizing us up, calculating, and judging whether we were friend or foe. It seemed certain that he had never seen people underwater before. Finally, the dolphin gave a powerful thrust of his tail to rejoin the pod as they followed the mackerel once more into the deep. We remained rooted to the spot for some time, as if bewitched by his gaze.

Acknowledgements

I am indebted to many members of the Historical Diving Society (UK) for help, advice and enthusiasm in researching this book. The Chairman, Dr John Bevan, deserves special mention, as do Reg Vallintine, Adrian Barak and Nigel Phillips, all of whom have been generous with their time and have allowed me access to their remarkable book collections. Kevin Casey, at Sub Aqua Prints, made his extensive collection of early diving cartoons and sketches available. Members of the HDS (USA) have been similarly kind, especially its president, Leslie Leaney, who put me in touch with so many of the key figures in diving on that continent. In Paris, Capitaine Philippe Rousseau was an invaluable source of information on the early French pioneers of underwater exploration. I would also like to thank Professor Dr Hans Hass and his wife Lotte for their kindness and hospitality in Vienna, and Jacques Cousteau's son Jean-Michel at Ocean Futures in California. In London, thanks go to Clare Valentine of the Natural History Museum and Joanna Corden, archivist at the Royal Society.

For their time and reminiscences I am also very grateful to Dickie Greenland in England, Dottie Frazier in Los Angeles, Neal Watson in Fort Lauderdale and George Billiris in Tarpon Springs. Nick Toth deserves special thanks for historical assistance and for introducing me to the Greek community in Tarpon. Further north on the Gulf Coast, Chief Quartermaster Bob Barth at the US Navy

Experimental Diving Unit in Panama City has been a faithful and omniscient source of material on the Sealab experiments, and put me in touch with so many people who played a part in the underwater habitat programmes, including Walt Mazzone and George Bond (son of the late Dr George Bond). In Key Largo, I must thank Ian Koblick, president of the Marine Resources Development Foundation and owner of La Chalupa, as well as Dr Lance Rennka, for their time and expertise in an almost forgotten science.

Thanks also go to Captain Keith Plaskett and his wife Cindi for Southern hospitality and blue crabs in Pensacola, as well as diving guidance in the Cayman Islands. Diving in Papua New Guinea would not have been possible without the assistance of Peter Hughes and his team from the *Dancer* fleet. In the Bahamas, my thanks go to Stuart and Michelle Cove, and in Fiji to Curly Carswell, Lorne and Doug Cammick and Zak Qereqeretabua. My research and experiments in free diving would have been impossible without the kindness of Stefania and Umberto Pelizzari in Sardinia, as well as physiological advice from Dr Claes Lundgren, Director of the Centre for Research in Special Environments at New York State University at Buffalo. Also in New York, Bob Croft has been exceedingly generous with his time and reminiscences about the early days of breath-hold diving experiments.

Gratitude is also due to my agents Joanna Weinberg and Natasha Fairweather at A. P. Watt for encouraging me to write this book, and to Rowland White for his enthusiastic editorship from within Michael Joseph.

Last I would like to thank the hundreds of diving buddies who have shared my underwater experiences and in particular some of the actual events described in *Neutral Buoyancy*, including: Gary Baptiste, Wayne Burke, Janine Driessel, Giles Ecott, David Imelman, Emry Oxford, Harald Pek, Carlos Ruiz, Adrian Tyte and Geoff Weg.

Select Bibliography

Allen, Gerald, and Roger Steene, *Indo-Pacific Coral Reef Field Guide*, Singapore, 1994.

Anonymous, *Angliae Tutamen*, London, 1695.

Anonymous, *Die Taucher Maschine*, Leipzig, 1805.

Bacon, Francis, *Novum Organum* (Translation, Peter Shaw), London, 1802.

Beebe, William, *Beneath Tropic Seas: A Record of Diving among the Coral Reefs of Haiti*, Putnams, New York, 1928.

Bevan, John, *The Infernal Diver*, Submex, London, 1996.

Bond, George F., *Papa Topside: The Sealab Chronicles of Captain George F. Bond*, Edited by Helen Siiteri, Naval Institute Press, Maryland, 1993.

—, *Sealab III Chronicle*, Unpublished journal, June 1968, USN Experimental Diving Unit Library.

Borelli, G. A., *De Motu Animalium* (2 volumes), Rome, 1680/81.

Boyle, Robert, 'New Pneumatical Experiments about Respiration', *Philosophical Transactions*, Journal of the Royal Society, London, August 1670.

—, 'Tracts . . . About the Cosmicall Qualities of Things', Oxford, 1671.

Brown, Joseph E., *The Golden Sea, Man's Underwater Adventures*, Cassell, London, 1974.

Churchill, Winston, *The Second World War, Vol. IV, The Hinge of Fate*, Cassell, London, 1949.

Cousteau, Jacques-Yves, 'Fish Men Explore a New World Undersea', *National Geographic Magazine*, vol. cii, no. 4, Washington, 1952.

Cousteau, J. Y. and Frédéric Dumas, *The Silent World*, Harper & Rowe, New York, 1953.

Cowan, Zélide, *Early Divers*, Treasure World Publishing, Great Yarmouth, 1977.

Davis, Robert H., *Deep Diving and Submarine Operations*, Siebe, Gorman & Company, Cwmbran, 1981.

Diolé, Philippe, *The Undersea Adventure*, Sidgwick and Jackson, London, 1953.

Drieberg, Frédéric de, *Mémoire sur une Nouvelle Machine à Plonger*, Paris, 1811.

Dugan, James, *Man Explores the Sea*, Hamish Hamilton, London, 1956.

Ellis, Richard, *Deep Atlantic*, Lyons Press, New York, 1996.

Falck, N. D., *A Philosophical Dissertation on the Diving Vessel Projected by Mr Day, and Sunk in Plymouth Sound*, London, 1775.

Fleming, Ian, *Live and Let Die*, Jonathan Cape, London, 1954.

—, *Thunderball*, Hodder and Stoughton, London, 1989.

Flynn, Errol, *My Wicked, Wicked Ways*, Heinemann, London, 1960.

Gent, — , *De l'Emploi Thérapeutique de l'Air Comprimé dans l'Astme et l'Emphysème*, Bulletin, Académie de Médécine, Paris, 1869, Vol. 34, pp. 1119–20.

Gilpatric, Guy, *The Compleat Goggler*, USA, 1938.

Haldane, J. S. and J. G. Priestley, *Respiration*, Yale University Press, 1922.

Halley, Edmund, 'The Art of Living Underwater: Or, a Discourse concerning the Means of furnishing Air at the Bottom of the

Sea, in any ordinary Depths', *Philosophical Transactions*, Royal Society, London, July–September 1716.

Harris, Gary L., *Ironsuit*, Best Publishing Company, Arizona, 1994.

Hass, Hans, *Diving to Adventure*, Jarrolds, London, 1952.

—, *Under the Red Sea*, Jarrolds, London, 1953.

—, *Conquest of the Underwater World*, David & Charles, London, 1975.

Heinke, John W., *A History of Diving*, Heinke and Davis, London, 1876.

Hill, Leonard, *Caisson Sickness*, London, 1912.

Hussain, Farooq, *Living Underwater*, November Books, London, 1970.

Hutton, J. Bernard, *Frogman Extraordinary*, Neville Spearman, London, 1960.

Kelly-Bourges, M., *A Fool's Guide to Sponge Taxonomy*, Natural History Museum, London, 1994.

Kenyon, Ley, *Pocket Guide to the Undersea World*, Collins, London, 1956.

Klingert, Karl H., *Beschreibung einer in allen Flussen brauchbaren Tauchermaschine*, Breslau, 1797.

Kolar, Bohumil and Oldrich Unger, *Explorers of the Deep*, Hamlyn, London, 1976.

Larson, Howard E., *A History of Self-Contained Diving and Underwater Swimming*, National Academy of Sciences Committee on Underwater Warfare, Washington, 1955.

de Latil, Pierre and Jean Rivoire, *Man and the Underwater World*, Jarrolds, London, 1956.

—, *Sunken Treasure*, Rupert Hart-Davis, London, 1962.

Lévi, Claude, *Sponges of the New Caledonian Lagoon*, Editions de l'Orstrom, Paris, 1998.

Lieske, Ewald and Robert Myers, *Coral Reef Fishes (Indo-Pacific and Caribbean)*, HarperCollins, London, 1994.

Lilly, J. C., *Man and Dolphin*, Victor Gollancz, London, 1962.

Lorini, Buonaiuto, *Delle Fortificationi*, Venice, 1597.

Lundgren, Claes E. G. and John N. Miller, *The Lung at Depth*, Marcel Dekker, New York, 1999.

MacCurdy, Edward, *The Notebooks of Leonardo Da Vinci*, Jonathan Cape, London, 1948.

Madsen, Axel, *Cousteau: An Unauthorised Biography*, Robson, London, 1986.

Maraini, Fosco, *Hekura: The Diving Girls' Island*, Hamish Hamilton, London, 1962.

Martin, Lawrence, *Scuba Diving Explained*, Best Publishing, Arizona, 1997.

Marx, Robert F., *The History of Underwater Exploration*, Dover Publications, New York, 1990.

Mather, Cotton, *The Life of Sir William Phips*, New York, 1929.

Maugham, W. Somerset, *The World Over*, Collected Stories Vol. 1, The Reprint Society, London, 1951.

Mayol, Jacques, *Homo Delphinus*, Idelson-Gnocchi, Naples, 2000.

Miller, James W. and Ian G. Koblick, *Living and Working in the Sea*, Five Corners Publications, Plymouth, USA, 1995.

Munson, Richard, *Cousteau – The Captain and his World*, Robert Hale, London, 1991.

Pelizzari, Umberto, *Profondamente*, Mondadori, Milan, 1997.

Pent, Robert F., *History of Tarpon Springs*, Great Outdoors Publishing, St Petersburg, USA, 1964.

Phillips, John L., *The Bends*, Yale University Press, New Haven, USA, 1998.

Le Prieur, Yves, *Premier de Plongée*, Editions France Empire, Paris, 1956.

Pugh, Marshall, *Commander Crabb*, Macmillan & Co., London, 1956.

Siebe, Henry, *The Conquest of the Sea*, Chatto and Windus, London, 1874.

Sipperly, David and Terry Maas, *Freedive!*, BlueWater Freedivers, California, 1998.

Smith, Hugh M., *The Florida Commercial Sponges*, US Fish Commission Bulletin for 1897, Washington, Government Printing Office, 1898.

Snell, Dr E. Hugh, *Compressed Air Illness*, London, 1896.

Snyderman, Marty and Clay Wiseman, *Guide to Marine Life, Caribbean, Bahamas, Florida*, Aqua Quest, New York, 1996.

Storrs, Sir Ronald, *Dunlop in War and Peace*, Hutchinson, London, 1946.

Tailliez, Philippe, *To Hidden Depths*, William Kimber, London, 1954.

Tartaglia, Niccolo, *Regola generale da sulevare con regione e misura non solamente ogni affondata nave*, Venice, 1551.

Ufano, Diego, *Artillerie*, Zutphen, 1621.

Vegetius, *De Re Militari*, Erfurt, 1511.

Verne, Jules, *20,000 Leagues Under the Sea*, Hetzel, Paris, 1870.

Veron, J. E. N., *Corals of Australia and the Indo Pacific*, Angus & Robertson, London, 1986.

Waldron, T. J. and James Gleeson, *The Frogmen*, Pan Books, London, 1954.

Warren, C. E. T. and James Benson, *Above Us the Waves: The Story of Midget Submarines and Human Torpedoes*, Harrap, London, 1953.

Welham, M. G. & J., *Frogman Spy*, W. H. Allen, London, 1990.

Williamson, J. E., *Twenty Years Under the Sea*, Hale, Cushman & Flint, Boston, 1936.